A DICTIONARY OF
MUSICAL THEMES

A DICTIONARY OF
MUSICAL THEMES

By

HAROLD BARLOW

and

SAM MORGENSTERN

Introduction by

JOHN ERSKINE

LONDON & TONBRIDGE

ERNEST BENN LIMITED

First published in Great Britain 1949
by Williams and Norgate Limited
Second Impression 1949
Third Impression 1950

Published by Ernest Benn Limited
25 New Street Square · Fleet Street
London · EC4A 3JA
& Sovereign Way · Tonbridge · Kent
Fourth Impression 1952
Fifth Impression 1955
Sixth Impression 1958
Seventh Impression 1963
Eighth Impression 1967
Ninth (Corrected) Impression 1970
Tenth Impression 1972
Eleventh Impression 1974
© Crown Publishers Inc. U.S.A.
ISBN 0 510-35501-3

CONTENTS

* *Bach's Fugue in G Minor, Organ " The Little Fugue " appears on page 526.*

Elgar's Symphony No. 2 in E flat (Op. 63) appears on page 526.

Tschaikowsky Melodie, Op. 42, No. 3 from Souvenir D'Un Lieu, Cher, Vn. & Pft. appears on page 526.

INTRODUCTION

By John Erskine

THIS dictionary of musical themes, by Harold Barlow and Sam Morgenstern, supplies an aid which students of music have long needed. When the authors showed me the plan of it a year ago, or somewhat earlier, I applauded at once, and agreed to write a word of preface. We should now have something in musical literature to parallel Bartlett's *Familiar Quotations*. Whenever a musical theme haunted us, but refused to identify itself no matter how much we scraped our memory, all we should have to do would be to look up the tune in Barlow and Morgenstern, where those ingenious dictionary-makers would assemble some ten thousand musical themes, with a notation-index or theme-finder, to locate the name of the composition from which the haunting fragment came, and the name of the composer.

After a brief but exciting conversation, Mr. Barlow and Mr. Morgenstern went off with my promise of a preface, as it were, in their pocket, leaving me very thoughtful — and inclined to become more thoughtful with each passing hour. I knew there had already been attempts to index music, and I was fairly familiar with the difficulties which had in the past tripped up bold experimenters. A dictionary such as Bartlett's can classify quotations according to the subject with which they deal, and can arrange them in the usual index method by the letter-order of the opening words. But no method has been hit on to index musical sounds, nor the variations in pitch by which a theme is articulated. No method, that is, which permits the musical material of a theme to remain strictly musical.

I understood what Mr. Barlow and Mr. Morgenstern would try to do; since letters can easily be indexed, and musical notes cannot be, they would try to translate the notes into letters. After much thought I feared this would prove a task far beyond even their enthusiasm, and the result might be less useful than they hoped. But they put an end to my doubts by bringing to my study one day a section of the theme index, and challenging me to give them a theme they couldn't speedily locate. My conversion was prompt. I am glad to record here my confidence in the theory of this book, and my admiration for the manner in which the theory has been worked out.

As the authors are more than ready to admit, the ten thousand themes, more or less, which can be identified quickly and easily with the help of this book, do not encompass the entire literature of music, but they do include practically all the themes which can be found in compositions that have been recorded. It is hardly likely that a music student will be haunted by a theme from a composition not yet considered worthy of recording.

The authors believe, and I agree with them, that their dictionary of musical themes will be useful to the trained musician, even to the professional performer, who is more likely than the beginner or the amateur to have a firm grasp of the musical material which has gone into well-known masterpieces.

The book is divided into two parts. The first part contains ten thousand or more musical themes arranged by composers. The second part is the notation-index or theme-finder. If we consult the dictionary in order to locate a theme, we shall begin with the second part of the book, and conclude with the passage in the first part which gives the answer we have been looking for. But there are many occasions when a musician needs to refresh his memory about the themes in a given composition. Though he knows the name of the composition and of the composer, he may need to remind himself of the theme in the first movement, or the second, or the third. Of course he can go to his music shelves and consult his copy of the complete work. That is, if his music shelves are large enough to contain the scores of ten thousand sonatas or symphonies. I suspect that the convenience of the Barlow-Morgenstern dictionary will soon be recognized by serious students of musical literature.

How enormous that body of literature is, and how rapidly it increases, we sometimes forget. It is well within the truth to say that no pianist, no violinist, and no singer, pretends to have in his repertoire all the important compositions for piano, violin, or voice. Each musician has probably read over hundreds of pieces he would gladly include in his repertoire if life were long enough. A pianist who keeps in his repertoire, and in condition for performance, a thousand pieces of respectable length and difficulty, is an unusual artist. If his repertoire were three times as large, he would still be something of a specialist; the piano repertory has long since grown beyond human capacity to master completely. If recital programs do not seem more repetitious than they sometimes are, it is because of the helpful capacity of audiences to forget music which they themselves do not play. Sometimes they wish to recall at least a theme or two of what they have forgotten. From now on they will probably consult the Barlow and Morgenstern dictionary of themes.

The present volume does not contain themes from vocal music. To cover vocal as well as instrumental compositions, another volume would be needed as large as this.*

I have been speaking of trained musicians as well as of the average music lover. Both can use this dictionary without difficulty. The theme index is ingenious and, as I now believe, simple. If a theme or a tune is running through your head, and if your musical ear is good enough for you to pick out the theme on the white notes of the scale, you will find that you have transposed the theme automatically into the key of C — or perhaps into A minor — or perhaps, with the help of a black note here or there, into C minor. If you write down the letters by which the white notes are named, and find the resulting letter sequence in the index, you will be directed at once to the name of the original work and the name of its composer.

It is this process of identifying the theme when it is played by ear on the white keys that seemed to me at first complicated and likely to discourage those who consult the dictionary. But I am confident now that once we have tried the method for ourselves, we shall find it extraordinarily simple.

Like any other dictionary of quotations, this book will perhaps be most useful to the young. Music is now a well-established subject in American education. Though many children in our schools are fortunately taught to play and sing, all of them — and

---

* *A Dictionary of Vocal Themes,* Ernest Benn, London

this is equally their good fortune — are put in the way of listening to recorded music, to great masterpieces performed by great artists of yesterday and today. Not so long ago school children used to go along the street humming a snatch of ragtime or jazz. Nowadays the youngsters are just as likely to hum a passage from Schubert or Tschaikovsky, or whoever was the composer who last spoke to them from the disc in the music class.

"What is that you are humming?"

Sometimes the children remember, but more often, like the elders, they forget. But when they have learned to consult this dictionary, they will place the passage at once.

I believe this book is destined to a wide and increasing usefulness, both to mature music lovers now and to the army of children whom our schools are training to be the music lovers of tomorrow.

PREFACE

WHEN we began the research for this book, we both felt like the Sorcerer's Apprentice, for each theme that we found seemed to loose a crowd of others waiting for us. It looked as if this one book might stretch into volumes. However, the limits we set ourselves made the completion of the work seem possible within a lifetime.

This work contains about 10,000 themes. They have been chosen primarily from recorded, instrumental pieces. No vocal works, excepting those which in instrumental arrangement have become better known than their originals, have been included. We feel that the book contains almost all the themes the average and even the more erudite listener might want to look up.

Certain works we omitted because the scores were unavailable in libraries, and publishers who were more than helpful could not supply them. A few other works we left out because we could not, after great effort, secure copyrights. Though the book does not exhaust the subject, by far, we feel that we have compiled a fairly complete index of themes, not only first themes, but every important theme, introduction, and salient rememberable phrase of the works included. In certain modern works where a number of varied phrases could be construed as thematic, we tried to present them all. Naturally, in the development of a work certain phrases occur which are as rememberable as the themes themselves. To include these would amount to reprinting the pieces in their entirety. A few ultra-modern works we left out. We felt that anyone likely to remember their themes, or more aptly their combinations of notes, would in all probability know their source. Consequently, these works would hardly fit into the scope of this volume.

Careful search through so many hundreds of works by different composers living in different eras in divers countries leads the research student to rather interesting generalizations. Permeating the work of many of the great and prolific composers we find certain combinations of notes, a certain "melos." This "melos" or melodic line seems to be a strong ingredient of their style. Schubert, Beethoven, Mozart, each has his ever-recurring theme song, but so disguised that it makes for artistic variety rather than monotony.

Many themes in compositions of the same period seem to possess similar melodic lines. In our notation key we had to carry some themes to seven or eight letters before their lines began to diverge. It is not that the composers were necessarily imitative. Melodic thinking of the period simply took on certain characteristics, rhythm and harmonic background giving these almost identical lines their variety.

Since the folk tune plays such an integral part in serious composition, one finds special national characteristics in the melodic lines of composers of various lands. Certain interval as well as rhythmic combinations make for Spanish, Russian, German, and French themes, and those of other countries too, of course. Identical motives are used again and again by composers, both consciously and unconsciously. The famous Mannheim motive (G C Eb G C Eb D C B C) as found in Beethoven's First Piano Sonata, Mozart's G Minor Symphony, and Mendelssohn's E Minor String Quartet, is probably the most obvious example of this. We found a rather wry footnote to the first page of one of Clementi's Bb Major Piano Sonatas, stating that when he played this piece for Kaiser Franz Joseph, Mozart was in the audience. The theme of the Sonata is identical with the overture of The Magic Flute, which appeared a few years later. Mozart was famous for his phenomenal memory.

Parody quotations of themes, such as the Tristan Prelude in Debussy's Golliwogg's Cake Walk, are both plentiful and amusing. The Lullaby in Strauss's Domestic Symphony is a steal from a Venetian Boat Song by Mendelssohn, and whether Prokofieff knows it or not, the last half of the second theme in the second movement of his Sixth Piano Sonata bears more than a sneaking resemblance to Mendelssohn's Spring Song.

And so the research student becomes a tone sleuth.

The book should prove useful not only to those who are bothered by a theme and can't remember its source, but also to those who know the source but can't remember the theme. We ourselves shall certainly use it in both capacities.

A book of these dimensions could never have appeared without the aid and encouragement of a great many interested people. We owe a debt of deep and sincere gratitude first to Miss Gladys Chamberlain, Director of the 58th St. Music Library of New York City, who turned over the entire resources of that splendid organization to us, and gave us unreservedly of her time and advice. We want to thank the members of her staff, Miss Mary Lee Daniels, Miss Eleanor Chasan, Miss Lilly Goldberg, Mrs. Hilda Stolov, Mrs. Leah Silton, Mrs. Elsa Hollister, who were more than helpful.

In the music division of the main library of New York City, we wish to thank Mr. Philip Miller, and two of his indefatigable pages, George Klinger and Noel Schwartz.

Our thanks for the special kindness of James Blish, Mrs. Rose Gandal, Alex. M. Kramer, Robert Lowndes, Ben Meiselman, Dr. Rudolf Nissim, Herbert Weinstock, and the many music publishers and copyright owners who gave us assistance. We are indebted to Robert Simon, of Crown Publishers, for his constant encouragement in the undertaking; and to Miss Elizabeth Galvin, his assistant, without whom this book would probably never have appeared.

S. M.

New York, N. Y.
April, 1948

ACKNOWLEDGEMENTS

The Publishers have to acknowledge the following copyright permissions:

Items A 29, E 49, F 124—7, F 214—5, G 185—201, H 723—91, K 90—118, M 396—400, P 66, P 78—84, P 100—7, R 123—4, R 155—6, R 162 S 1523—34, S 1534a—g, S 1535—40, S 1546—7, S 1599—1608, T 119—22c, T 301—2, T 315—20 by permission of Schott & Co. Ltd., London, for all countries with the exception of Germany (Where these works are controlled by B. Schott's Sohne, Mainz) and the U.S.A. (where these works are controlled by The Associated Music Publishers Inc., New York).

Items B 1728—37, C 584—8, D 269—94, D 300—38, D 350—425, D 434—69, S 145—61, S 166—71, S 1609—15 by permission of N. Simrock—Richard Shauer, London.

Items B 434—6, P 163—4, R 285—92 by permission of D. Rahter—Richard Shauer, London.
Permission is also acknowledged from Messrs. Alfred Lengnick & Co. Ltd. as publishers for the British Empire for the following :—
Items C 584, D 292—4, D 357—73, D 466—9.

Items S 812-5 by permission of Elkin & Co. Ltd., London. Permission is also acknowledged from Elkin & Co. Ltd., as publishers for the British Empire for the following :— M 18—20, M 23—26, M 37—45.

The call for a further impression has provided the opportunity, wherever possible, to revise the dates of birth and death of composers, and to make a few other corrections.   1970

ADAM, Adolphe (1803-1856)

La Poupée de Nuremberg
(The Nuremberg Doll)
Overture

1st Theme — AI

2nd Theme — A2

3rd Theme — A3

4th Theme — A4

Si J'Étais Roi
Overture

1st Theme — A5

2nd Theme — A6

3rd Theme — A7

4th Theme — A8

ALBÉNIZ, Isaac M. F. (1860-1909)

Suite Española, Pft.
Cadiz (Saeta)
By permission of Associated
Music Publishers, Inc.

1st Theme — A9

2nd Theme — A10

Cuba

— A11

Seguidillas

1st Theme — A12

2nd Theme — A13

Sevillanas

— A14

Iberia I, Pft.
Evocación
By permission of Associated
Music Publishers, Inc.

— A15

Fête Dieu à Seville

1st Theme — A16

2nd Theme — A17

Iberia II, Pft.
Triana
By permission of Associated
Music Publishers, Inc.

1st Theme — A18

2nd Theme — A19

Iberia III, Pft.
El Albaicin (El Polo)
By permission of Associated
Music Publishers, Inc.

A20

Iberia IV, Pft.
Jerez
By permission of Associated
Music Publishers, Inc.

A21

Malaga

A22

Cordoba (Nocturne), Pft.
By permission of Associated
Music Publishers, Inc.

1st Theme — A23

2nd Theme — A24

Pavana-Capricho, Op. 12,
Pft.
By permission of Associated
Music Publishers, Inc.

1st Theme — A25

2nd Theme — A26

Sous Le Palmier, in E Flat
(Tango Flamenco), Pft.
By permission of Associated
Music Publishers, Inc.

1st Theme — A27

2nd Theme — A28

Tango in D, Pft.
By permission of Associated
Music Publishers, Inc.

A29

ALFVÉN, Hugo (1872-1960)

Midsommarvarka
(Swedish Rhapsody), Op. 19,
Orch.
By permission of Associated
Music Publishers, Inc.

1st Theme — A30

2nd Theme — A31

3rd Theme — A32

4th Theme — A33

ARENSKY, Anton (1861-1906)

Suite No. 1, Op. 15,
2 Pfts.
Copyright by the Oxford
University Press
Reproduced by permission.

I. Romance
1st Theme — A34

2nd Theme — A35

II. Valse
1st Theme — A36

Trio in D Minor, Op. 32, Vn., Pft., & Vcl.
By permission of International Music Co.

2nd Theme — A37

1st Movement 1st Theme — A38

1st Movement 2nd Theme — A39

2nd Movement 1st Theme — A40

2nd Movement 2nd Theme — A41

3rd Movement (Elégie) 1st Theme — A42

3rd Movement 2nd Theme — A43

4th Movement 1st Theme — A44

4th Movement 2nd Theme — A45

ATTERBERG, Kurt (1887-)

Symphony No. 6, in C, Op. 31
By permission of Associated Music Publishers, Inc.

1st Movement 1st Theme — A46

1st Movement 2nd Theme — A47

1st Movement 3rd Theme — A48

2nd Movement 1st Theme — A49

2nd Movement 2nd Theme — A50

3rd Movement 1st Theme — A51

3rd Movement 2nd Theme — A52

AUBER, Daniel François (1782-1871)

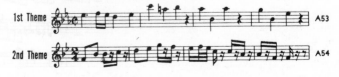

Le Cheval de Bronze Overture

1st Theme — A53

2nd Theme — A54

3rd Theme — A55

Le Domino Noir
Overture — 1st Theme — A56

2nd Theme — A57

3rd Theme — A58

4th Theme — A59

Fra Diavolo
Overture — 1st Theme — A60

2nd Theme — A61

3rd Theme — A62

La Muette De Portici
Overture — 1st Theme — A63

2nd Theme — A64

AUBERT, Louis (1877-1968)

Habañera, Orch. — 1st Theme — A65
Permission for reprint granted
by Durand & Cie, Paris.
Elkan-Vogel Co., Inc. Philadelphia,
Copyright Owners — 2nd Theme — A66

Suite Breve, Op. 6, Orch.
I. Menuet — 1st Theme — A67
Permission for reprint granted
by Durand & Cie, Paris.
Elkan-Vogel Co., Inc.
Philadelphia, Copyright Owners, — 2nd Theme — A68

II. Berceuse — A69

III. Air de Ballet — 1st Theme — A70

2nd Theme — A71

3rd Theme — A72

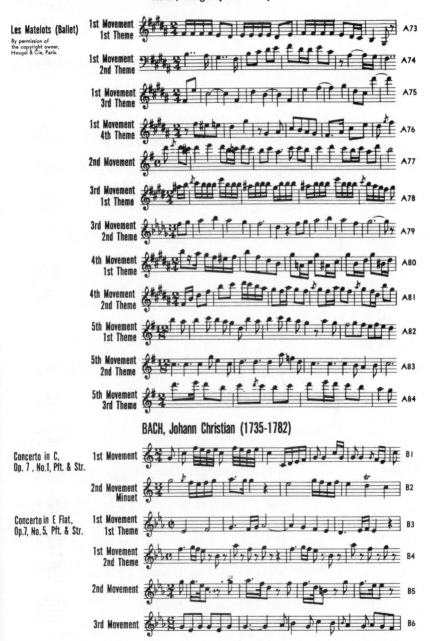

AURIC, Georges (1899-)

Les Matelots (Ballet)
By permission of
the copyright owner,
Heugel & Cie, Paris.

1st Movement 1st Theme — A73
1st Movement 2nd Theme — A74
1st Movement 3rd Theme — A75
1st Movement 4th Theme — A76
2nd Movement — A77
3rd Movement 1st Theme — A78
3rd Movement 2nd Theme — A79
4th Movement 1st Theme — A80
4th Movement 2nd Theme — A81
5th Movement 1st Theme — A82
5th Movement 2nd Theme — A83
5th Movement 3rd Theme — A84

BACH, Johann Christian (1735-1782)

Concerto in C,
Op. 7 , No.1, Pft. & Str.

1st Movement — B1
2nd Movement Minuet — B2

Concerto in E Flat,
Op.7, No.5, Pft. & Str.

1st Movement 1st Theme — B3
1st Movement 2nd Theme — B4
2nd Movement — B5
3rd Movement — B6

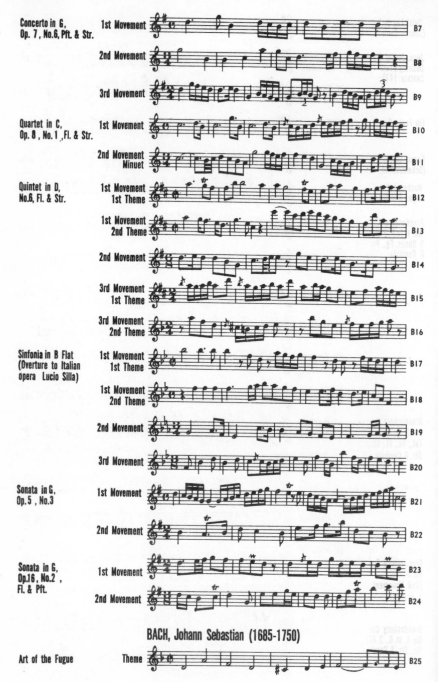

Concerto in G,
Op. 7, No.6, Pft. & Str.   1st Movement   B7

2nd Movement   B8

3rd Movement   B9

Quartet in C,
Op. 8 , No.1 , Fl. & Str.   1st Movement   B10

2nd Movement
Minuet   B11

Quintet in D,
No.6, Fl. & Str.   1st Movement
1st Theme   B12

1st Movement
2nd Theme   B13

2nd Movement   B14

3rd Movement
1st Theme   B15

3rd Movement
2nd Theme   B16

Sinfonia in B Flat
(Overture to Italian
opera Lucio Silla)   1st Movement
1st Theme   B17

1st Movement
2nd Theme   B18

2nd Movement   B19

3rd Movement   B20

Sonata in G,
Op.5 , No.3   1st Movement   B21

2nd Movement   B22

Sonata in G,
Op.16, No.2 ,
Fl. & Pft.   1st Movement   B23

2nd Movement   B24

BACH, Johann Sebastian (1685-1750)

Art of the Fugue   Theme   B25

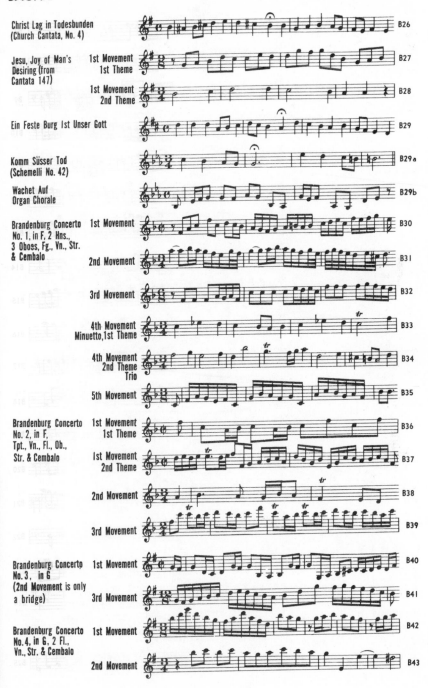

Christ Lag in Todesbunden
(Church Cantata, No. 4)　　　　　　　　　　　　　　　　　　B26

Jesu, Joy of Man's　1st Movement　　　　　　　　　　　　B27
Desiring (from　　1st Theme
Cantata 147)

　　　　　　　　1st Movement　　　　　　　　　　　　B28
　　　　　　　　2nd Theme

Ein Feste Burg Ist Unser Gott　　　　　　　　　　　　　B29

Komm Süsser Tod
(Schemelli No. 42)　　　　　　　　　　　　　　　　　　B29a

Wachet Auf
Organ Chorale　　　　　　　　　　　　　　　　　　　B29b

Brandenburg Concerto　1st Movement　　　　　　　　　B30
No. 1, in F, 2 Hns.,
3 Oboes, Fg., Vn., Str.
& Cembalo　　　　2nd Movement　　　　　　　　　　B31

　　　　　　　　3rd Movement　　　　　　　　　　　B32

　　　　　　　　4th Movement　　　　　　　　　　　B33
　　　　Minuetto,1st Theme

　　　　　　　　4th Movement　　　　　　　　　　　B34
　　　　　　　　2nd Theme
　　　　　　　　　Trio
　　　　　　　　5th Movement　　　　　　　　　　　B35

Brandenburg Concerto　1st Movement　　　　　　　　　B36
No. 2, in F,　　　1st Theme
Tpt., Vn., Fl., Ob.,
Str. & Cembalo　　1st Movement　　　　　　　　　　B37
　　　　　　　　2nd Theme

　　　　　　　　2nd Movement　　　　　　　　　　B38

　　　　　　　　3rd Movement　　　　　　　　　　B39

Brandenburg Concerto　1st Movement　　　　　　　　B40
No. 3, in G
(2nd Movement is only
a bridge)　　　　3rd Movement　　　　　　　　　　B41

Brandenburg Concerto　1st Movement　　　　　　　　B42
No. 4, in G, 2 Fl.,
Vn., Str. & Cembalo
　　　　　　　　2nd Movement　　　　　　　　　　B43

3rd Movement B44

Brandenburg Concerto
No. 5 , in D
Fl., Vn., Str. & Cembalo

1st Movement B45

2nd Movement B46

3rd Movement B47

Brandenburg Concerto
No.6 in B Flat, Viola
Solos & Strings

1st Movement B48

2nd Movement B49

3rd Movement B50

Concerto No. 8 ,
in A Minor, Fl., Vn.,
Pft. & Orch.

1st Movement B51

2nd Movement B52

3rd Movement B53

Concerto No. 1, in
D Minor, Pft. & Orch.

1st Movement B54

2nd Movement B55

3rd Movement B56

Concerto No.2 , in
D, Pft. & Orch.

1st Movement B57

2nd Movement B58

3rd Movement B59

Concerto No. 4 , in
A, Pft. & Orch.

1st Movement B60

2nd Movement B61

Concerto No. 5 , in
F Minor, Pft. & Orch.

1st Movement B62

2nd Movement B63

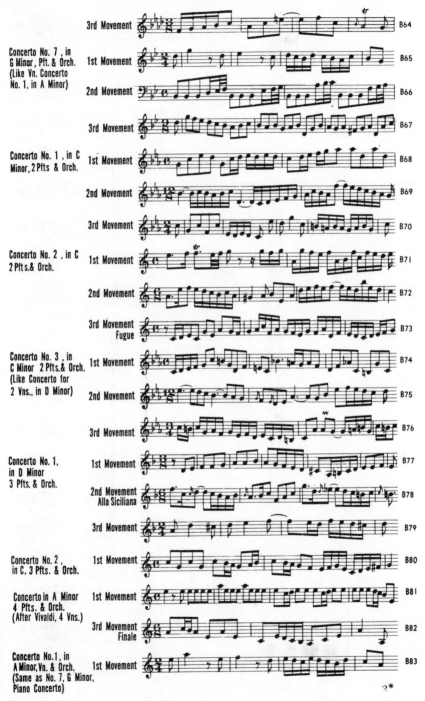

3rd Movement — B64

Concerto No. 7 , in G Minor , Pft. & Orch. (Like Vn. Concerto No. 1, in A Minor) — 1st Movement — B65

2nd Movement — B66

3rd Movement — B67

Concerto No. 1 , in C Minor, 2 Pfts & Orch. — 1st Movement — B68

2nd Movement — B69

3rd Movement — B70

Concerto No. 2 , in C 2 Pfts.& Orch. — 1st Movement — B71

2nd Movement — B72

3rd Movement Fugue — B73

Concerto No. 3 , in C Minor 2 Pfts.& Orch. (Like Concerto for 2 Vns., in D Minor) — 1st Movement — B74

2nd Movement — B75

3rd Movement — B76

Concerto No. 1, in D Minor 3 Pfts. & Orch. — 1st Movement — B77

2nd Movement Alla Siciliana — B78

3rd Movement — B79

Concerto No. 2 , in C, 3 Pfts. & Orch. — 1st Movement — B80

Concerto in A Minor 4 Pfts. & Orch. (After Vivaldi, 4 Vns.) — 1st Movement — B81

3rd Movement Finale — B82

Concerto No.1, in A Minor,Vn. & Orch. (Same as No. 7, G Minor, Piano Concerto) — 1st Movement — B83

2*

* For Fugue in G Minor, Organ, B 99 a, see Page 526

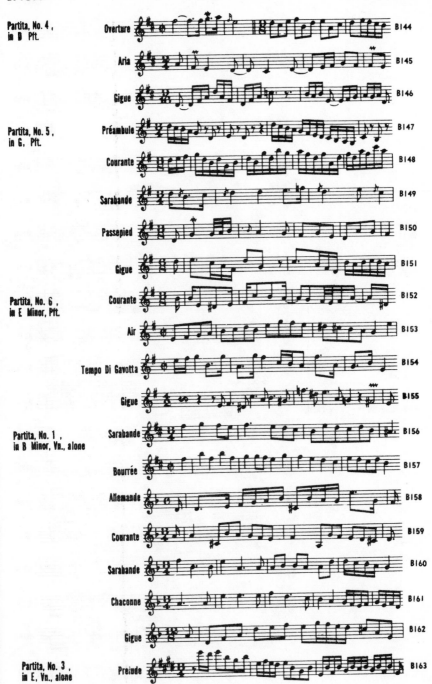

Partita, No. 4,
in B Pft.

Overture — B144

Aria — B145

Gigue — B146

Partita, No. 5,
in G, Pft.

Préambule — B147

Courante — B148

Sarabande — B149

Passepied — B150

Gigue — B151

Partita, No. 6,
in E Minor, Pft.

Courante — B152

Air — B153

Tempo Di Gavotta — B154

Gigue — B155

Partita, No. 1,
in B Minor, Vn., alone

Sarabande — B156

Bourrée — B157

Allemande — B158

Courante — B159

Sarabande — B160

Chaconne — B161

Gigue — B162

Partita, No. 3,
in E, Vn., alone

Prelude — B163

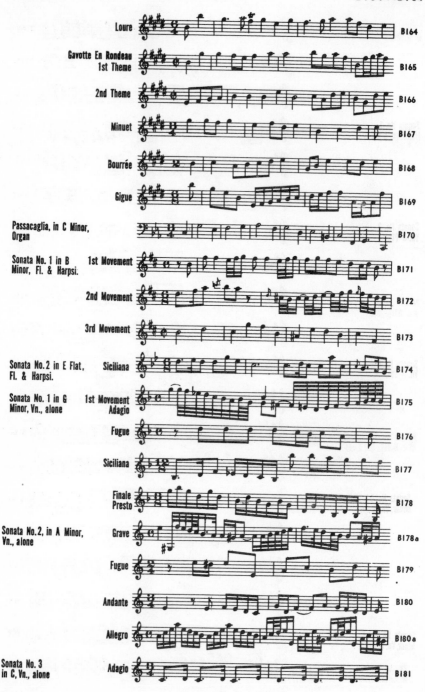

Loure   B164

Gavotte En Rondeau
1st Theme   B165

2nd Theme   B166

Minuet   B167

Bourrée   B168

Gigue   B169

Passacaglia, in C Minor,
Organ   B170

Sonata No. 1 in B   1st Movement   B171
Minor, Fl. & Harpsi.

                         2nd Movement   B172

                         3rd Movement   B173

Sonata No. 2 in E Flat, Siciliana   B174
Fl. & Harpsi.

Sonata No. 1 in G   1st Movement   B175
Minor, Vn., alone   Adagio

                         Fugue   B176

                         Siciliana   B177

                         Finale   B178
                         Presto

Sonata No. 2, in A Minor, Grave   B178a
Vn., alone

                         Fugue   B179

                         Andante   B180

                         Allegro   B180a

Sonata No. 3   Adagio   B181
in C, Vn., alone

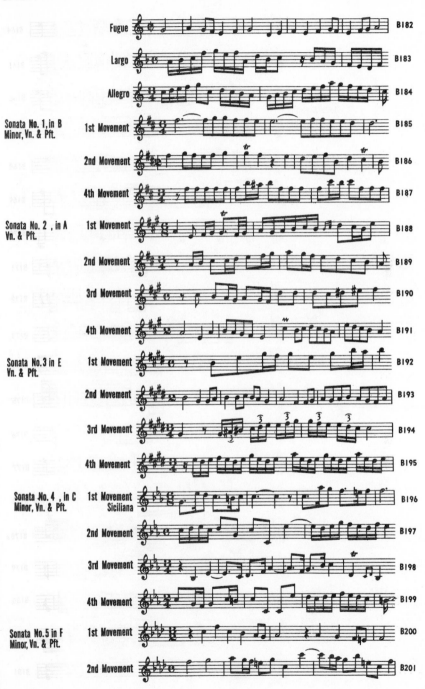

Fugue   B182
Largo   B183
Allegro   B184

Sonata No. 1, in B Minor, Vn. & Pft.
1st Movement   B185
2nd Movement   B186
4th Movement   B187

Sonata No. 2, in A Vn. & Pft.
1st Movement   B188
2nd Movement   B189
3rd Movement   B190
4th Movement   B191

Sonata No. 3 in E Vn. & Pft.
1st Movement   B192
2nd Movement   B193
3rd Movement   B194
4th Movement   B195

Sonata No. 4, in C Minor, Vn. & Pft.
1st Movement Siciliana   B196
2nd Movement   B197
3rd Movement   B198
4th Movement   B199

Sonata No. 5 in F Minor, Vn. & Pft.
1st Movement   B200
2nd Movement   B201

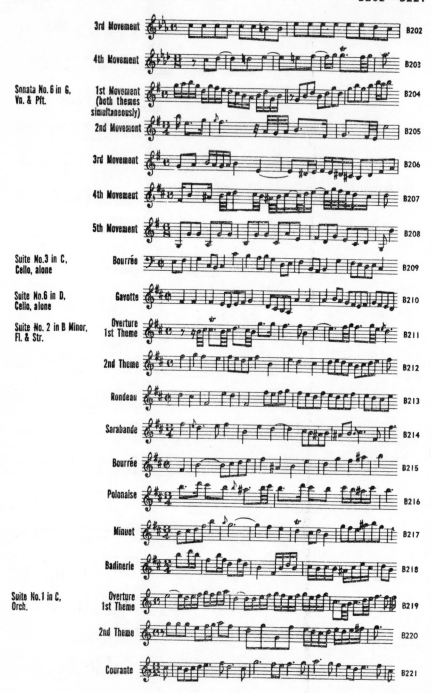

	3rd Movement	B202
	4th Movement	B203
Sonata No. 6 in G, Vn. & Pft.	1st Movement (both themes simultaneously)	B204
	2nd Movement	B205
	3rd Movement	B206
	4th Movement	B207
	5th Movement	B208
Suite No.3 in C, Cello, alone	Bourrée	B209
Suite No.6 in D, Cello, alone	Gavotte	B210
Suite No. 2 in B Minor, Fl. & Str.	Overture 1st Theme	B211
	2nd Theme	B212
	Rondeau	B213
	Sarabande	B214
	Bourrée	B215
	Polonaise	B216
	Minuet	B217
	Badinerie	B218
Suite No.1 in C, Orch.	Overture 1st Theme	B219
	2nd Theme	B220
	Courante	B221

Gavotte — B222
Forlane — B223
Minuet — B224
Bourrée — B225
Passepied — B226

Suite No.3 in D, Orch.
Overture 1st Theme — B227
2nd Theme — B228

"Air for the G String"
Air — B229

Gavotte 1st Theme — B230
2nd Theme — B231
Bourrée — B232
Gigue — B233

English Suite, No. 1, in A, Pft.
Sarabande — B234
Bourrée 1st Theme — B235
2nd Theme — B236
Gigue — B237

English Suite, No.2, in A Minor, Pft.
Prelude — B238
Allemande — B239
Courante — B240
Sarabande — B241

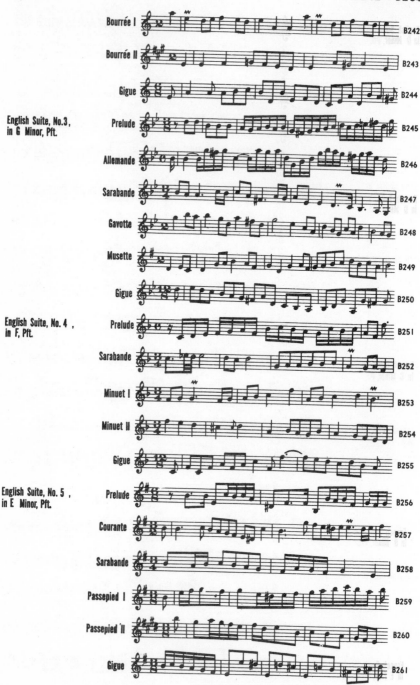

Bourrée I — B242

Bourrée II — B243

Gigue — B244

English Suite, No.3, in G Minor, Pft.

Prelude — B245

Allemande — B246

Sarabande — B247

Gavotte — B248

Musette — B249

Gigue — B250

English Suite, No. 4, in F, Pft.

Prelude — B251

Sarabande — B252

Minuet I — B253

Minuet II — B254

Gigue — B255

English Suite, No. 5, in E Minor, Pft.

Prelude — B256

Courante — B257

Sarabande — B258

Passepied I — B259

Passepied II — B260

Gigue — B261

English Suite, No. 6, in D Minor, Pft. — Courante — B262

Sarabande — B263

Gavotte I — B264

Gavotte II — B265

Gigue — B266

French Suite, No. 1, in D Minor, Pft. — Courante — B267

Sarabande — B268

Minuet I — B269

Minuet II — B270

Gigue — B271

French Suite, No. 2, in C Minor, Pft. — Courante — B272

Sarabande — B273

Air — B274

Minuet — B275

Gigue — B276

French Suite, No. 3, in B Minor, Pft. — Allemande — B277

Sarabande — B278

Minuetto — B279

Anglaise — B280

French Suite, No. 4, in E Flat, Pft. — Sarabande — B281

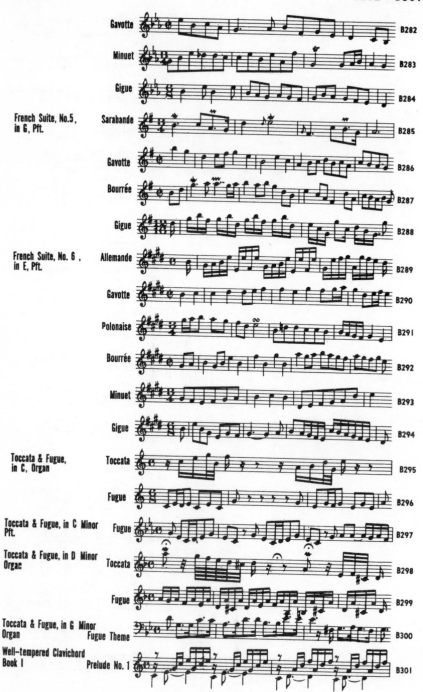

Gavotte — B282

Minuet — B283

Gigue — B284

French Suite, No.5, in G, Pft. — Sarabande — B285

Gavotte — B286

Bourrée — B287

Gigue — B288

French Suite, No. 6, in E, Pft. — Allemande — B289

Gavotte — B290

Polonaise — B291

Bourrée — B292

Minuet — B293

Gigue — B294

Toccata & Fugue, in C, Organ — Toccata — B295

Fugue — B296

Toccata & Fugue, in C Minor Pft. — Fugue — B297

Toccata & Fugue, in D Minor Organ — Toccata — B298

Fugue — B299

Toccata & Fugue, in G Minor Organ — Fugue Theme — B300

Well-tempered Clavichord Book I — Prelude No. 1 — B301

Fugue No.1 — B302
Prelude No.2 — B303
Fugue No.2 — B304
Prelude No.3 — B305
Fugue No.3 — B306
Prelude No.4 — B307
Fugue No.4 — B308
Prelude No.5 — B309
Fugue No.5 — B310
Prelude No.6 — B311
Fugue No.6 — B312
Prelude No.7 — B313
Fugue No.7 — B314
Prelude No.8 — B315
Fugue No.8 — B316
Prelude No.9 — B317
Fugue No.9 — B318
Prelude No.10 — B319
Fugue No.10 — B320
Prelude No.11 — B321

Fugue No. 11 — B322
Prelude No. 12 — B323
Fugue No. 12 — B324
Prelude No. 13 — B325
Fugue No. 13 — B326
Prelude No. 14 — B327
Fugue No. 14 — B328
Prelude No. 15 — B329
Fugue No. 15 — B330
Prelude No. 16 — B331
Fugue No. 16 — B332
Prelude No. 17 — B333
Fugue No. 17 — B334
Prelude No. 18 — B335
Fugue No. 18 — B336
Prelude No. 19 — B337
Fugue No. 19 — B338
Prelude No. 20 — B339
Fugue No. 20 — B340
Prelude No. 21 — B341

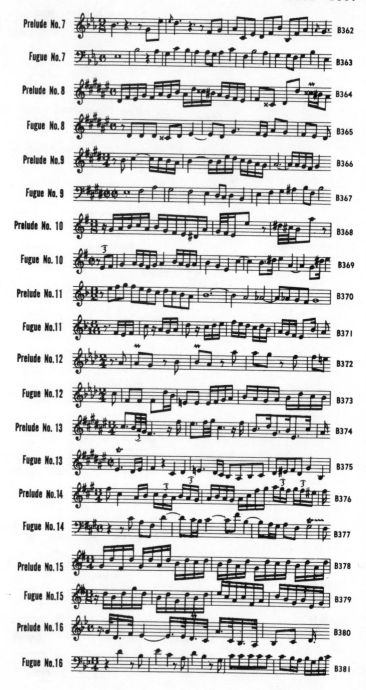

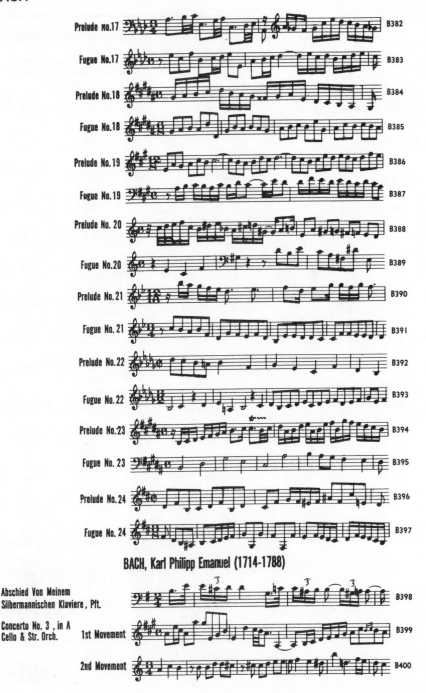

Prelude No.17   B382

Fugue No.17   B383

Prelude No.18   B384

Fugue No.18   B385

Prelude No.19   B386

Fugue No.19   B387

Prelude No.20   B388

Fugue No.20   B389

Prelude No.21   B390

Fugue No.21   B391

Prelude No.22   B392

Fugue No.22   B393

Prelude No.23   B394

Fugue No.23   B395

Prelude No.24   B396

Fugue No.24   B397

BACH, Karl Philipp Emanuel (1714-1788)

Abschied Von Meinem
Silbermannischen Klaviere, Pft.   B398

Concerto No. 3 , in A
Cello & Str. Orch.   1st Movement   B399

2nd Movement   B400

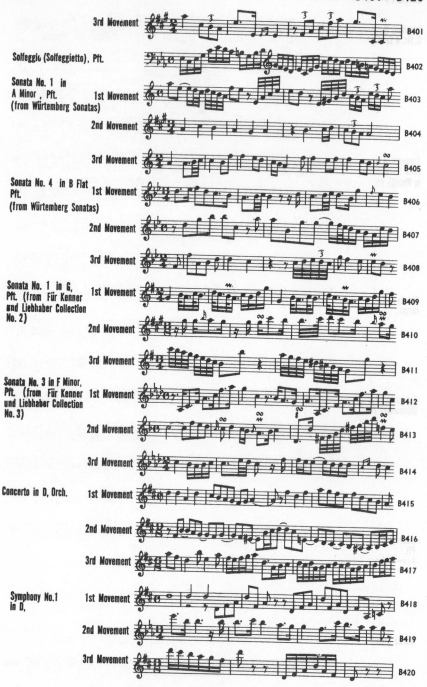

3rd Movement — B401

Solfeggio (Solfeggietto), Pft. — B402

Sonata No. 1 in A Minor, Pft. (from Würtemberg Sonatas) — 1st Movement — B403

2nd Movement — B404

3rd Movement — B405

Sonata No. 4 in B Flat Pft. (from Würtemberg Sonatas) — 1st Movement — B406

2nd Movement — B407

3rd Movement — B408

Sonata No. 1 in G, Pft. (from Für Kenner und Liebhaber Collection No. 2) — 1st Movement — B409

2nd Movement — B410

3rd Movement — B411

Sonata No. 3 in F Minor, Pft. (from Für Kenner und Liebhaber Collection No. 3) — 1st Movement — B412

2nd Movement — B413

3rd Movement — B414

Concerto in D, Orch. — 1st Movement — B415

2nd Movement — B416

3rd Movement — B417

Symphony No.1 in D, — 1st Movement — B418

2nd Movement — B419

3rd Movement — B420

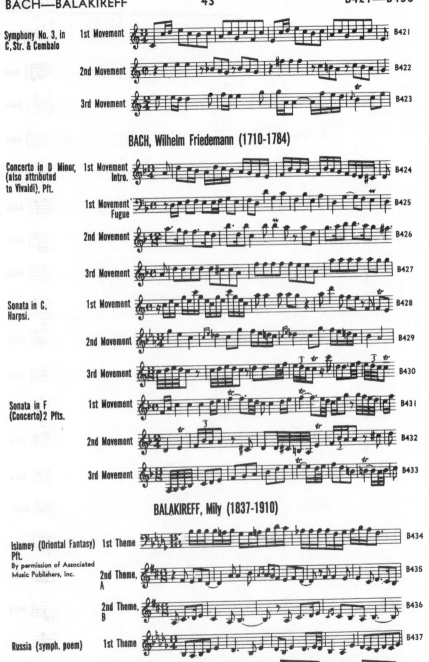

Symphony No. 3, in
C, Str. & Cembalo — 1st Movement — B421

2nd Movement — B422

3rd Movement — B423

BACH, Wilhelm Friedemann (1710-1784)

Concerto in D Minor,
(also attributed
to Vivaldi), Pft. — 1st Movement Intro. — B424

1st Movement Fugue — B425

2nd Movement — B426

3rd Movement — B427

Sonata in C,
Harpsi. — 1st Movement — B428

2nd Movement — B429

3rd Movement — B430

Sonata in F
(Concerto) 2 Pfts. — 1st Movement — B431

2nd Movement — B432

3rd Movement — B433

BALAKIREFF, Mily (1837-1910)

Islamey (Oriental Fantasy)
Pft.
By permission of Associated
Music Publishers, Inc. — 1st Theme — B434

2nd Theme, A — B435

2nd Theme, B — B436

Russia (symph. poem) — 1st Theme — B437

2nd Theme — B438

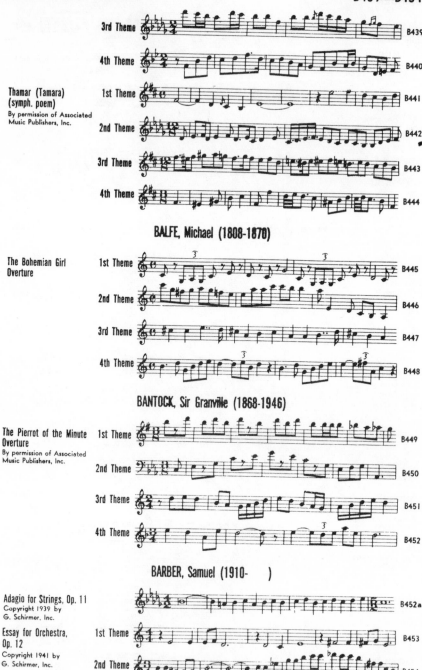

3rd Theme — B439

4th Theme — B440

Thamar (Tamara)
(symph. poem)
By permission of Associated
Music Publishers, Inc.

1st Theme — B441

2nd Theme — B442

3rd Theme — B443

4th Theme — B444

BALFE, Michael (1808-1870)

The Bohemian Girl
Overture

1st Theme — B445

2nd Theme — B446

3rd Theme — B447

4th Theme — B448

BANTOCK, Sir Granville (1868-1946)

The Pierrot of the Minute
Overture
By permission of Associated
Music Publishers, Inc.

1st Theme — B449

2nd Theme — B450

3rd Theme — B451

4th Theme — B452

BARBER, Samuel (1910-   )

Adagio for Strings, Op. 11
Copyright 1939 by
G. Schirmer, Inc.

— B452a

Essay for Orchestra,
Op. 12
Copyright 1941 by
G. Schirmer, Inc.

1st Theme — B453

2nd Theme — B454

First Symphony Op. 9
Copyright 1943 by G. Schirmer, Inc.

1st Theme — B454a
2nd Theme — B454b
3rd Theme — B454c
4th Theme — B454d
5th Theme — B454e
6th Theme — B454f
7th Theme — B454g

The School for Scandal Overture
Copyright 1941 by G. Schirmer, Inc.

1st Theme — B455
2nd Theme — B456

BARTÓK, Béla (1881-1945)

Allegro Barbaro, Pft.
By permission of the copyright owner, Boosey and Hawkes, Inc.

1st Theme — B457
2nd Theme — B458

Bagatelle, Op.2, Pft. — B459

Burlesque (A Bit Drunk) Op.8c, No.2 — B460

Concerto for Vn. & Orch.
By permission of the copyright owner, Boosey and Hawkes, Inc.

1st Movement 1st Theme — B461
1st Movement 2nd Theme — B462
2nd Movement — B463
3rd Movement 1st Theme — B464
3rd Movement 2nd Theme — B465

Contrasts, Vn.. Cl. & Pft.
By permission of the copyright owner, Boosey and Hawkes, Inc.

1st Movement 1st Theme Recruiting Dance — B466

Hungarian Folk Songs
Ungarische Volksweisen
(Arranged by Szigeti),
Vn. & Pft.
By permission of the
copyright owner, Boosey
and Hawkes, Inc.

Hungarian Sketches, No. 1
(Est a Szeklyeknel)

Quartet No. 1,
Op. 7, Str.
By permission of the
copyright owner, Boosey
and Hawkes, Inc.

1st Movement
2nd Theme — B467

2nd Movement
Relaxation — B468

3rd Movement
1st Theme
Fast Dance — B469

3rd Movement
2nd Theme — B470

3rd Movement
3rd Theme — B471

1st Movement
1st Theme — B472

1st Movement
2nd Theme — B473

1st Movement
3rd Theme — B474

2nd Movement
1st Theme — B475

2nd Movement
2nd Theme — B476

3rd Movement
1st Theme — B477

3rd Movement
2nd Theme — B478

1st Movement
An Evening
in the Village
1st Theme — B479

2nd Theme — B480

2nd Movement
Bear Dance — B481

1st Movement — B482

2nd Movement
Intro. — B483

2nd Movement
1st Theme — B484

2nd Movement
2nd Theme — B485

3rd Movement
Intro. — B486

Quartet No.2,
Op.17, Str.

3rd Movement 1st Theme — B487
3rd Movement 2nd Theme — B488
1st Movement — B489
2nd Movement Intro. — B490
2nd Movement 1st Theme — B491
2nd Movement 2nd Theme — B492
3rd Movement 1st Theme — B493
3rd Movement 2nd Theme — B494

Rhapsody No. 1
(Folk Dances), Vn. & Orch.

1st Movement 1st Theme — B495
1st Movement 2nd Theme — B496
2nd Movement 1st Theme — B497
2nd Movement 2nd Theme — B498

Rumanian Folk Dances
Pft.
By permission of the
copyright owner, Boosey
and Hawkes, Inc.

1st Movement — B499
2nd Movement — B500
3rd Movement — B501
4th Movement — B502
5th Movement — B503
6th Movement 1st Theme — B504
6th Movement 2nd Theme — B505
6th Movement 3rd Theme — B506

BAX, Sir Arnold Trevor (1883-1953)

Fantasy-Sonata, Viola & Harp
Copyright 1922 Murdock, Murdock & Co., London. Carl Fischer, Inc., N. Y., Sole Agents for the U.S.A..

1st Movement 1st Theme — B507

1st Movement 2nd Theme — B508

2nd Movement — B509

3rd Movement — B510

4th Movement — B511

Mediterranean, Orch.
Copyright 1923 Murdock, Murdock & Co., London. Carl Fischer. Inc.. N. Y.. Sole Agents for the U. S. A.

B512

Overture to a Picaresque Comedy
Copyright 1934 Murdock, Murdbck & Co., London. Carl Fischer, Inc., N. Y., Sole Agents for the U. S. A.

1st Theme — B513

2nd Theme — B514

3rd Theme — B515

Sonata, Viola & Pft.
Copyright 1923 Murdock, Murdock & Co., London. Carl Fischer, Inc., N. Y., Sole Agents for the U.S.A.

1st Movement 1st Theme — B516

1st Movement 2nd Theme — B517

2nd Movement 1st Theme — B518

2nd Movement 2nd Theme — B519

3rd Movement — B520

BEETHOVEN, Ludwig Van (1770-1827)

Andante Favori, F

B521

Concerto No. 1, in C Op.15, Pft.

1st Movement 1st Theme — B522

1st Movement 2nd Theme — B523

2nd Movement 1st Theme — B524

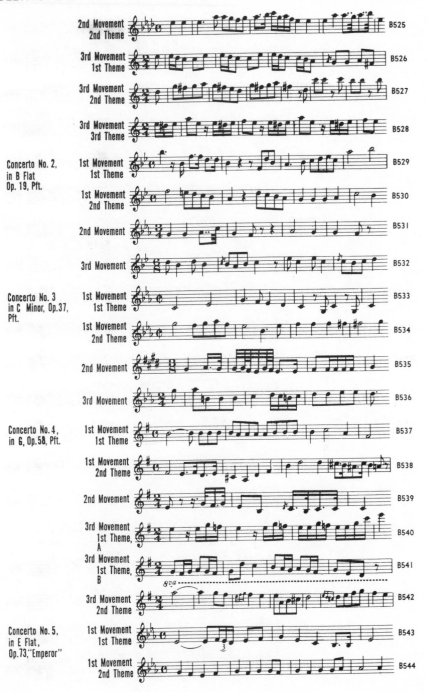

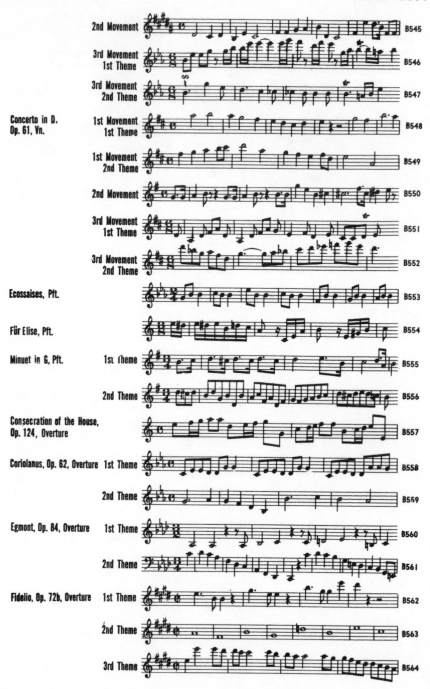

	2nd Movement	B545
	3rd Movement 1st Theme	B546
	3rd Movement 2nd Theme	B547
Concerto in D, Op. 61, Vn.	1st Movement 1st Theme	B548
	1st Movement 2nd Theme	B549
	2nd Movement	B550
	3rd Movement 1st Theme	B551
	3rd Movement 2nd Theme	B552
Ecossaises, Pft.		B553
Für Elise, Pft.		B554
Minuet in G, Pft.	1st Theme	B555
	2nd Theme	B556
Consecration of the House, Op. 124, Overture		B557
Coriolanus, Op. 62, Overture	1st Theme	B558
	2nd Theme	B559
Egmont, Op. 84, Overture	1st Theme	B560
	2nd Theme	B561
Fidelio, Op. 72b, Overture	1st Theme	B562
	2nd Theme	B563
	3rd Theme	B564

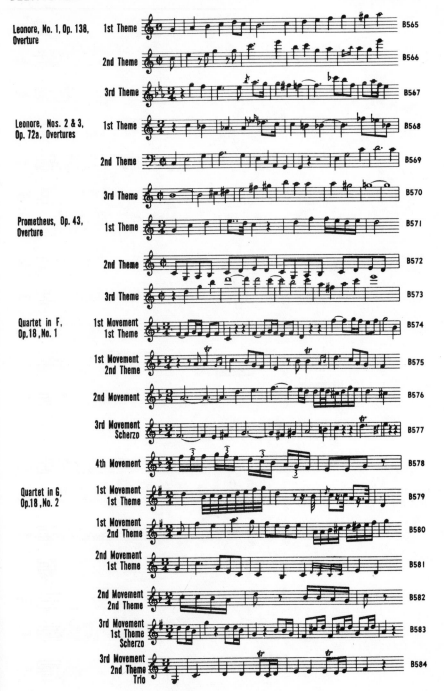

Leonore, No. 1, Op. 138, Overture — 1st Theme — B565
2nd Theme — B566
3rd Theme — B567

Leonore, Nos. 2 & 3, Op. 72a, Overtures — 1st Theme — B568
2nd Theme — B569
3rd Theme — B570

Prometheus, Op. 43, Overture — 1st Theme — B571
2nd Theme — B572
3rd Theme — B573

Quartet in F, Op.18, No. 1 — 1st Movement 1st Theme — B574
1st Movement 2nd Theme — B575
2nd Movement — B576
3rd Movement Scherzo — B577
4th Movement — B578

Quartet in G, Op.18, No. 2 — 1st Movement 1st Theme — B579
1st Movement 2nd Theme — B580
2nd Movement 1st Theme — B581
2nd Movement 2nd Theme — B582
3rd Movement 1st Theme Scherzo — B583
3rd Movement 2nd Theme Trio — B584

4th Movement 1st Theme — B585
4th Movement 2nd Theme — B586
Quartet in D, Op.18, No. 3 — 1st Movement — B587
2nd Movement — B588
3rd Movement — B589
4th Movement 1st Theme — B590
4th Movement 2nd Theme — B591
Quartet in C Minor, Op.18, No. 4 — 1st Movement 1st Theme — B592
1st Movement 2nd Theme — B593
2nd Movement 1st Theme — B594
2nd Movement 2nd Theme — B595
3rd Movement Minuet — B596
4th Movement 1st Theme — B597
4th Movement 2nd Theme — B598
Quartet in A, Op.18, No.5 — 1st Movement 1st Theme — B599
1st Movement 2nd Theme — B600
2nd Movement Minuet — B601
3rd Movement — B602
4th Movement 1st Theme — B602 a
4th Movement 2nd Theme — B603

Quartet in E Flat, Op.74, "Harp" — 1st Movement Intro. — B624

1st Movement — B625

2nd Movement — B626

3rd Movement — B627

4th Movement — B628

Quartet in F Minor, Op.95, — 1st Movement — B629

2nd Movement 1st Theme — B630

2nd Movement 2nd Theme — B631

3rd Movement — B632

4th Movement Intro. — B633

4th Movement — B634

Quartet in E Flat, Op.127 — 1st Movement 1st Theme — B635

1st Movement 2nd Theme — B636

2nd Movement — B637

3rd Movement — B638

4th Movement 1st Theme — B639

4th Movement 2nd Theme — B640

Quartet in B Flat, Op.130 "Scherzoso" — 1st Movement Intro. — B641

1st Movement — B642

2nd Movement — B643

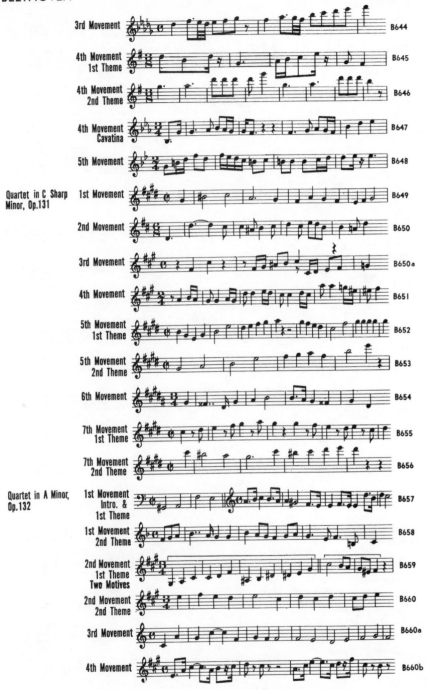

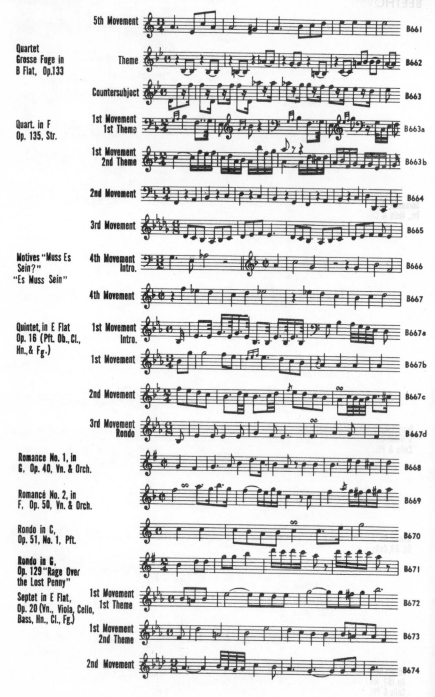

3rd Movement	B675
4th Movement	B676
5th Movement	B677
6th Movement	B678
7th Movement	B679
Serenade, Op. 8, Vn., Viola & Cello — 1st Movement	B679a
2nd Movement	B679b
3rd Movement Minuet	B679c
4th Movement 1st Theme	B679d
4th Movement 2nd Theme	B679e
5th Movement Alla Polacca	B679f
6th Movement	B679g
Sonata No. 2, in G Minor, Op. 5, No. 2, Cello & Pft. — 1st Movement Intro.	B679h
1st Movement	B680
2nd Movement	B680a
Sonata No. 3 in A, Op. 69, Cello & Pft. — 1st Movement	B681
2nd Movement 1st Theme	B682
2nd Movement 2nd Theme	B683
3rd Movement	B684
Sonata No. 4, in C, Op. 102, No. 1, Cello & Pft. — 1st Movement Intro.	B685

3*

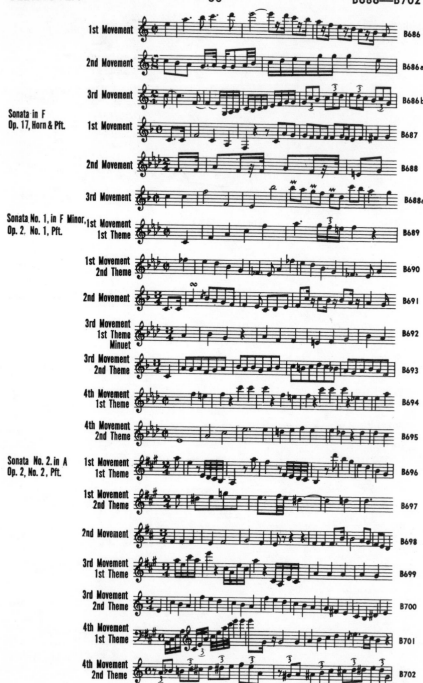

1st Movement — B686
2nd Movement — B686a
3rd Movement — B686b
Sonata in F Op. 17, Horn & Pft. — 1st Movement — B687
2nd Movement — B688
3rd Movement — B688a
Sonata No. 1, in F Minor, Op. 2, No. 1, Pft. — 1st Movement 1st Theme — B689
1st Movement 2nd Theme — B690
2nd Movement — B691
3rd Movement 1st Theme Minuet — B692
3rd Movement 2nd Theme — B693
4th Movement 1st Theme — B694
4th Movement 2nd Theme — B695
Sonata No. 2. in A Op. 2, No. 2, Pft. — 1st Movement 1st Theme — B696
1st Movement 2nd Theme — B697
2nd Movement — B698
3rd Movement 1st Theme — B699
3rd Movement 2nd Theme — B700
4th Movement 1st Theme — B701
4th Movement 2nd Theme — B702

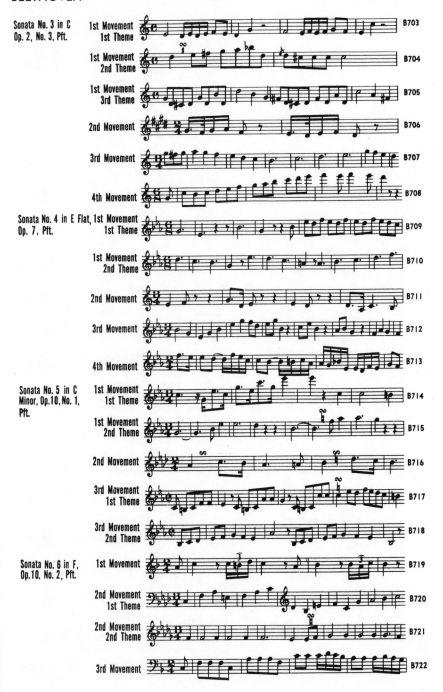

Sonata No. 3 in C
Op. 2, No. 3, Pft.

1st Movement / 1st Theme   B703

1st Movement / 2nd Theme   B704

1st Movement / 3rd Theme   B705

2nd Movement   B706

3rd Movement   B707

4th Movement   B708

Sonata No. 4 in E Flat,
Op. 7, Pft.

1st Movement / 1st Theme   B709

1st Movement / 2nd Theme   B710

2nd Movement   B711

3rd Movement   B712

4th Movement   B713

Sonata No. 5 in C
Minor, Op. 10, No. 1,
Pft.

1st Movement / 1st Theme   B714

1st Movement / 2nd Theme   B715

2nd Movement   B716

3rd Movement / 1st Theme   B717

3rd Movement / 2nd Theme   B718

Sonata No. 6 in F,
Op. 10, No. 2, Pft.

1st Movement   B719

2nd Movement / 1st Theme   B720

2nd Movement / 2nd Theme   B721

3rd Movement   B722

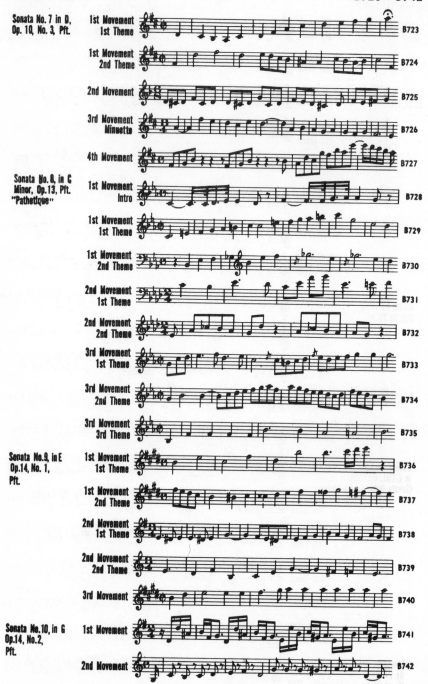

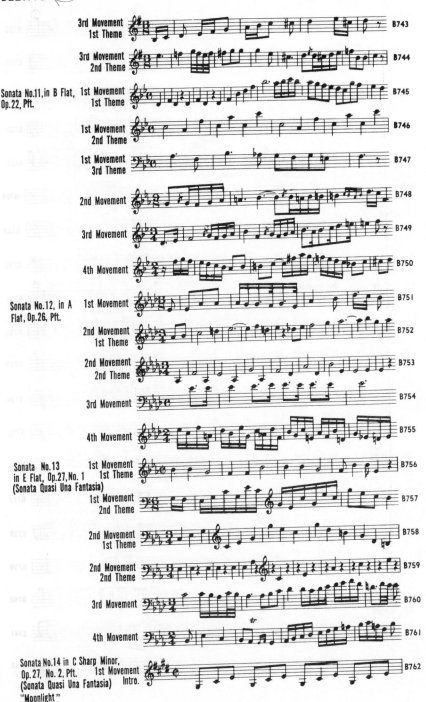

3rd Movement 1st Theme — B743

3rd Movement 2nd Theme — B744

Sonata No.11, in B Flat, Op.22, Pft. 1st Movement 1st Theme — B745

1st Movement 2nd Theme — B746

1st Movement 3rd Theme — B747

2nd Movement — B748

3rd Movement — B749

4th Movement — B750

Sonata No.12, in A Flat, Op.26, Pft. 1st Movement — B751

2nd Movement 1st Theme — B752

2nd Movement 2nd Theme — B753

3rd Movement — B754

4th Movement — B755

Sonata No.13 in E Flat, Op.27, No.1 (Sonata Quasi Una Fantasia) 1st Movement 1st Theme — B756

1st Movement 2nd Theme — B757

2nd Movement 1st Theme — B758

2nd Movement 2nd Theme — B759

3rd Movement — B760

4th Movement — B761

Sonata No.14 in C Sharp Minor, Op.27, No.2, Pft. (Sonata Quasi Una Fantasia) "Moonlight" 1st Movement Intro. — B762

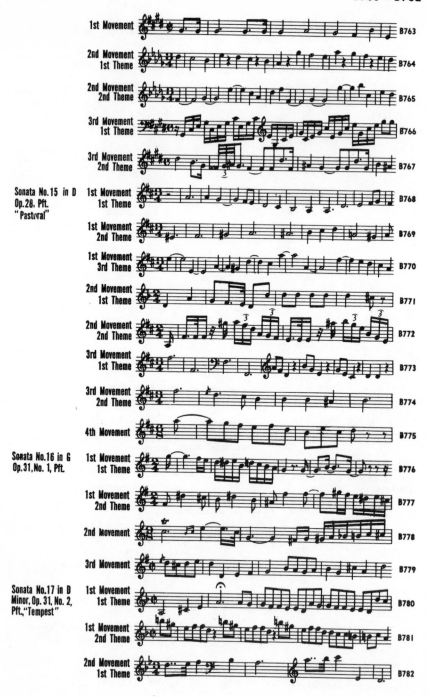

1st Movement — B763

2nd Movement
1st Theme — B764

2nd Movement
2nd Theme — B765

3rd Movement
1st Theme — B766

3rd Movement
2nd Theme — B767

Sonata No.15 in D
Op.28, Pft.
"Pastoral"

1st Movement
1st Theme — B768

1st Movement
2nd Theme — B769

1st Movement
3rd Theme — B770

2nd Movement
1st Theme — B771

2nd Movement
2nd Theme — B772

3rd Movement
1st Theme — B773

3rd Movement
2nd Theme — B774

4th Movement — B775

Sonata No.16 in G
Op.31,No. 1, Pft.

1st Movement
1st Theme — B776

1st Movement
2nd Theme — B777

2nd Movement — B778

3rd Movement — B779

Sonata No.17 in D
Minor, Op. 31, No. 2,
Pft.,"Tempest"

1st Movement
1st Theme — B780

1st Movement
2nd Theme — B781

2nd Movement
1st Theme — B782

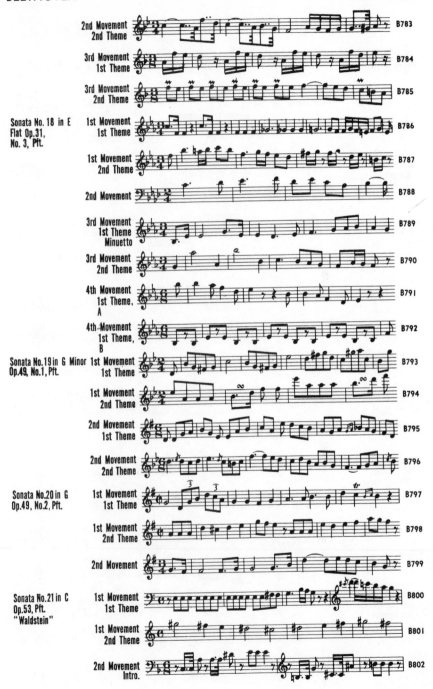

2nd Movement 2nd Theme	B783
3rd Movement 1st Theme	B784
3rd Movement 2nd Theme	B785
Sonata No. 18 in E Flat Op.31, No. 3, Pft. 1st Movement 1st Theme	B786
1st Movement 2nd Theme	B787
2nd Movement	B788
3rd Movement 1st Theme Minuetto	B789
3rd Movement 2nd Theme	B790
4th Movement 1st Theme, A	B791
4th Movement 1st Theme, B	B792
Sonata No.19 in G Minor Op.49, No.1, Pft. 1st Movement 1st Theme	B793
1st Movement 2nd Theme	B794
2nd Movement 1st Theme	B795
2nd Movement 2nd Theme	B796
Sonata No.20 in G Op.49, No.2, Pft. 1st Movement 1st Theme	B797
1st Movement 2nd Theme	B798
2nd Movement	B799
Sonata No.21 in C Op.53, Pft. "Waldstein" 1st Movement 1st Theme	B800
1st Movement 2nd Theme	B801
2nd Movement Intro.	B802

2nd Movement Rondo — B803

Sonata No. 22 in F Op. 54, Pft. — 1st Movement 1st Theme — B804

1st Movement 2nd Theme — B805

2nd Movement — B806

Sonata No. 23 in F Minor, Op. 57, Pft. "Appassionata" — 1st Movement 1st Theme — B807

1st Movement 2nd Theme — B808

1st Movement 3rd Theme — B809

2nd Movement — B810

3rd Movement 1st Theme — B811

3rd Movement 2nd Theme — B812

Sonata No. 24 in F Sharp, Op. 78, Pft. — 1st Movement 1st Theme — B813

1st Movement 2nd Theme — B814

2nd Movement — B815

Sonata No. 25, in G Op. 79, Pft. (Alla Tedesca) — 1st Movement — B816

2nd Movement 1st Theme — B817

2nd Movement 2nd Theme — B818

3rd Movement — B819

Sonata No. 26 in E Flat, Op. 81a, Pft. Les Adieux — 1st Movement Intro. — B820

1st Movement 1st Theme, A — B821

1st Movement 1st Theme, B — B822

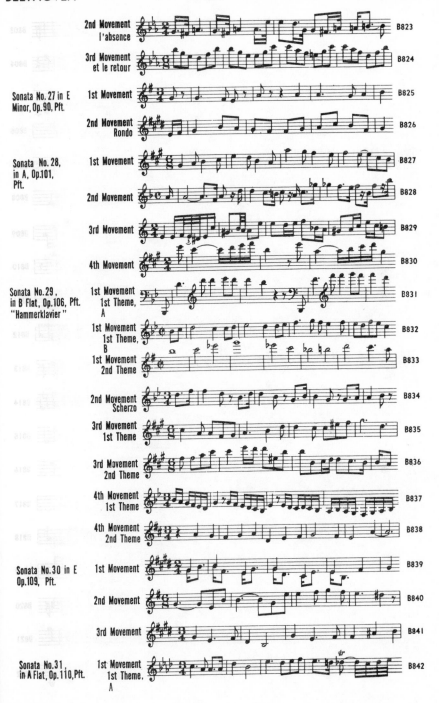

2nd Movement l'absence	B823
3rd Movement et le retour	B824
Sonata No. 27 in E Minor, Op. 90, Pft. — 1st Movement	B825
2nd Movement Rondo	B826
Sonata No. 28, in A, Op. 101, Pft. — 1st Movement	B827
2nd Movement	B828
3rd Movement	B829
4th Movement	B830
Sonata No. 29, in B Flat, Op. 106, Pft. "Hammerklavier" — 1st Movement 1st Theme, A	B831
1st Movement 1st Theme, B	B832
1st Movement 2nd Theme	B833
2nd Movement Scherzo	B834
3rd Movement 1st Theme	B835
3rd Movement 2nd Theme	B836
4th Movement 1st Theme	B837
4th Movement 2nd Theme	B838
Sonata No. 30 in E Op. 109, Pft. — 1st Movement	B839
2nd Movement	B840
3rd Movement	B841
Sonata No. 31, in A Flat, Op. 110, Pft. — 1st Movement 1st Theme, A	B842

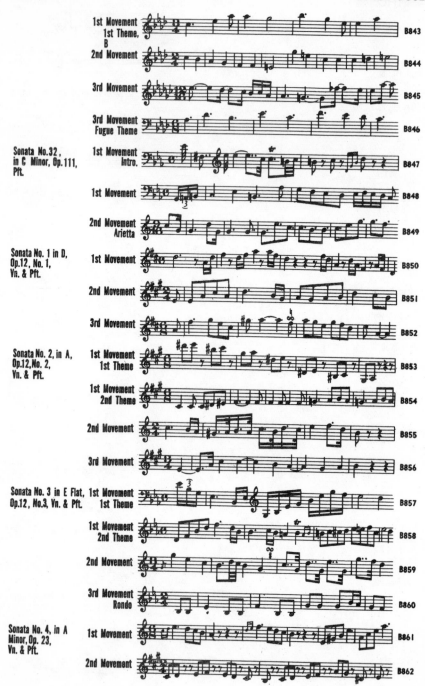

	1st Movement 1st Theme, B	B843
	2nd Movement	B844
	3rd Movement	B845
	3rd Movement Fugue Theme	B846
Sonata No.32, in C Minor, Op.111, Pft.	1st Movement Intro.	B847
	1st Movement	B848
	2nd Movement Arietta	B849
Sonata No. 1 in D, Op.12, No. 1, Vn. & Pft.	1st Movement	B850
	2nd Movement	B851
	3rd Movement	B852
Sonata No. 2, in A, Op.12, No. 2, Vn. & Pft.	1st Movement 1st Theme	B853
	1st Movement 2nd Theme	B854
	2nd Movement	B855
	3rd Movement	B856
Sonata No. 3 in E Flat, Op.12, No.3, Vn. & Pft.	1st Movement 1st Theme	B857
	1st Movement 2nd Theme	B858
	2nd Movement	B859
	3rd Movement Rondo	B860
Sonata No. 4, in A Minor, Op. 23, Vn. & Pft.	1st Movement	B861
	2nd Movement	B862

3rd Movement — B863

Sonata No. 5, Op. 24
Vn. & Pft., "Spring"

1st Movement — B864

2nd Movement — B865

3rd Movement
Scherzo — B866

4th Movement — B867

Sonata No. 6 , in A
Op. 30, No. 1,
Vn. & Pft.

1st Movement
1st Theme — B868

1st Movement
2nd Theme — B869

2nd Movement — B870

3rd Movement — B871

Sonata No. 7 in C
Minor, Op. 30, No. 2
Vn. & Pft.

1st Movement
1st Theme — B872

1st Movement
2nd Theme — B873

2nd Movement — B874

3rd Movement
1st Theme — B875

3rd Movement
2nd Theme — B876

4th Movement — B877

Sonata No. 8 in G
Op. 30, No. 3
Vn. & Pft.

1st Movement — B878

2nd Movement — B879

3rd Movement — B880

Sonata No. 9 in A, Op. 47,
Vn. & Pft.
"Kreutzer"

1st Movement
Intro. — B881

1st Movement — B882

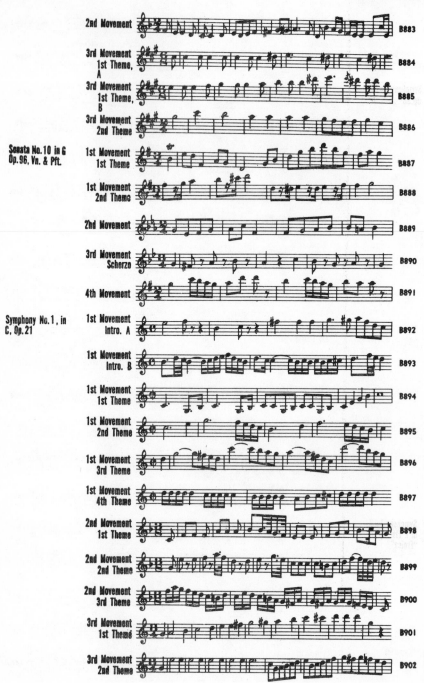

Sonata No. 10 in G Op. 96, Vn. & Pft.

Symphony No. 1, in C, Op. 21

2nd Movement — B883

3rd Movement 1st Theme, A — B884

3rd Movement 1st Theme, B — B885

3rd Movement 2nd Theme — B886

1st Movement 1st Theme — B887

1st Movement 2nd Theme — B888

2nd Movement — B889

3rd Movement Scherzo — B890

4th Movement — B891

1st Movement Intro. A — B892

1st Movement Intro. B — B893

1st Movement 1st Theme — B894

1st Movement 2nd Theme — B895

1st Movement 3rd Theme — B896

1st Movement 4th Theme — B897

2nd Movement 1st Theme — B898

2nd Movement 2nd Theme — B899

2nd Movement 3rd Theme — B900

3rd Movement 1st Theme — B901

3rd Movement 2nd Theme — B902

4th Movement 1st Theme — B903

4th Movement 2nd Theme — B904

Symphony No.2, in D Op.36 — 1st Movement Intro. — B905

1st Movement 1st Theme — B906

1st Movement 2nd Theme — B907

2nd Movement 1st Theme, A — B908

2nd Movement 1st Theme, B — B909

2nd Movement 2nd Theme — B910

2nd Movement 3rd Theme — B911

2nd Movement 4th Theme — B912

3rd Movement 1st Theme — B913

3rd Movement 2nd Theme — B914

4th Movement 1st Theme — B915

4th Movement 2nd Theme — B916

4th Movement 3rd Theme — B917

Symphony No.3, in E Flat, Op.55 "Eroica" — 1st Movement 1st Theme — B918

1st Movement 2nd Theme — B919

1st Movement 3rd Theme — B920

1st Movement 4th Theme — B921

1st Movement 5th Theme — B922

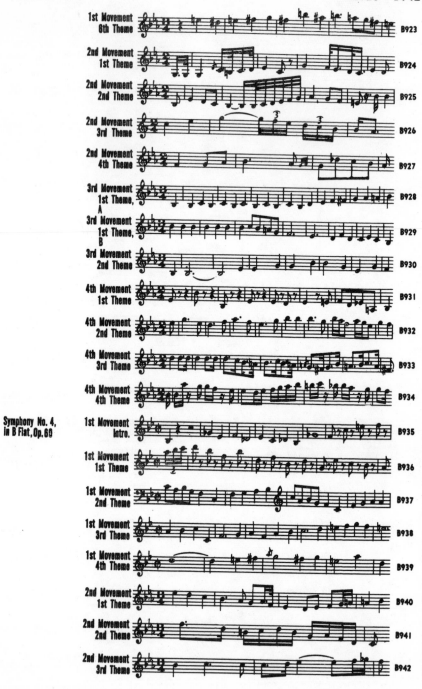

1st Movement / 6th Theme — B923
2nd Movement / 1st Theme — B924
2nd Movement / 2nd Theme — B925
2nd Movement / 3rd Theme — B926
2nd Movement / 4th Theme — B927
3rd Movement / 1st Theme, A — B928
3rd Movement / 1st Theme, B — B929
3rd Movement / 2nd Theme — B930
4th Movement / 1st Theme — B931
4th Movement / 2nd Theme — B932
4th Movement / 3rd Theme — B933
4th Movement / 4th Theme — B934

Symphony No. 4, In B Flat, Op. 60

1st Movement / Intro. — B935
1st Movement / 1st Theme — B936
1st Movement / 2nd Theme — B937
1st Movement / 3rd Theme — B938
1st Movement / 4th Theme — B939
2nd Movement / 1st Theme — B940
2nd Movement / 2nd Theme — B941
2nd Movement / 3rd Theme — B942

Symphony No. 5, in C
Minor, Op. 67
"Fate"

3rd Movement 1st Theme — B943
3rd Movement 2nd Theme — B944
4th Movement 1st Theme — B945
4th Movement 2nd Theme — B946
4th Movement 3rd Theme — B947
1st Movement 1st Theme, A — B948
1st Movement 1st Theme, B — B949
1st Movement 1st Theme, C — B950
1st Movement 2nd Theme — B951
1st Movement 3rd Theme — B952
1st Movement 4th Theme — B953
2nd Movement 1st Theme — B954
2nd Movement 2nd Theme — B955
2nd Movement Coda — B956
3rd Movement 1st Theme — B957
3rd Movement 2nd Theme — B958
3rd Movement 3rd Theme — B959
4th Movement 1st Theme — B960
4th Movement 2nd Theme — B961
4th Movement 3rd Theme — B962

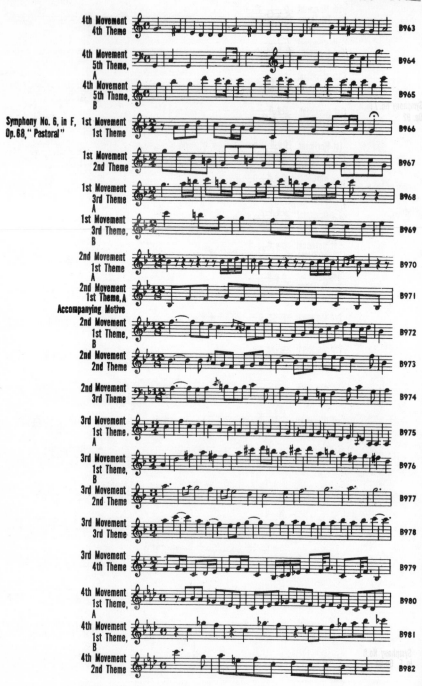

4th Movement
4th Theme — B963

4th Movement
5th Theme, A — B964

4th Movement
5th Theme, B — B965

Symphony No. 6, in F,
Op. 68," Pastoral"

1st Movement
1st Theme — B966

1st Movement
2nd Theme — B967

1st Movement
3rd Theme A — B968

1st Movement
3rd Theme, B — B969

2nd Movement
1st Theme A — B970

2nd Movement
1st Theme, A
Accompanying Motive — B971

2nd Movement
1st Theme, B — B972

2nd Movement
2nd Theme — B973

2nd Movement
3rd Theme — B974

3rd Movement
1st Theme, A — B975

3rd Movement
1st Theme, B — B976

3rd Movement
2nd Theme — B977

3rd Movement
3rd Theme — B978

3rd Movement
4th Theme — B979

4th Movement
1st Theme, A — B980

4th Movement
1st Theme, B — B981

4th Movement
2nd Theme — B982

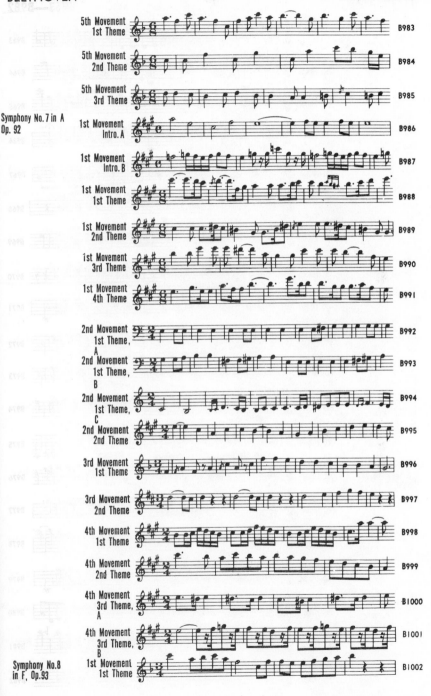

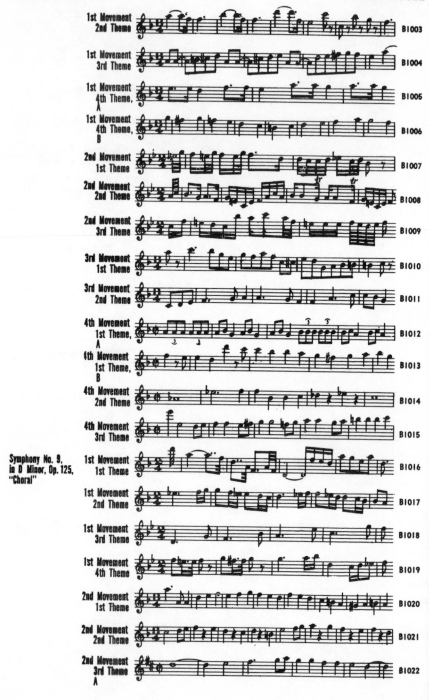

1st Movement 2nd Theme — B1003
1st Movement 3rd Theme — B1004
1st Movement 4th Theme, A — B1005
1st Movement 4th Theme, B — B1006
2nd Movement 1st Theme — B1007
2nd Movement 2nd Theme — B1008
2nd Movement 3rd Theme — B1009
3rd Movement 1st Theme — B1010
3rd Movement 2nd Theme — B1011
4th Movement 1st Theme, A — B1012
4th Movement 1st Theme, B — B1013
4th Movement 2nd Theme — B1014
4th Movement 3rd Theme — B1015

Symphony No. 9, in D Minor, Op. 125, "Choral"

1st Movement 1st Theme — B1016
1st Movement 2nd Theme — B1017
1st Movement 3rd Theme — B1018
1st Movement 4th Theme — B1019
2nd Movement 1st Theme — B1020
2nd Movement 2nd Theme — B1021
2nd Movement 3rd Theme A — B1022

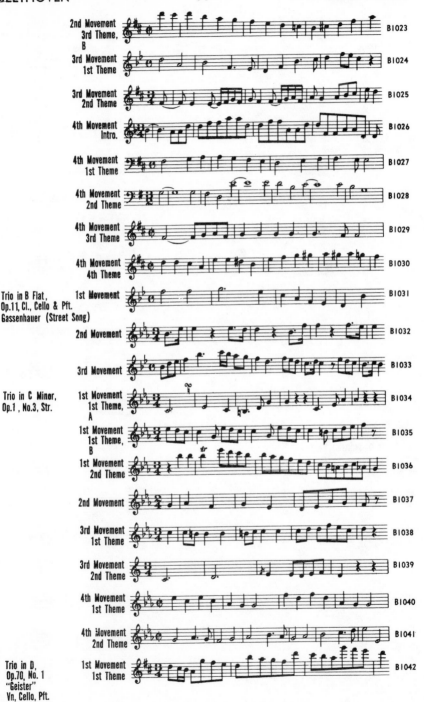

2nd Movement 3rd Theme, B	B1023
3rd Movement 1st Theme	B1024
3rd Movement 2nd Theme	B1025
4th Movement Intro.	B1026
4th Movement 1st Theme	B1027
4th Movement 2nd Theme	B1028
4th Movement 3rd Theme	B1029
4th Movement 4th Theme	B1030
Trio in B Flat, **Op.11, Cl., Cello & Pft.** **Gassenhauer (Street Song)** — 1st Movement	B1031
2nd Movement	B1032
3rd Movement	B1033
Trio in C Minor, **Op.1 , No.3, Str.** — 1st Movement 1st Theme, A	B1034
1st Movement 1st Theme, B	B1035
1st Movement 2nd Theme	B1036
2nd Movement	B1037
3rd Movement 1st Theme	B1038
3rd Movement 2nd Theme	B1039
4th Movement 1st Theme	B1040
4th Movement 2nd Theme	B1041
Trio in D, **Op.70, No. 1** **"Geister"** **Vn, Cello, Pft.** — 1st Movement 1st Theme	B1042

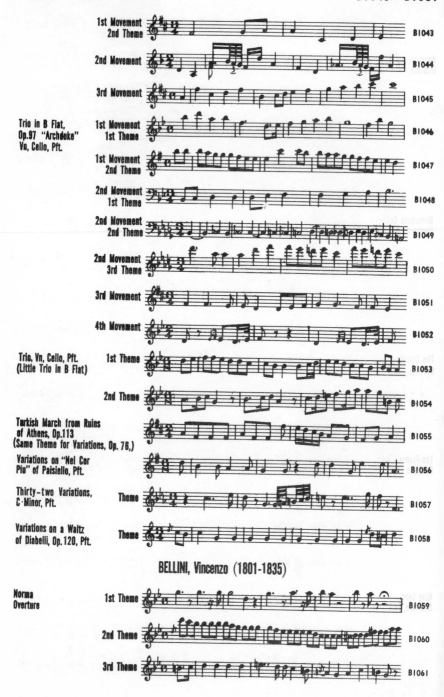

1st Movement
2nd Theme — B1043

2nd Movement — B1044

3rd Movement — B1045

Trio in B Flat,
Op.97 "Archduke"
Vn, Cello, Pft.

1st Movement
1st Theme — B1046

1st Movement
2nd Theme — B1047

2nd Movement
1st Theme — B1048

2nd Movement
2nd Theme — B1049

2nd Movement
3rd Theme — B1050

3rd Movement — B1051

4th Movement — B1052

Trio, Vn, Cello, Pft.
(Little Trio in B Flat)

1st Theme — B1053

2nd Theme — B1054

Turkish March from Ruins
of Athens, Op.113
(Same Theme for Variations, Op. 76,) — B1055

Variations on "Nel Cor
Piu" of Paisiello, Pft. — B1056

Thirty-two Variations,
C-Minor, Pft.   Theme — B1057

Variations on a Waltz
of Diabelli, Op.120, Pft.   Theme — B1058

BELLINI, Vincenzo (1801-1835)

Norma
Overture   1st Theme — B1059

2nd Theme — B1060

3rd Theme — B1061

BERLIOZ, Hector (1803-1869)

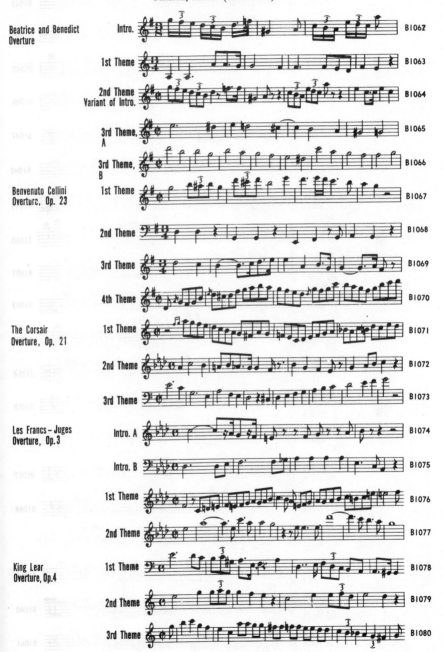

Beatrice and Benedict Overture — Intro. — B1062

1st Theme — B1063

2nd Theme Variant of Intro. — B1064

3rd Theme, A — B1065

3rd Theme, B — B1066

Benvenuto Cellini Overture, Op. 23 — 1st Theme — B1067

2nd Theme — B1068

3rd Theme — B1069

4th Theme — B1070

The Corsair Overture, Op. 21 — 1st Theme — B1071

2nd Theme — B1072

3rd Theme — B1073

Les Francs – Juges Overture, Op.3 — Intro. A — B1074

Intro. B — B1075

1st Theme — B1076

2nd Theme — B1077

King Lear Overture, Op.4 — 1st Theme — B1078

2nd Theme — B1079

3rd Theme — B1080

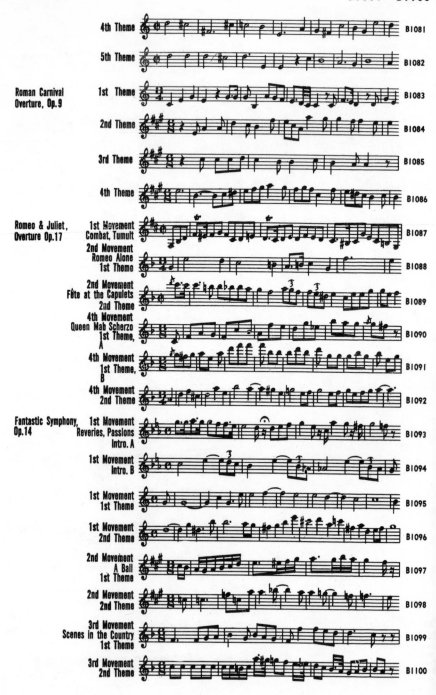

4th Movement
March to the Scaffold
1st Theme — B1101

4th Movement
2nd Theme — B1102

5th Movement
Witches' Sabbath
1st Theme — B1103

5th Movement
2nd Theme
Dies Irae — B1104

5th Movement
3rd Theme — B1105

Harold in Italy, Op.16 1st Movement
Orch. Harold in the Mountains
Intro. A1 — B1106

1st Movement
Intro. A 2 — B1107

1st Movement
Intro. B — B1108

1st Movement
1st Theme — B1109

1st Movement
2nd Theme — B1110

1st Movement
3rd Theme — B1111

2nd Movement
March of the Pilgrims — B1112

3rd Movement
Serenade
1st Theme — B1113

3rd Movement
2nd Theme — B1114

4th Movement
Orgy of the Brigands
1st Theme — B1115

4th Movement
2nd Theme — B1116

4th Movement
3rd Theme — B1117

BERNSTEIN, Leonard (1918-)

Fancy Free
Ballet
Copyright 1946 by
Harms, Inc.
Reprinted by
special permission.

Opening Dance — B1117a

At the Bar
Intro. — B1117b

Theme — B1117c
Pas de Deux — B1117d
Variation 1 / 1st Theme — B1117e
2nd Theme — B1117f
Variation 2 — B1117g
Variation 3 / 1st Theme — B1117h
2nd Theme — B1117i
Finale — B1117j

Jeremiah, Symphony
Copyright 1943 by
Harms, Inc.
Reprinted by
special permission.

1st Movement / Prophecy / 1st Theme — B1117k
1st Movement / 2nd Theme — B1117l
1st Movement / 3rd Theme — B1117m
2nd Movement / 1st Theme — B1117n
2nd Movement / 2nd Theme — B1117o
3rd Movement / 1st Theme — B1117p
3rd Movement / 2nd Theme — B1117q
3rd Movement / 3rd Theme — B1117r

BIZET, Georges (1838-1875)

L'Arlesienne
Suite No.1, Orch.

Overture / 1st Theme — B1118
2nd Theme — B1119
Minuetto / 1st Theme — B1120

2nd Theme — B1121

Countertheme to 2nd Theme — B1122

Adagietto — B1123

Carillon 1st Theme — B1124

2nd Theme — B1125

L'Arlesienne Suite No. 2, Orch.

Pastorale 1st Theme — B1126

2nd Theme — B1127

Intermezzo 1st Theme — B1128

2nd Theme — B1129

Minuetto — B1130

Farandole — B1131

Carmen, Opera

Prelude to Act 1 1st Theme — B1132

2nd Theme — B1133

3rd Theme (Toreador Song) — B1134

4th Theme (Fate Motive) — B1135

1st Intermezzo 1st Theme — B1136

2nd Theme — B1137

(Act II) Danse Bohème — B1138

2nd Intermezzo — B1139

3rd Intermezzo — B1140

Petite Suite, Op. 22
"Jeux D'Enfants"
Orch.

Marche — B1141

Berceuse (Doll) — B1142

Impromptu — B1143

Duo (Petit Mari,
Petite Femme) — B1144

Galop (Le Bal) — B1145

Symphony No. 1,
in C

1st Movement
1st Theme,
A — B1146

1st Movement
1st Theme,
B — B1147

1st Movement
2nd Theme — B1148

2nd Movement
1st Theme — B1149

2nd Movement
2nd Theme — B1150

3rd Movement — B1151

4th Movement
1st Theme — B1152

4th Movement
2nd Theme — B1153

4th Movement
3rd Theme — B1154

BLOCH, Ernest (1880-1959)

Baal Shem, (Three
Pictures of Chassidic
Life) Vn. & Pft.

Vidui (Contrition)
Copyright 1924
by Carl Fischer,
Inc., N. Y. — B1155

Nigun (Improvisation)
1st Theme
Copyright 1924 by Carl Fischer,
Inc., N. Y. — B1156

2nd Theme — B1157

Simchas Torah
Copyright 1924 by Carl Fischer,
Inc., N. Y. — B1158

Concerto grosso
Str. Orch. & Pft.
Obbligato
By permission of C. C. Birchard &
Co., owners of the copyright.

1st Movement
(Prelude) — B1159

2nd Movement (Dirge) 1st Theme A   B1160

1st Theme B   B1161

2nd Theme   B1162

3rd Theme   B1163

3rd Movement Pastorale & Rustic Dances 1st Theme   B1164

3rd Movement 2nd Theme   B1165

3rd Movement 3rd Theme   B1166

3rd Movement 4th Theme   B1167

3rd Movement 5th Theme   B1168

4th Movement Fugue 1st Theme   B1169

4th Movement 2nd Theme   B1170

1st Movement 1st Theme   B1171

1st Movement 2nd Theme   B1172

1st Movement 3rd Theme   B1173

2nd Movement 1st Theme   B1174

2nd Movement 2nd Theme   B1175

2nd Movement 3rd Theme   B1176

3rd Movement 1st Theme   B1177

3rd Movement 2nd Theme   B1178

4th Movement 1st Theme   B1179

Quartet, Str.
Copyright renewal
assigned 1946 to
G. Schirmer, Inc.

4th Movement 2nd Theme — B1180

4th Movement 3rd Theme — B1181

Quintet, Pft. & Str.
Copyright 1924
by G. Schirmer, Inc.

1st Movement 1st Theme — B1182

1st Movement 2nd Theme — B1183

2nd Movement 1st Theme — B1184

2nd Movement 2nd Theme — B1185

3rd Movement — B1186

Schelomo (Hebrew Rhapsody), Cello & Orch.
Copyright renewal assigned 1945 to G. Schirmer, Inc.

1st Theme — B1187

2nd Theme — B1188

3rd Theme — B1189

4th Theme — B1190

5th Theme — B1191

6th Theme — B1192

Sonata, Vn. & Pft.
Copyright 1922
by G. Schirmer, Inc.

1st Movement — B1193

2nd Movement — B1194

3rd Movement — B1195

Suite, Viola & Orch.
Copyright 1921
by G. Schirmer, Inc.

1st Movement 1st Theme — B1196

1st Movement 2nd Theme — B1197

1st Movement 3rd Theme — B1198

2nd Movement 1st Theme — B1199

2nd Movement
2nd Theme — B1200

3rd Movement — B1201

4th Movement — B1202

Israel, Symphony
Copyright 1925
by G. Schirmer, Inc.

1st Theme — B1203

2nd Theme — B1204

3rd Theme — B1205

4th Theme — B1206

5th Theme — B1207

Three Nocturnes,
Vn., Cello, & Pft.
Copyright by Carl Fischer, Inc., N. Y.
Reprinted by permisssion.

I — B1208

II — B1209

III — B1210

BOCCHERINI, Luigi (1743-1805)

Concerto in B Flat
Cello & Orch.

1st Movement
1st Theme — B1211

1st Movement
2nd Theme — B1212

2nd Movement — B1213

3rd Movement — B1214

Concerto No.2 in D
Cello & Orch.

1st Movement — B1215

2nd Movement
1st Theme — B1216

2nd Movement
2nd Theme — B1217

3rd Movement
1st Theme,
A — B1218

B1220
B1221
B1222
B1223
B1224
B1225
B1226
B1227
B1228
B1229
B1230
B1231
B1232
B1233
B1234
B1235
B1236
B1237
B1238

Quintet in D,
Op.37, Str.   1st Movement   B1239

2nd Movement   B1240

3rd Movement
1st Theme   B1241

3rd Movement
2nd Theme   B1242

Rondo, Cello & Pft.   1st Theme   B1243

2nd Theme   B1244

3rd Theme   B1245

Sonata No. 2
in C, Cello & Pft.   1st Movement   B1246

2nd Movement   B1247

3rd Movement   B1248

Sonata No. 6
in A, Cello & Pft.   1st Movement   B1249

2nd Movement
1st Theme   B1250

2nd Movement
2nd Theme   B1251

3rd Movement
1st Theme   B1252

3rd Movement
2nd Theme   B1253

Sonata in B Flat,
Cello & Pft.   1st Movement   B1254

2nd Movement   B1255

3rd Movement
1st Theme   B1256

3rd Movement
2nd Theme   B1257

Sonata in C,
Cello & Pft.   1st Movement   B1258

2nd Movement   B1259

3rd Movement   B1260

BOËLLMANN, Leon (1862-1897)

Suite Gothique,
Op. 25, Organ   1st Movement   Introduction-Choral   B1261
Permission for reprint
granted by Durand
& Cie, Paris.   2nd Movement   Menuet Gothique   B1262
Elkan-Vogel Co., Inc.
Philadelphia, Copyright
Owners   3rd Movement   B1263

4th Movement
Toccata   B1264

Variations Symphoniques,
Op. 63, Cello & Orch.   Intro.   B1265
Permission for reprint granted
by Durand & Cie, Paris.
Elkan-Vogel Co., Inc. Philadelphia,
Copyright Owners   Theme   B1266

BOÏELDIEU, Francois (1775-1834)

Le Calife De Bagdad
Overture   1st Theme   B1267

2nd Theme   B1268

3rd Theme   B1269

La Dame Blanche,
Overture,   1st Theme   B1270

2nd Theme   B1271

3rd Theme   B1272

BORODIN, Alexander (1833-1887)

On the Steppes of
Central Asia, Orch.   1st Theme   B1273

2nd Theme   B1274

Polovetsian Dances
from Prince Igor   1st Theme   B1275

BORODIN

	2nd Theme	B1276
	3rd Theme	B1277
	3rd Theme	B1278
	4th Theme	B1279
Quartet No.1, in A, Str.	1st Movement Intro.	B1280
	1st Movement 1st Theme	B1281
	1st Movement 2nd Theme	B1282
	2nd Movement 1st Theme	B1283
	2nd Movement 2nd Theme	B1284
	2nd Movement 3rd Theme Fugato	B1285
	3rd Movement 1st Theme	B1286
	3rd Movement 2nd Theme	B1287
	4th Movement 1st Theme	B1288
	4th Movement 2nd Theme	B1289
Quartet No.2 in D, Str.	1st Movement 1st Theme	B1290
	1st Movement 2nd Theme	B1291
	1st Movement 3rd Theme	B1292
	2nd Movement 1st Theme	B1293
	2nd Movement 2nd Theme	B1294
	3rd Movement 1st Theme Notturno	B1295

4*

Symphony No. 1
in E Flat

Symphony No. 2
in B Minor

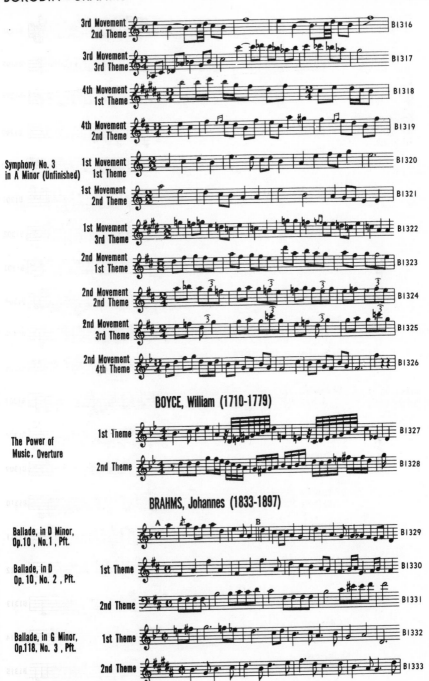

3rd Movement / 2nd Theme — B1316
3rd Movement / 3rd Theme — B1317
4th Movement / 1st Theme — B1318
4th Movement / 2nd Theme — B1319

Symphony No. 3 in A Minor (Unfinished)
1st Movement / 1st Theme — B1320
1st Movement / 2nd Theme — B1321
1st Movement / 3rd Theme — B1322
2nd Movement / 1st Theme — B1323
2nd Movement / 2nd Theme — B1324
2nd Movement / 3rd Theme — B1325
2nd Movement / 4th Theme — B1326

BOYCE, William (1710-1779)

The Power of Music, Overture
1st Theme — B1327
2nd Theme — B1328

BRAHMS, Johannes (1833-1897)

Ballade, in D Minor, Op.10 , No.1 , Pft. — B1329

Ballade, in D Op. 10 , No. 2 , Pft.
1st Theme — B1330
2nd Theme — B1331

Ballade, in G Minor, Op.118, No. 3 , Pft.
1st Theme — B1332
2nd Theme — B1333

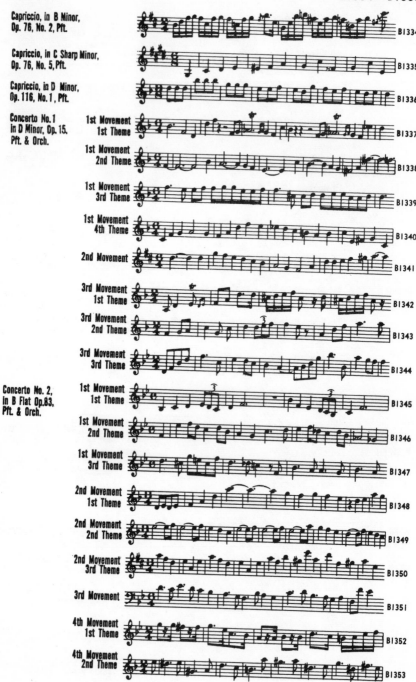

Capriccio, in B Minor, Op. 76, No. 2, Pft. — B1334

Capriccio, in C Sharp Minor, Op. 76, No. 5, Pft. — B1335

Capriccio, in D Minor, Op. 116, No. 1, Pft. — B1336

Concerto No. 1 in D Minor, Op. 15, Pft. & Orch.
1st Movement 1st Theme — B1337
1st Movement 2nd Theme — B1338
1st Movement 3rd Theme — B1339
1st Movement 4th Theme — B1340
2nd Movement — B1341
3rd Movement 1st Theme — B1342
3rd Movement 2nd Theme — B1343
3rd Movement 3rd Theme — B1344

Concerto No. 2, in B Flat Op. 83, Pft. & Orch.
1st Movement 1st Theme — B1345
1st Movement 2nd Theme — B1346
1st Movement 3rd Theme — B1347
2nd Movement 1st Theme — B1348
2nd Movement 2nd Theme — B1349
2nd Movement 3rd Theme — B1350
3rd Movement — B1351
4th Movement 1st Theme — B1352
4th Movement 2nd Theme — B1353

2nd Theme — B1374

No. 5, in F Sharp Minor
1st Theme — B1375

2nd Theme — B1376

No. 6, in D Flat — B1377

No. 7, in A — B1378

No.12, in D Minor — B1379

Intermezzo, in A Flat,
Op. 76, No.3, Pft. — B1380

Intermezzo, in A Minor,
Op. 76, No.7, Pft. — B1381

Intermezzo, in A Minor,
Op.116, No.2, Pft. — B1382

Intermezzo, in C Sharp
Minor, Op.116, No.3, Pft. — B1383

Intermezzo, in E,
Op.116, No.4, Pft. — B1384

Intermezzo, in E Flat,
Op.117, No. 1, Pft. — B1385

Intermezzo, in B Flat
Minor, Op.117, No.2, Pft. 1st Theme — B1386

2nd Theme — B1387

Intermezzo, in A Minor,
Op.118, No.1, Pft. — B1388

Intermezzo, in A,
Op.118, No.2, Pft. 1st Movement — B1389

2nd Movement — B1390

Intermezzo, in E Flat 1st Movement
Minor, Op.118, No.6, Pft. — B1391

2nd Movement — B1392

Intermezzo, in B Minor,
Op.119, No.1, Pft. — B1393

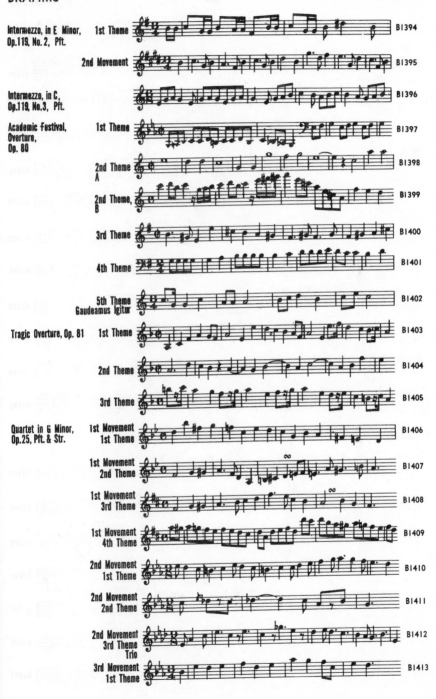

Intermezzo, in E Minor, Op.119, No.2, Pft. — 1st Theme — B1394

2nd Movement — B1395

Intermezzo, in C, Op.119, No.3, Pft. — B1396

Academic Festival, Overture, Op. 80 — 1st Theme — B1397

2nd Theme A — B1398

2nd Theme, B — B1399

3rd Theme — B1400

4th Theme — B1401

5th Theme Gaudeamus Igitur — B1402

Tragic Overture, Op. 81 — 1st Theme — B1403

2nd Theme — B1404

3rd Theme — B1405

Quartet in G Minor, Op.25, Pft. & Str. — 1st Movement 1st Theme — B1406

1st Movement 2nd Theme — B1407

1st Movement 3rd Theme — B1408

1st Movement 4th Theme — B1409

2nd Movement 1st Theme — B1410

2nd Movement 2nd Theme — B1411

2nd Movement 3rd Theme Trio — B1412

3rd Movement 1st Theme — B1413

Quartet in A,
Op. 26, Pft. & Str.

3rd Movement
2nd Theme — B1414

4th Movement
1st Theme — B1415

4th Movement
2nd Theme — B1416

4th Movement
3rd Theme — B1417

1st Movement
1st Theme — B1418

1st Movement
2nd Theme — B1419

2nd Movement — B1420

3rd Movement
1st Theme — B1421

3rd Movement
2nd Theme
Trio — B1422

4th Movement — B1423

Quartet in C Minor
Op. 51, No. 1, Str.

1st Movement
1st Theme — B1424

1st Movement
2nd Theme — B1425

2nd Movement — B1426

3rd Movement
1st Theme — B1427

3rd Movement
2nd Theme — B1428

4th Movement
1st Theme — B1429

4th Movement
2nd Theme — B1430

4th Movement
3rd Theme — B1431

4th Movement
4th Theme — B1432

Quartet in A Minor
Op. 51, No. 2, Str.

1st Movement
1st Theme — B1433

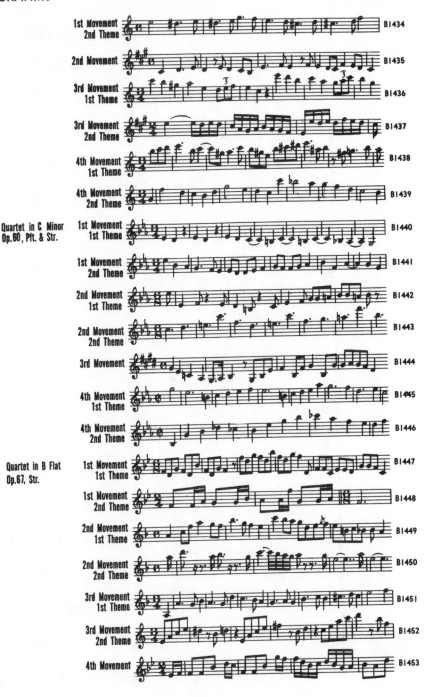

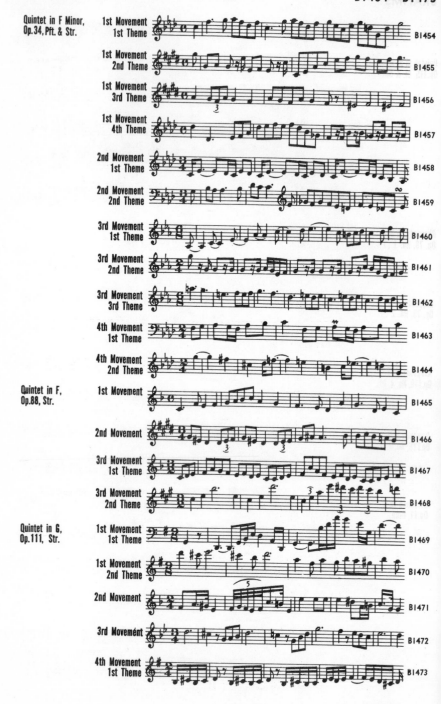

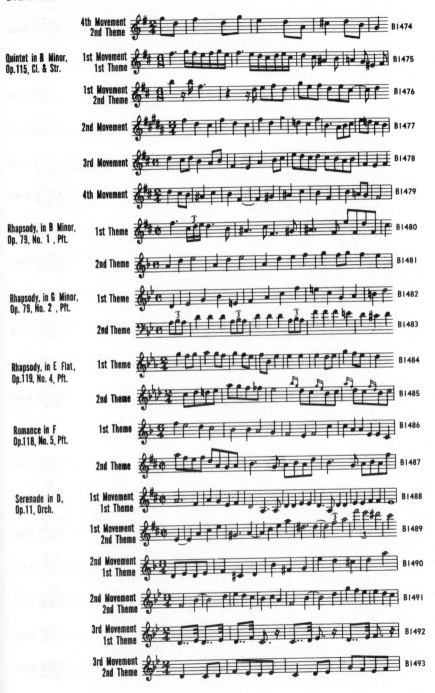

4th Movement / 2nd Theme   B1474

Quintet in B Minor, Op.115, Cl. & Str.   1st Movement / 1st Theme   B1475

1st Movement / 2nd Theme   B1476

2nd Movement   B1477

3rd Movement   B1478

4th Movement   B1479

Rhapsody, in B Minor, Op. 79, No. 1 , Pft.   1st Theme   B1480

2nd Theme   B1481

Rhapsody, in G Minor, Op. 79, No. 2 , Pft.   1st Theme   B1482

2nd Theme   B1483

Rhapsody, in E Flat, Op.119, No. 4, Pft.   1st Theme   B1484

2nd Theme   B1485

Romance in F Op.118, No. 5, Pft.   1st Theme   B1486

2nd Theme   B1487

Serenade in D, Op.11, Orch.   1st Movement / 1st Theme   B1488

1st Movement / 2nd Theme   B1489

2nd Movement / 1st Theme   B1490

2nd Movement / 2nd Theme   B1491

3rd Movement / 1st Theme   B1492

3rd Movement / 2nd Theme   B1493

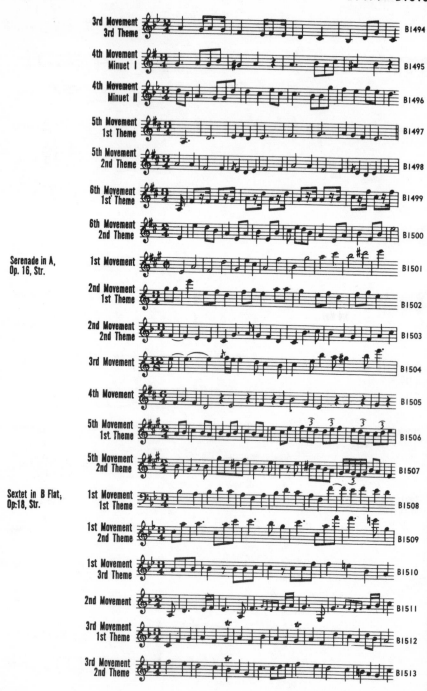

3rd Movement / 3rd Theme — B1494
4th Movement / Minuet I — B1495
4th Movement / Minuet II — B1496
5th Movement / 1st Theme — B1497
5th Movement / 2nd Theme — B1498
6th Movement / 1st Theme — B1499
6th Movement / 2nd Theme — B1500

Serenade in A, Op. 16, Str.
1st Movement — B1501
2nd Movement / 1st Theme — B1502
2nd Movement / 2nd Theme — B1503
3rd Movement — B1504
4th Movement — B1505
5th Movement / 1st Theme — B1506
5th Movement / 2nd Theme — B1507

Sextet in B Flat, Op. 18, Str.
1st Movement / 1st Theme — B1508
1st Movement / 2nd Theme — B1509
1st Movement / 3rd Theme — B1510
2nd Movement — B1511
3rd Movement / 1st Theme — B1512
3rd Movement / 2nd Theme — B1513

Symphony No.1
in C Minor
Op.68

4th Movement — B1574

1st Movement Intro. A 1 — B1575

Both Themes Simultaneous Intro. A 2 — B1576

1st Movement Intro. B — B1577

1st Movement 1st Theme, A — B1578

1st Movement 1st Theme, B — B1579

1st Movement 1st Theme, C — B1580

1st Movement 2nd Theme — B1581

1st Movement 3rd Theme — B1582

1st Movement 4th Theme — B1583

2nd Movement 1st Theme — B1584

2nd Movement 2nd Theme — B1585

2nd Movement 3rd Theme — B1586

2nd Movement 4th Theme — B1587

3rd Movement 1st Theme — B1588

3rd Movement 2nd Theme — B1589

3rd Movement 3rd Theme, A — B1590

3rd Movement 3rd Theme, B — B1591

3rd Movement 4th Theme — B1592

4th Movement Intro. A — B1593

3rd Movement 4th Theme — B1614
4th Movement 1st Theme, A — B1615
4th Movement 1st Theme, B — B1616
4th Movement 2nd Theme — B1617
4th Movement 3rd Theme — B1618

Symphony No. 3 in F Op. 90

1st Movement 1st Theme — B1619
1st Movement 2nd Theme — B1620
1st Movement 3rd Theme — B1621
1st Movement 4th Theme — B1622
2nd Movement 1st Theme — B1623
2nd Movement 2nd Theme — B1624
2nd Movement 3rd Theme — B1625
3rd Movement 1st Theme — B1626
3rd Movement 2nd Theme — B1627
3rd Movement 3rd Theme — B1628
4th Movement 1st Theme A — B1629
4th Movement 1st Theme B — B1630
4th Movement 2nd Theme — B1631
4th Movement 3rd Theme — B1632
4th Movement 4th Theme — B1633

Symphony No. 4
in E Minor, Op. 98

4th Movement
6th Theme

4th Movement
7th Theme

Trio in A Minor
Op.114, Cl. or Viola,
Cello & Pft.

1st Movement
1st Theme

1st Movement
2nd Theme

2nd Movement

3rd Movement

4th Movement
1st Theme

4th Movement
2nd Theme

4th Movement
3rd Theme

Trio in B
Op.8 Vn., Cello &
Pft.

1st Movement
1st Theme

1st Movement
2nd Theme

2nd Movement
1st Theme

2nd Movement
2nd Theme

3rd Movement
1st Theme

3rd Movement
2nd Theme

4th Movement
1st Theme

4th Movement
2nd Theme

Trio in C
Op.87, Vn., Cello &
Pft.

1st Movement
1st Theme

1st Movement
2nd Theme

1st Movement
3rd Theme

2nd Movement — B1674

3rd Movement
1st Theme — B1675

3rd Movement
2nd Theme — B1676

4th Movement
1st Theme — B1677

4th Movement
2nd Theme — B1678

4th Movement
3rd Theme — B1679

Trio in C Minor,
Op.101, Vn., Cello
& Pft.

1st Movement
1st Theme — B1680

1st Movement
2nd Theme — B1681

1st Movement
3rd Theme — B1682

2nd Movement — B1683

3rd Movement
1st Theme — B1684

3rd Movement
2nd Theme — B1685

4th Movement
1st Theme — B1686

4th Movement
2nd Theme — B1687

Trio in E Flat,
Op. 40, Vn., Hn. & Pft.

1st Movement
1st Theme — B1688

1st Movement
2nd Theme — B1689

2nd Movement
1st Theme — B1690

2nd Movement
2nd Theme — B1691

2nd Movement
3rd Theme — B1692

3rd Movement
1st Theme — B1693

3rd Movement 2nd Theme — B1694

4th Movement 1st Theme — B1695

4th Movement 2nd Theme — B1696

Variations on a Theme of Haydn, Op.56a, Orch. — Theme — B1697

Variations on a Theme of Schumann, Op. 23, Pft. 4 Hands — B1698

Waltzes, Op. 39, Pft.

No. 1 — B1699

No. 2 — B1700

No. 3 — B1701

No. 4 — B1702

No. 7 — B1703

No. 8 — B1704

No. 9 — B1705

No. 10 — B1706

No. 11 — B1707

No. 12 — B1708

No. 14 — B1709

No. 15 — B1710

No. 16 — B1711

BRITTEN, Benjamin (1913-   )

Peter Grimes, Four Sea Interludes, Op. 33a, Orch. — 1st Interlude Dawn — B1711a

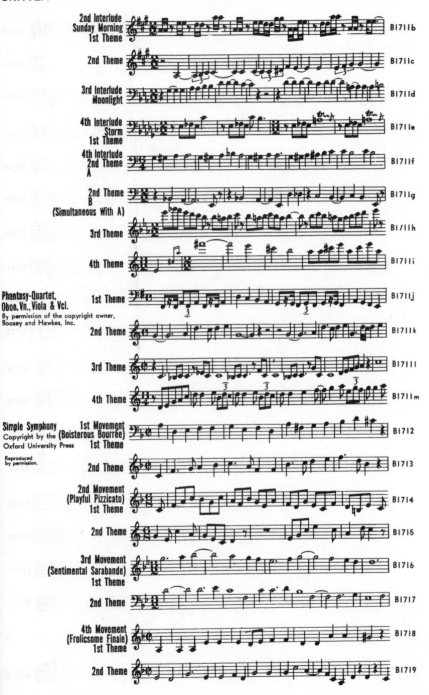

2nd Interlude
Sunday Morning
1st Theme — B1711b

2nd Theme — B1711c

3rd Interlude
Moonlight — B1711d

4th Interlude
Storm
1st Theme — B1711e

4th Interlude
2nd Theme
A — B1711f

2nd Theme
B
(Simultaneous With A) — B1711g

3rd Theme — B1711h

4th Theme — B1711i

Phantasy-Quartet,
Oboe, Vn., Viola & Vcl.
1st Theme — B1711j

2nd Theme — B1711k

3rd Theme — B1711l

4th Theme — B1711m

Simple Symphony
1st Movement
(Boisterous Bourrée)
1st Theme — B1712

2nd Theme — B1713

2nd Movement
(Playful Pizzicato)
1st Theme — B1714

2nd Theme — B1715

3rd Movement
(Sentimental Sarabande)
1st Theme — B1716

2nd Theme — B1717

4th Movement
(Frolicsome Finale)
1st Theme — B1718

2nd Theme — B1719

Variations on a Theme of Frank Bridge, Op. 10, Orch. — Theme
By permission of the copyright owner, Boosey and Hawkes, Inc.

BRUCH, Max (1838-1920)

Concerto No.1 in G Minor, Vn. & Orch. — 1st Movement Intro.

Permission for reprint granted by Durand & Cie, Paris. Elkan-Vogel Co.,Inc. Philadelphia, Copyright Owners.

1st Movement 1st Theme

1st Movement 2nd Theme

1st Movement 2nd Theme

2nd Movement 1st Theme, A

2nd Movement 1st Theme, B

3rd Movement 1st Theme

3rd Movement 2nd Theme

Concerto No. 2 in D Minor, Vn. & Orch. — 1st Movement 1st Theme
By permission of Associated Music Publishers, Inc.

1st Movement 2nd Theme

2nd Movement 1st Theme

2nd Movement 2nd Theme

3rd Movement 1st Theme, A

3rd Movement 1st Theme, B

3rd Movement 2nd Theme

Kol Nidrei (Based on Traditional Hebrew Themes) Vn. & Pft. — 1st Theme
By permission of Associated Music Publishers, Inc. — 2nd Theme

3rd Theme

BRUCKNER, Anton (1824-1896)

Overture in G Minor
By permission of Associated
Music Publishers, Inc.

1st Theme — B1738

2nd Theme — B1739

3rd Theme — B1740

Quintet in F, Str.
By permission of
International Music Co.

1st Movement 1st Theme — B1741

1st Movement 2nd Theme — B1742

2nd Movement 1st Theme — B1743

2nd Movement 2nd Theme — B1744

3rd Movement — B1745

4th Movement — B1746

Symphony No. 3
in D Minor
Copyright by Lienau,
Licensed by
SESAC, Inc., N. Y.

1st Movement 1st Theme — B1747

1st Movement 2nd Theme — B1748

1st Movement 3rd Theme — B1749

1st Movement 4th Theme — B1750

2nd Movement 1st Theme — B1751

2nd Movement 2nd Theme — B1752

2nd Movement 3rd Theme — B1753

3rd Movement 1st Theme — B1754

3rd Movement 2nd Theme, A — B1755

3rd Movement 2nd Theme B — B1756

4th Movement 1st Theme — B1757

4th Movement 2nd Theme — B1758

4th Movement 3rd Theme — B1759

Symphony No.4. in E Flat, "Romantic"
By permission of Associated Music Publishers, Inc.

1st Movement 1st Theme — B1760

1st Movement 2nd Theme — B1761

1st Movement 3rd Theme — B1762

2nd Movement 1st Theme — B1763

2nd Movement 2nd Theme — B1764

3rd Movement 1st Theme — B1765

3rd Movement 2nd Theme — B1766

3rd Movement 3rd Theme — B1767

4th Movement 1st Theme — B1768

4th Movement 2nd Theme — B1769

4th Movement 3rd Theme — B1770

4th Movement 4th Theme — B1771

Symphony No.5, in B Flat,
By permission of Associated Music Publishers, Inc.

1st Movement Intro. — B1772

1st Movement 1st Theme — B1773

1st Movement 2nd Theme — B1774

2nd Movement 1st Theme — B1775

2nd Movement 2nd Theme — B1776

Symphony No.7,
in E
By permission of Associated
Music Publishers, Inc.

Symphony No.9,
in D Minor
By permission of Associated
Music Publishers, Inc.

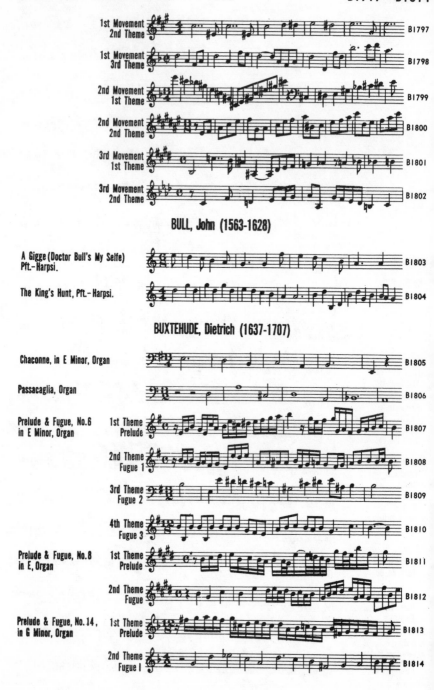

1st Movement 2nd Theme — B1797

1st Movement 3rd Theme — B1798

2nd Movement 1st Theme — B1799

2nd Movement 2nd Theme — B1800

3rd Movement 1st Theme — B1801

3rd Movement 2nd Theme — B1802

BULL, John (1563-1628)

A Gigge (Doctor Bull's My Selfe) Pft.-Harpsi. — B1803

The King's Hunt, Pft.-Harpsi. — B1804

BUXTEHUDE, Dietrich (1637-1707)

Chaconne, in E Minor, Organ — B1805

Passacaglia, Organ — B1806

Prelude & Fugue, No.6 in E Minor, Organ — 1st Theme Prelude — B1807

2nd Theme Fugue 1 — B1808

3rd Theme Fugue 2 — B1809

4th Theme Fugue 3 — B1810

Prelude & Fugue, No.8 in E, Organ — 1st Theme Prelude — B1811

2nd Theme Fugue — B1812

Prelude & Fugue, No.14, in G Minor, Organ — 1st Theme Prelude — B1813

2nd Theme Fugue I — B1814

3rd Theme
Fugue II — B1815

Toccata No. 20 in F,
Organ   1st Theme — B1816

                    2nd Theme — B1817

Toccata No. 21 in F,
Organ   1st Theme — B1818

                    2nd Theme — B1819

Toccata No. 22 in G
Organ — B1820

BYRD, William (1543-1623)

The Bells
Fitzwilliam Virginal Book
No. 69, Harpsi.   1st Theme — B1821

                    2nd Theme — B1822

                    3rd Theme — B1823

The Carman's Whistle
Fitzwilliam Virginal Book, No. 58
Variations for Harpsi. — B1824

Galliard
Fitzwilliam Virginal Book No. 92
Harpsi. — B1825

Galliard, The Earl of Salisbury
from The Parthenia, Harpsi. — B1826

Sir John Grayes' Galliard
Fitzwilliam Virginal Book No. 191,
Harpsi. — B1827

Miserere Fitzwilliam
Virginal Book No. 177
Organ or Harpsi.   1st Theme — B1828

                    2nd Theme — B1829

O Mistris Myne Fitzwilliam Virginal
Book No. 66, Variations for Harpsi. — B1830

Pavan, The Earl of Salisbury
from The Parthenia
Harpsi.   Theme,
                    A — B1831

                    Theme,
                    B — B1832

Rowland, Harpsi.
Fitzwilliam Virginal Book No. 160 — B1833

Sellenger's Round, Harpsi.
Fitzwilliam Virginal Book No. 64   B1834

La Volta, Harpsi.
Fitzwilliam Virginal Book No. 155   B1835

Wolsey's Wilde, Harpsi.
Fitzwilliam Virginal Book No. 157   B1836

CABANILLAS, Juan (1644-1712)

Passacalles in D Minor, Organ   C1

Tiento De Falsas, Del 4° Tomo, Organ   C2

CABÉZON, Antonio de (1510-1566)

Tiento, Del 1° Tomo, Organ   C3

Tiento, Del 4° Tomo, Organ   C4

Variations on "El Canto Del Caballero"   C5

CADMAN, Charles Wakefield (1881-1946)

Thunderbird Suite, Orch.
(Music for a Production
of Norman Bel Geddes)
(Based on American
Indian Tunes)
Copyright by
White-Smith
Music Publishers
Co., Boston.

1st Movement
From the
Village   C6

2nd Movement
Before the Sunrise   C7

3rd Movement
Nuwana's Love Song
(Blackfeet Indian Tune)   C8

4th Movement
Night Song (Blackfeet Indian Tune)   C9

5th Movement
Wolf Song (War Dance)   C10

CAIX d'HERVELOIS, Louis de (1670-1760)

Suite No. 1, in A,
Cello & Pft.

1st Movement
La Milanese   C11

2nd Movement
Sarabande   C12

3rd Movement
Minuet   C13

3rd Movement
3rd Theme — C32

3rd Movement
4th Theme — C33

3rd Movement
5th Theme — C34

4th Movement
The Lake — C35

5th Movement
Dogs
1st Theme — C36

5th Movement
2nd Theme — C37

6th Movement
Dreams — C38

Quartet in A Minor, Str.
Copyright 1928 by
G. Schirmer, Inc.

1st Movement
Intro. — C39

1st Movement
1st Theme — C40

1st Movement
2nd Theme — C41

2nd Movement — C42

3rd Movement
1st Theme — C43

3rd Movement
2nd Theme — C44

CASELLA, Alfredo (1883-1947)

Il Convento Veneziano, Ballet
Copyright 1919 by
G. Ricordi & Co., Inc.

Ronde D'Enfants
1st Theme — C45

2nd Theme — C46

Pas Des
Vieilles Dames — C47

La Giara, Ballet
By permission of Associated
Music Publishers, Inc.

Sicilian Dance
"Chiovu" — C48

General Dance — C49

Finale — C50

Pupazzetti, Orch.
By permission of the copyright holders, J. & W. Chester, Ltd., 11 Great Marlborough Street, London, W. 1.

1st Movement 1st Theme Marcietta — C51

1st Movement 2nd Theme — C52

2nd Movement Berceuse — C53

3rd Movement Serenata — C54

4th Movement Notturnino — C55

5th Movement 1st Theme Polka — C56

5th Movement 2nd Theme — C57

Serenata
Cl., Fg., Tpt., Vn. & Cello
By permission of Associated Music Publishers, Inc.

1st Movement Marcia — C58

2nd Movement Minuet — C59

3rd Movement 1st Theme Notturno — C60

3rd Movement 2nd Theme — C61

4th Movement 1st Theme Gavotte — C62

4th Movement 2nd Theme Musette — C63

5th Movement Cavatina — C64

6th Movement Finale-Tarantella — C65

Siciliana E Burlesca,
Vn., Cello, Pft.
Copyright 1919 by G. Ricordi & Co., Inc.

1st Movement Siciliana — C66

2nd Movement Burlesca — C67

CHABRÍER, Alexis Emmanuel (1841-1894)

Bourrée Fantasque,
Pft., Arr. for Orch., F. Mottl
By permission of M M Enoch & Cie., Music Publishers, 27 Boulevard des Italiens, Paris.

1st Theme — C68

2nd Theme A — C69

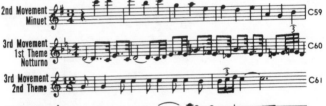

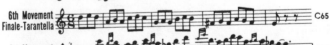

5*

Espana,
Rhapsody for Orch.
By permission of
M M Enoch & Cie.,
Music Publishers,
27 Boulevard
des Italiens, Paris.

2nd Theme B — C70

1st Theme — C71

2nd Theme — C72

3rd Theme — C73

4th Theme — C74

5th Theme — C75

Habanera, Pft. or Orch.
By permission of M M Enoch & Cie.,
Music Publishers,
27 Boulevard des Italiens, Paris.

— C76

Joyeuse Marche, Orch.
By permission of
M M Enoch & Cie.,
Music Publishers,
27 Boulevard
des Italiens, Paris.

Intro. — C77

1st Theme — C78

2nd Theme — C79

3rd Theme — C80

Gwendoline,
Overture
By permission of
M M Enoch & Cie.,
Music Publishers,
27 Boulevard
des Italiens, Paris.

1st Theme — C81

2nd Theme — C82

3rd Theme — C83

Pieces Pittoresques, Pft.
By permission of
M M Enoch & Cie.,
Music Publishers,
27 Boulevard
des Italiens, Paris.

No. 4
Sous Bois — C84

No. 6
Idylle — C85

No. 7
Danse Villageoise
1st Theme — C86

2nd Theme — C87

No. 8 , Improvisation — C88

No. 10 Scherzo-Valse
1st Theme — C89

2nd Theme — C90

3rd Theme — C91

Le Roi Malgré Lui, Orch.
By permission of
M M Enoch & Cie.,
Music Publishers,
27 Boulevard
des Italiens, Paris.

Prelude — C92

Danse Slave
1st Theme — C93

2nd Theme — C94

Fête Polonaise
1st Theme — C95

2nd Theme — C96

3rd Theme — C97

CHADWICK, George W. (1854-1931)

Symphonic Sketches
Copyright renewal assigned
1935 to G. Schirmer, Inc.

I. Jubilee
1st Theme — C98

2nd Theme — C99

3rd Theme, A — C100

3rd Theme, B — C101

4th Theme — C102

II. Nöel — C103

CHAMINADE, Cécile (1857-1944)

Air de Ballet, Pft.
By permission of
M M Enoch & Cie.,
Music Publishers,
27 Boulevard
des Italiens, Paris.
Callirhoë, in G
Air de Ballet. Pft.
By permission of M M Enoch & Cie., Music Publishers,
27 Boulevard des Italiens, Paris.
The Flatterer, Pft.

Scarf Dance, Pft.
By permission of
M M Enoch & Cie.,
Music Publishers,
27 Boulevard
des Italiens, Paris.

C104

C105

C106

1st Theme   2nd Theme — C107

3rd Theme (Orch. Version) — C108

Serenade, Pft.
By permission of M M Enoch & Cie.,
Music Publishers, 27 Boulevard des Italiens, Paris. — C109

Spanish Serenade, Vn. & Pft.
Arr. by Kreisler
By permission of
M M Enoch & Cie.,
Music Publishers,
27 Boulevard
des Italiens, Paris. — C110

CHAUSSON, Ernest (1855-1899)

Concerto in D
Pft., Vn. &
Str. Quartet
Op. 21
Copyright by Editions
Salabert Editions Salabert,
22 Rue Chaucat, Paris
Salabert, Inc.,
1 East 57 St., N. Y.

1st Movement 1st Theme — C111
1st Movement 2nd Theme — C112
2nd Movement Sicilienne — C113
3rd Movement 1st Theme — C114
3rd Movement 2nd Theme — C115
4th Movement 1st Theme — C116
4th Movement 2nd Theme — C117

Poème, Op. 25, Vn. & Orch.
By permission of Associated
Music Publishers, Inc.

Intro. — C118
1st Theme — C119
2nd Theme — C120
3rd Theme — C121

Quartet, Op. 30
Str. & Pft.
By permission of
International Music Co.

1st Movement 1st Theme — C122
1st Movement 2nd Theme — C123
1st Movement 3rd Theme — C124
2nd Movement 1st Theme — C125
2nd Movement 2nd Theme — C126

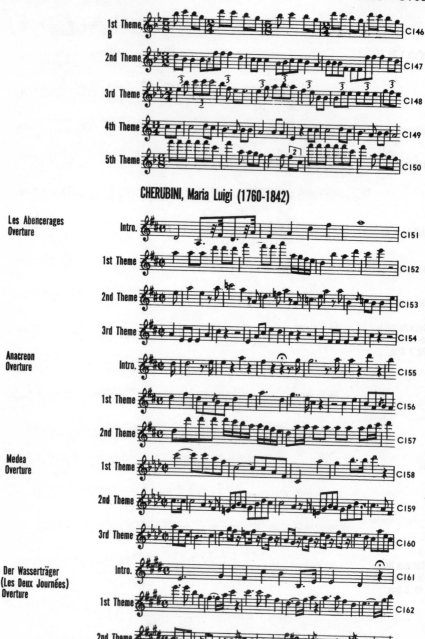

CHERUBINI, Maria Luigi (1760-1842)

Les Abencerages
Overture

Anacreon
Overture

Medea
Overture

Der Wasserträger
(Les Deux Journées)
Overture

CHOPIN, Frédéric (1810-1849)

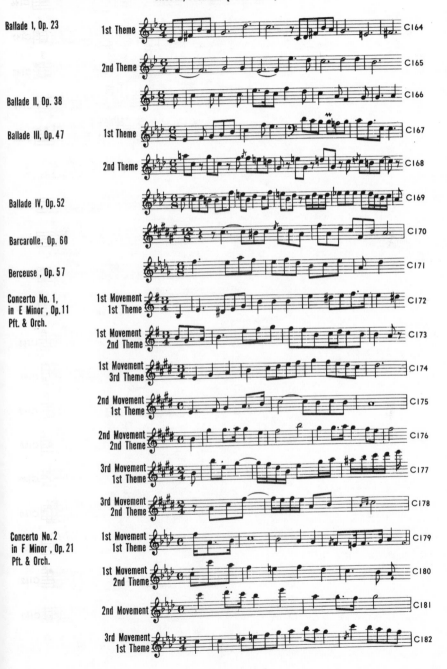

Ballade I, Op. 23 — 1st Theme — C164

2nd Theme — C165

Ballade II, Op. 38 — C166

Ballade III, Op. 47 — 1st Theme — C167

2nd Theme — C168

Ballade IV, Op. 52 — C169

Barcarolle, Op. 60 — C170

Berceuse, Op. 57 — C171

Concerto No. 1, in E Minor, Op. 11 Pft. & Orch. — 1st Movement 1st Theme — C172

1st Movement 2nd Theme — C173

1st Movement 3rd Theme — C174

2nd Movement 1st Theme — C175

2nd Movement 2nd Theme — C176

3rd Movement 1st Theme — C177

3rd Movement 2nd Theme — C178

Concerto No. 2 in F Minor, Op. 21 Pft. & Orch. — 1st Movement 1st Theme — C179

1st Movement 2nd Theme — C180

2nd Movement — C181

3rd Movement 1st Theme — C182

3rd Movement 2nd Theme — C183

Ecossaise, No. 1, Op. 72, No. 3 — C184

Ecossaise, No. 2, Op. 72, No. 4 — C185

Études, Op. 10
No. 1 in C — C186

No. 2 in A Minor — C187

No. 3 in E — C188

No. 4 in C Sharp Minor — C189

No. 5 in G Flat "Black Key" — C190

No. 6 in E Flat Minor — C191

No. 7 in C — C192

No. 8 in F Simultaneous { 1st Theme — C193 / 2nd Theme — C194

No. 9 in F Minor — C195

No. 10 in A Flat — C196

No. 11 in E Flat — C197

No. 12 in C Minor "Revolutionary" — C198

Etudes, Op. 25
No. 1 in A Flat "Harp" — C198a

No. 2 in F Minor — C199

No. 3 in F — C200

No. 4 in A Minor — C201

No. 5 in E Minor — 1st Theme — C202

2nd Theme — C203

No. 6 in G Sharp Minor — C204

No. 7 in C Sharp Minor — C205

No. 8 in D Flat — C206

No. 9 in G Flat "Butterfly" — C207

No. 10 in B Minor — Intro. — C208

1st Theme — C209

2nd Theme — C210

No. 11 in A Minor "Winter Wind" — C211

No. 12 in C Minor — C212

Posth. Etudes — No. 1 in F Minor — C213

No. 2 in D Flat — C214

No. 3 in A Flat — C215

Fantaisie in F Minor, Op. 49 — 1st Theme — C216

2nd Theme — C217

3rd Theme — C218

4th Theme — C219

Impromptu, Op. 29 — 1st Theme — 2nd Theme — C220

3rd Theme — C221

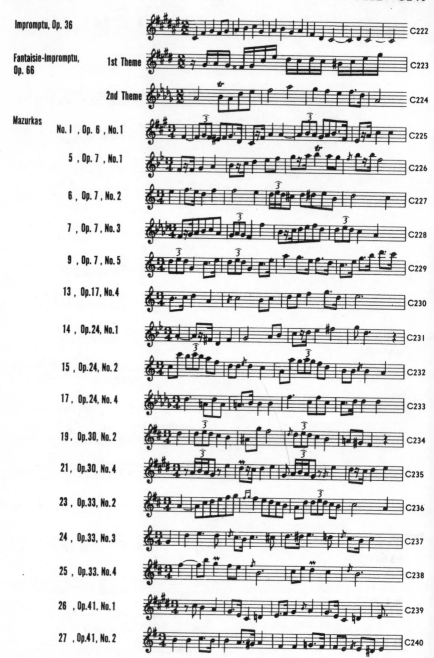

Impromptu, Op. 36 — C222

Fantaisie-Impromptu, Op. 66   1st Theme — C223

2nd Theme — C224

Mazurkas

No. 1 , Op. 6 , No. 1 — C225

5 , Op. 7 , No. 1 — C226

6 , Op. 7 , No. 2 — C227

7 , Op. 7 , No. 3 — C228

9 , Op. 7 , No. 5 — C229

13 , Op. 17, No. 4 — C230

14 , Op. 24, No. 1 — C231

15 , Op. 24, No. 2 — C232

17 , Op. 24, No. 4 — C233

19 , Op. 30, No. 2 — C234

21 , Op. 30, No. 4 — C235

23 , Op. 33, No. 2 — C236

24 , Op. 33, No. 3 — C237

25 , Op. 33, No. 4 — C238

26 , Op. 41, No. 1 — C239

27 , Op. 41, No. 2 — C240

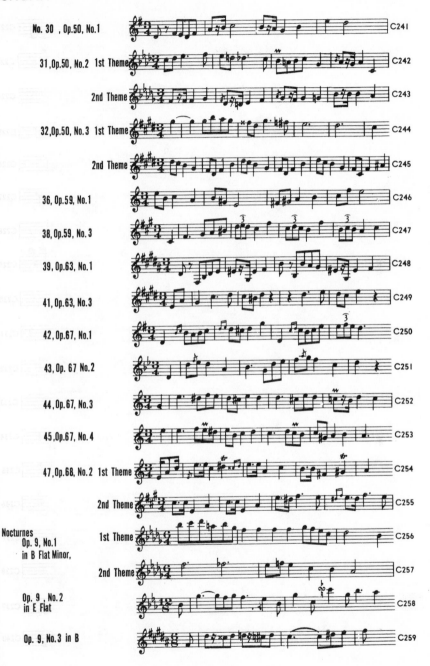

Op.15 , No.1 in F — C260

Op.15 , No.2 in F Sharp — C261

Op.15 , No.3 in G Minor — C262

Op.27, No.1 in C Sharp Minor — C263

Op.27, No.2 in D Flat — C264

Op.32, No.1 in B — C265

Op.32, No.2 in A Flat — C266

Op.37, No.1 in G Minor — C267

Op.37. No.2 in G — C268

Op.48 , No.1 in C Minor — 1st Theme — C269

2nd Theme — C270

Op.48, No.2 in F Sharp Minor — C271

Op.55 , No.1 in F Minor — C272

Op.55 , No.2 in E Flat — C273

Op.62, No.1 in B — C274

Op.62 , No.2 in E — C275

Op.72, No.1 in E Minor — C276

Andante Spianato & Polonaise, Op. 22 — 1st Theme Andante — C277

2nd Theme Polonaise — C278

Polonaises
Op. 26, No. 1 in C Sharp Minor   C279

Op. 40, No. 1 in A   1st Theme   C280

2nd Theme   C281

Op. 40, No. 2 in C Minor   C282

Op. 44 in F Sharp Minor   C283

Op. 53 in A Flat   1st Theme   C284

2nd Theme   C285

Preludes, Op. 28, No. 1   C286

2   C287

3   C288

4   C289

5   C290

6   C291

7   C292

8   C293

9   C294

10   C295

11   C296

12   C297

13   C298

14   C299

15   "Raindrop" 1st Theme   C300

2nd Theme   C301

16   C302

17   C303

18   C304

19   C305

20   C306

21   C307

22   C308

23   C309

24   C310

Scherzo in B Minor, Op. 20   1st Theme   C310a

2nd Theme   C311

Scherzo in B Flat Minor, Op.31   1st Theme   C312

2nd Theme   C313

Scherzo in C Sharp Minor Op. 39   1st Theme   C314

2nd Theme   C315

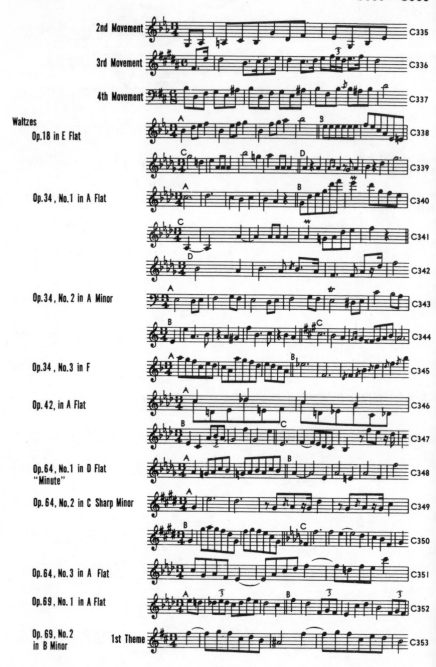

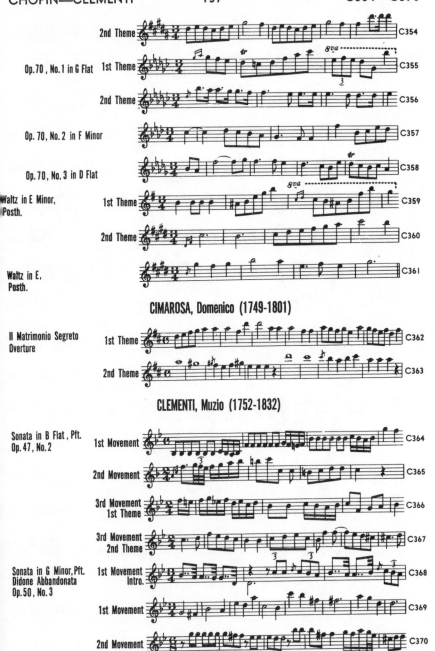

2nd Theme — C354

Op.70 , No.1 in G Flat — 1st Theme — C355

2nd Theme — C356

Op. 70 , No. 2 in F Minor — C357

Op.70 , No. 3 in D Flat — C358

Waltz in E Minor, Posth. — 1st Theme — C359

2nd Theme — C360

Waltz in E, Posth. — C361

CIMAROSA, Domenico (1749-1801)

Il Matrimonio Segreto Overture — 1st Theme — C362

2nd Theme — C363

CLEMENTI, Muzio (1752-1832)

Sonata in B Flat , Pft. Op. 47, No.2 — 1st Movement — C364

2nd Movement — C365

3rd Movement 1st Theme — C366

3rd Movement 2nd Theme — C367

Sonata in G Minor, Pft. Didone Abbandonata Op. 50, No. 3 — 1st Movement Intro. — C368

1st Movement — C369

2nd Movement — C370

3rd Movement — C371

Sonata No.1 in B Flat
2 Pianos, 4 Hands — 1st Movement 1st Theme — C372

1st Movement 2nd Theme — C373

2nd Movement — C374

3rd Movement — C375

Sonata No. 2 in B Flat
2 Pianos, 4 Hands — 1st Movement 1st Theme — C376

1st Movement 2nd Theme — C377

2nd Movement Tempo Di Minuetto — C378

COLERIDGE-TAYLOR, Samuel (1875-1912)

Othello Suite, Orch. — 1st Movement Dance 1st Theme — C387

1st Movement 2nd Theme — C388

2nd Movement Children's Intermezzo 1st Theme — C389

2nd Movement 2nd Theme — C390

3rd Movement Funeral March 1st Theme — C391

3rd Movement 2nd Theme — C392

4th Movement Willow Song — C393

5th Movement Military March 1st Theme — C394

5th Movement 2nd Theme — C395

Petite Suite de Concert
Orch. — 1st Movement 1st Theme — C396
Le Caprice de Nanette
By permission of the copyright
owner, Boosey and Hawkes, Inc.

Demande et Réponse

Un Sonnet D'Amour

La Tarantelle Frétillante

COPLAND, Aaron (1900-   )

Appalachian Spring Ballet
By permission of the copyright owner, Boosey and Hawkes, Inc.

Shaker Melody "The Gift To Be Simple"

Billy the Kid, Ballet
The Open Prairie
By permission of the copyright owner, Boosey and Hawkes, Inc.

Street in a Frontier Town (Cowboy Tune)

The Streets of Laredo

(Cowboy Tune)

(Cowboy Tune)

The Card Game — Scene II, 1st Theme — C416

Macabre Dance — 3rd Theme — C417

Billy in Prison — 4th Theme — C418

Scene III — C419

Concerto for Orch. & Pft.
Copyright 1929.
Cos Cob Press, Inc.

1st Movement, 1st Theme, A — C420

1st Movement, 1st Theme, B — C421

1st Movement, 2nd Theme — C422

2nd Movement, 1st Theme — C423

2nd Movement, 2nd Theme — C424

2nd Movement, 3rd Theme — C425

2nd Movement, 4th Theme — C426

Dance Symphony
Copyright 1931,
Cos Cob Press, Inc.

Intro. — C427

1st Movement, 1st Theme — C428

1st Movement, 2nd Theme — C429

1st Movement, 3rd Theme — C430

2nd Movement, 1st Theme — C431

2nd Movement, 2nd Theme — C432

3rd Movement, 1st Theme — C433

3rd Movement, 2nd Theme — C434

3rd Movement, 3rd Theme — C435

Music for the Theatre, Small Orch.
Copyright 1932, Cos Cob Press, Inc.

1st Movement Prologue 1st Theme — C436

1st Movement 2nd Theme — C437

2nd Movement Dance 1st Theme — C438

2nd Movement 2nd Theme — C439

3rd Movement Interlude 1st Theme — C440

3rd Movement 2nd Theme — C441

4th Movement Burlesque 1st Theme — C442

4th Movement 2nd Theme — C443

Nocturne, Vn. & Pft.
By permission of the copyright owner, Boosey and Hawkes, Inc.

1st Theme — C444

2nd Theme — C445

Passacaglia, Pft.
By permission of the copyright owner, Boosey and Hawkes, Inc. — C446

Piano Variations
Copyright 1932, Cos Cob Press, Inc.

Theme — C447

El Salon Mexico, Orch.
By permission of the copyright owner, Boosey and Hawkes, Inc.

Intro. — C448

1st Theme — C449

2nd Theme Trumpet Solo — C450

3rd Theme — C451

4th Theme — C452

5th Theme — C453

6th Theme — C454

7th Theme Clarinet Solo — C455

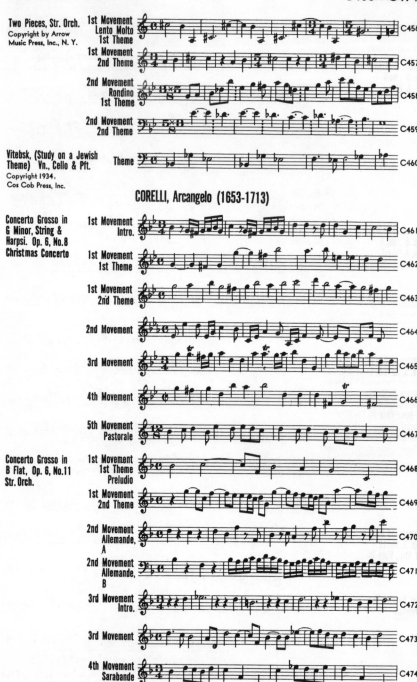

5th Movement Giga — C475

Sonata in G Minor, Op. 5 , No.5 Vn. & Harpsi.
1st Movement — C476
2nd Movement — C477
3rd Movement — C478
4th Movement — C479
5th Movement Gigue — C480

Sonata in E Minor, Op. 5 , No. 8 Vn. & Harpsi.
1st Movement Preludio — C481
2nd Movement Allemande — C482
3rd Movement Sarabande — C483
4th Movement Giga — C484

Sonata in D Minor, Op. 5, No. 12 "La Folia" — C485

Sonata Da Camera, B Flat , Op. 2, No.5 2 Vns., Viola Da Gamba, Harpsi.
1st Movement Preludio — C486
2nd Movement Allemande — C487
3rd Movement Sarabande — C488
4th Movement Tempo Di Gavotta — C489

Sonata Da Camera, G, Op. 2, No. 12 2 Vns., Viola Da Gamba, Harpsi. — C490

CORNELIUS, Peter (1824-1874)

Der Barbier Von Bagdad Overture
1st Theme — C491
2nd Theme — C492
3rd Theme — C493

COUPERIN, François (1668-1733)

Les Abeilles, Harpsi.   C494

La Bandoline, Harpsi.   C495

Les Baricades Misterieuses, Harpsi.   C496

Le Bavolet-Flotant, Harpsi.   C497

Les Bergeries, Harpsi.   Rondeau   C498

La Bersan, Harpsi.   C499

Les Calotins et Les Calotines, Harpsi.   C500

Le Carillon de Cythere, Harpsi.   C501

La Commére, Harpsi.   C502

Concert No. 8 in G,
Dans Le Goût Théatral   1st Movement / Overture / 1st Theme   C503

2nd Theme   C504

2nd Movement / Grande Retournele   C505

3rd Movement / Air No. 1   C506

4th Movement / Air Tendre No. 1   C507

5th Movement / Air Léger No. 1   C508

6th Movement / Loure   C509

7th Movement / Air No. 2   C510

8th Movement / Sarabande Brave / Et Tendre   C511

9th Movement / Air Leger No. 2   C512

10th Movement
Air Tendre No.2 C513

11th Movement
Air De Baccantes C514

Concert No.9, in E
Ritratto Deli' Amore
Chamber Orch.

1st Movement
Le Charme C515

2nd Movement
L'Enjouement C516

3rd Movement
Les Graces
(Courante Françoise) C517

4th Movement
Le Je Ne Scay Quoy C518

5th Movement
La Vivacité C519

6th Movement
La Noble Fierté
Sarabande C520

7th Movement
La Douceur C521

8th Movement
L'Et Coetera ou Minuets
1st Theme C522

2nd Theme C523

Concert No.13, in G
2 Cellos

1st Movement
Prelude C524

2nd Movement
Air C525

3rd Movement
Sarabande C526

4th Movement
Chaconne Legére C527

Concert Royal, No.2
Chamber Orch.

1st Movement
Prélude C528

2nd Movement
Allemande Fuguée C529

3rd Movement
Air Tendre C530

4th Movement
Air Contrefugué C531

5th Movement
Echo C532

6

Concert Royal, No. 4
in E Minor, Chamber Orch.
1st Movement Prelude — C533

2nd Movement Allemande — C534

3rd Movement Courante Françoise — C535

4th Movement Courante a L'Italiéne — C536

5th Movement Sarabande — C537

6th Movement Rigaudon — C538

7th Movement Forlane — C539

La Croûilli ou La Couperinéte, Harpsi. — C540

Le Dodo, Harpsi. — C541

Les Fastes de La Grande
et Ancienne Ménestrandises, Harpsi.
Act I (Les Notables et Jurés-Ménestrandises) — C542

Act II (Les Viéleux et Les Gueux) 1st Theme — C543

2nd Theme — C544

Act III (Les Jongleurs, Sauteurs, et Saltimbiques) — C545

Act IV (Les Invalides) — C546

Act V (Desordre et Deroute de Toute La Troupe) — C547

La Fleurie ou La Tendre Nanètte Harpsi. — C548

Les Folies Françaises Harpsi.
1st Movement La Virginité — C549

2nd Movement La Pudeur — C550

3rd Movement L'Ardeur — C551

4th Movement L'Esperance — C552

5th Movement La Fidelité — C553

6th Movement Le Perseverance — C554

7th Movement La Langueur — C555

8th Movement Le Coqueterie — C556

9th Movement Les Vieux Galans — C557

10th Movement Les Coucous Bénévoles — C558

11th Movement La Jalousie Taciturne — C559

12th Movement La Frénésie — C560

Le Gazouillement, Harpsi. — C561

L'Himen-Amour, Harpsi. — C562

La Julliet, Harpsi. or Fl., Cello & Harpsi. — C563

Les Langueurs-Tendres, Harpsi. — C564

Les Moissonneurs, Harpsi. — C565

Le Moucheron, Harpsi. — C566

Musétte de Choisi, Harpsi. — C567

Musétte de Taverni, Harpsi. — C568

La Nanète, Harpsi. — C569

Passacaille, Harpsi. 1st Theme, A — C570

1st Theme, B — C571

Les Petits Moulins à Vent Harpsi. — C572

Le Rossignol en Amour, Harpsi — C573

Soeur Monique, Harpsi. — C574

Les Tambourins, Harpsi. — C575

Le Tic-Toc-Chic ou Les Maillotins, Harpsi. — C576

Les Vergers Fleuris, Harpsi. — C577

Messe Pour Les Couvents, Organ
Offertoire Sur Les Grands Jeux — C578

Recit de Chromhorne — C579

Messe Pour Les Paroisses, Organ
Fugue on the Kyrie — C580

Recit de Chromhorne — C581

Offertoire Sur
Les Grands Jeux   1st Theme — C582

2nd Theme — C583

CUI, César (1835-1918)

Orientale, Op. 50, No.9, Vn. & Pft.
Copyright renewal assigned 1945
to G. Schirmer, Inc. — C584

Tarantella, Op. 12, Orch.   1st Theme
By permission of Associated
Music Publishers, Inc — C585

2nd Theme — C586

3rd Theme — C587

4th Theme — C588

DAQUIN, Louis Claude (1694-1772)

Le Coucou, Harpsi.   1st Theme — D1

2nd Theme — D2

La Guitarre, Harpsi. **D3**

L'Hirondelle, Harpsi. **D4**

Musette Et Tambourin
Harpsi. 1st Theme Musette **D5**

2nd Theme Tambourin **D6**

Noël No. 9, (Sur Les Flutes), Organ **D7**

Noël No. 10, Organ **D8**

DARGOMIJSKY, Alexander Sergeivich (1813-1869)

Roussalka, Opera Danse Slave **D9**

Gypsy Dance **D10**

Dance of the Nymphs
1st Theme **D11**

2nd Theme **D12**

DEBUSSY, Claude (1862-1918)

Prélude A L'Après-Midi
D'Un Faune 1st Theme **D13**
(Afternoon of A Faun)
Orch.
Permission for reprint granted 2nd Theme **D14**
by Jean Jobert, Paris. Elkan-Vogel Co.
Inc.,Philadelphia, Copyright Owners

Arabesque No. 1, 1st Theme, **D15**
in E, Pft. A
Permission for reprint granted
by Durand & Cie, Paris.
Elkan-Vogel Co.,Inc.,- 1st Theme, **D16**
Philadelphia, Copyright Owners B

2nd Theme **D17**

Arabesque No. 2, 1st Theme **D18**
in G, Pft.
Permission for reprint granted
by Durand & Cie, Paris.
Elkan-Vogel Co., Inc., 2nd Theme **D19**
Philadelphia, Copyright Owners.

Ballad Pft. 1st Theme **D20**
Permission for reprint granted
by Jean Jobert, Paris.
Elkan-Vogel Co., Philadelphia,Inc.
Copyright Owners.

2nd Theme — D21

Children's Corner Suite, Pft.
Permission for reprint granted by Durand & Cie, Paris. Elkan-Vogel Co., Inc., Philadelphia, Copyright Owners.

Doctor Gradus Ad Parnassum — D22

Jimbo's Lullaby — D23

Serenade of the Doll — D24

The Little Shepherd 1st Theme — D25

2nd Theme — D26

Golliwogg's Cake Walk 1st Theme — D27

2nd Theme — D28

3rd Theme (Parody on Tristan) — D29

Danses, Harp
Permission for reprint granted by Durand & Cie, Paris. Elkan-Vogel Co., Inc., Philadelphia, Copyright Owners.

I Danse Sacrée — D30

II Danse Profane — D31

Danse (Tarantelle Styrienne), Pft.
Permission for reprint granted by Jean Jobert, Paris. Elkan-Vogel Co., Inc. Philadelphia, Copyright Owners.

1st Theme — D32

2nd Theme — D33

Estampes, Pft.
Permission for reprint granted by Durand & Cie, Paris. Elkan-Vogel Co. Inc. Philadelphia, Copyright Owners.

Pagodes — D34

La Soirée dans Grenade 1st Theme — D35

2nd Theme — D36

3rd Theme — D37

Jardins Sous La Pluie (Gardens in the Rain) 1st Theme — D38

2nd Theme — D39

L'Isle Joyeuse, Pft.
Permission for reprint granted by Durand & Cie, Paris. Elkan-Vogel Co., Inc., Philadelphia, Copyright Owners.

Intro. — D40

1st Theme — D41

2nd Theme — D42

3rd Theme — D43

Gigues, from Images, Orch., No. 1
Permission for reprint granted by Durand & Cie, Paris. Elkan-Vogel Co., Inc. Philadelphia, Copyright Owners.

1st Theme — D44

2nd Theme — D45

3rd Theme — D46

Iberia, from Images, Orch., No. 2
Par Les Rues et Par Les Chemins (Along the Streets and Roads)
Permission for reprint granted by Durand & Cie, Paris. Elkan-Vogel Co., Inc. Philadelphia, Copyright Owners.

1st Movement 1st Theme — D47

1st Movement 2nd Theme — D48

1st Movement 3rd Theme — D49

1st Movement 4th Theme — D50

1st Movement 5th Theme — D51

1st Movement 6th Theme — D52

Les Parfums de La Nuit (Perfumes of the Night)

2nd Movement Intro. — D53

2nd Movement 1st Theme — D54

2nd Movement 2nd Theme — D55

2nd Movement 3rd Theme — D56

2nd Movement 4th Theme — D57

2nd Movement 5th Theme — D58

2nd Movement 6th Theme — D59

Le Matin D'Un Jour De Fête (The Morning of a Holiday)

3rd Movement 1st Theme — D60

3rd Movement 2nd Theme — D61

3rd Movement 3rd Theme — D62

I Reflets Dans L'Eau from Images—1st Series, Pft. — 1st Theme — D63
Permission for reprint granted by Durand & Cie, Paris. Elkan-Vogel Co., Inc. Philadelphia, Copyright Owners.

2nd Theme — D64

II Hommage à Rameau from Images—1st Series, Pft. — 1st Theme — D65
Permission for reprint granted by Durand & Cie, Paris. Elkan-Vogel Co., Inc. Philadelphia, Copyright Owners.

2nd Theme — D66

Poissons D'Or (Goldfish) from Images—2nd Series, Pft. — D67
Permission for reprint granted by Durand & Cie, Paris. Elkan-Vogel Co., Inc. Philadelphia, Copyright Owners.

Mazurka, Pft. — D68
Permission for reprint granted by Jean Jobert, Paris. Elkan-Vogel Co., Inc. Philadelphia, Copyright Owners.

La Mer, Orch. — 1st Movement 1st Theme — D69
De L'Aube A Midi Sur La Mer (From Dawn to Noon on the Sea) — 1st Movement 2nd Theme — D70
Permission for reprint granted by Durand & Cie, Paris. Elkan-Vogel Co., Inc. Philadelphia, Copyright Owners.

1st Movement 3rd Theme — D71

1st Movement 4th Theme — D72

1st Movement 5th Theme — D73

1st Movement 6th Theme — D74

Jeux De Vagues (Play of the Waves) — 2nd Movement 1st Theme — D75

2nd Movement 2nd Theme — D76

2nd Movement 3rd Theme — D77

Dialogue du Vent et de la Mer (Dialogue of the Wind and the Sea) — 3rd Movement 1st Theme — D78

3rd Movement 2nd Theme — D79

Nocturnes, Orch. — Nuages (Clouds) 1st Theme — D80
Permission for reprint granted by Jean Jobert, Paris. Elkan-Vogel Co., Inc. Philadelphia, Copyright Owners.

2nd Theme — D81
3rd Theme — D82
Fêtes 1st Theme — D83
2nd Theme — D84
3rd Theme — D85
4th Theme — D86
Sirènes 1st Theme — D87
2nd Theme — D88

Petite Suite, 2 Pianos
Permission for reprint granted by Durand & Cie, Paris. Elkan-Vogel Co., Inc. Philadelphia. Copyright Owners,

En Bateau 1st Theme — D89
2nd Theme — D90
Cortège 1st Theme — D91
2nd Theme — D92
Menuet 1st Theme — D93
2nd Theme — D94
Ballet 1st Theme — D95
2nd Theme — D96

Pour le Piano, Suite
Permission for reprint granted by Durand & Cie, Paris. Elkan-Vogel Co., Inc. Philadelphia, Copyright Owners,

Prelude 1st Theme — D97
2nd Theme — D98
Sarabande — D99
Toccata — D100

5 *

La Plus Que Lente, Waltz, Pft.   1st Theme   D101

Permission for reprint granted by Durand & Cie, Paris. Elkan-Vogel Co., Inc. Philadelphia, Copyright Owners.   2nd Theme   D102

Préludes, Book 1, Pft. Permission for reprint granted by Durand & Cie, Paris. Elkan-Vogel Co., Inc. Philadelphia, Copyright Owners,
No. 1
Danseuses De Delphes   D103

No. 2
Voiles (Veils)   1st Theme   D104

2nd Theme   D105

No. 5
Les Collines D'Anacapri (The Hills of Anacapri   D106

No. 8
La Fille Aux Cheveux De Lin (The Girl With the Flaxen Hair)   D107

No. 10
La Cathedrale Engloutie (The Sunken Cathedral)   1st Theme   D108

2nd Theme   D109

No. 11
La Danse De Puck   D110

No. 12
Minstrels   D111

Préludes, Book II, Pft. Permission for reprint granted by Durand & Cie, Paris. Elkan-Vogel Co., Inc. Philadelphia, Copyright Owners,
No. 3
La Puerta Del Vino   D112

No. 5
Bruyères (Heather)   D113

No. 6
General Lavine-Eccentric   D114

No. 9, Hommage à S. Pickwick, Esq., P.P.M.P.C. (Parody on God Save the King)   D115

Printemps Symphonic Suite, Orch.   1st Movement 1st Theme   D116

Permission for reprint granted by Durand & Cie, Paris. Elkan-Vogel Co., Inc. Philadelphia, Copyright Owners.   1st Movement 2nd Theme   D117

2nd Movement 1st Theme   D118

2nd Movement 2nd Theme   D119

Quartet in G Minor, Str.   1st Movement 1st Theme, A   D120

Permission for reprint granted by Durand & Cie, Paris. Elkan-Vogel Co., Inc. Philadelphia, Copyright Owners.

1st Movement 1st Theme, B — D121

1st Movement 2nd Theme — D122

2nd Movement 1st Theme, A — D123

2nd Movement 1st Theme, B — D124

3rd Movement 1st Theme — D125

3rd Movement 2nd Theme, A — D126

3rd Movement 2nd Theme, B — D127

4th Movement — D128

Rapsodie, Saxophone & Orch.
Permission for reprint granted by Durand & Cie, Paris. Elkan-Vogel Co., Inc. Philadelphia, Copyright Owners.

1st Theme — D129

2nd Theme — D130

3rd Theme — D131

Rapsodie, Clarinet & Orch.
Permission for reprint granted by Durand & Cie, Paris. Elkan-Vogel Co., Inc. Philadelphia, Copyright Owners.

1st Theme — D132

2nd Theme — D133

Rêverie, Pft.
By permisssion of The Boston Music Co., copyright owner.

1st Theme — D134

2nd Theme — D135

Sonata in G Minor, Vn. & Pft.
Permission for reprint granted by Durand & Cie, Paris. Elkan-Vogel Co., Inc. Philadelphia, Copyright Owners.

1st Movement 1st Theme — D136

1st Movement 2nd Theme — D137

2nd Movement 1st Theme — D138

2nd Movement 2nd Theme — D139

3rd Movement — D140

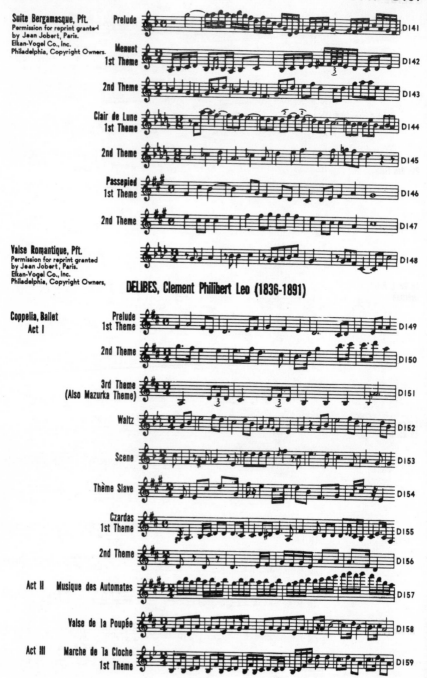

Suite Bergamasque, Pft.
Permission for reprint granted
by Jean Jobert, Paris.
Elkan-Vogel Co., Inc.
Philadelphia, Copyright Owners.

Prelude — D141

Menuet
1st Theme — D142

2nd Theme — D143

Clair de Lune
1st Theme — D144

2nd Theme — D145

Passepied
1st Theme — D146

2nd Theme — D147

Valse Romantique, Pft.
Permission for reprint granted
by Jean Jobert, Paris.
Elkan-Vogel Co., Inc.
Philadelphia, Copyright Owners,

— D148

DELIBES, Clement Philibert Leo (1836-1891)

Coppelia, Ballet
Act I

Prelude
1st Theme — D149

2nd Theme — D150

3rd Theme
(Also Mazurka Theme) — D151

Waltz — D152

Scene — D153

Thème Slave — D154

Czardas
1st Theme — D155

2nd Theme — D156

Act II Musique des Automates — D157

Valse de la Poupée — D158

Act III Marche de la Cloche
1st Theme — D159

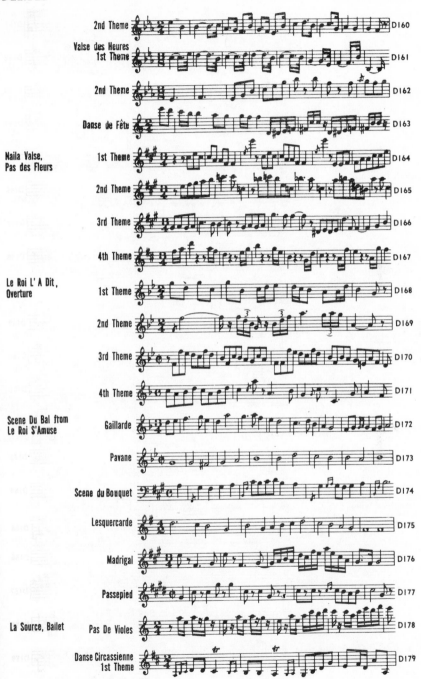

2nd Theme — D160
Valse des Heures
1st Theme — D161
2nd Theme — D162
Danse de Fête — D163
Naila Valse,
Pas des Fleurs
1st Theme — D164
2nd Theme — D165
3rd Theme — D166
4th Theme — D167
Le Roi L' A Dit,
Overture
1st Theme — D168
2nd Theme — D169
3rd Theme — D170
4th Theme — D171
Scene Du Bal from
Le Roi S'Amuse
Gaillarde — D172
Pavane — D173
Scene du Bouquet — D174
Lesquercarde — D175
Madrigal — D176
Passepied — D177
La Source, Ballet
Pas De Violes — D178
Danse Circassienne
1st Theme — D179

2nd Theme — D180

Scherzo—Polka — D181

Sylvia, Ballet   Prelude — D182

Les Chasseresses — D183

Valse Lente — D184

Marche de Bacchus
1st Theme — D185

2nd Theme — D186

Pizzicato — D187

DELIUS, Frederick (1862-1934)

Appalachia, Orch.
By permission of the
copyright owner,
Boosey and Hawkes, Inc.   Intro. — D188

1st Theme — D189

2nd Theme
(March Variant of
1st Theme) — D190

Brigg Fair, Orch.
By permission of the
copyright owner,
Boosey and Hawkes, Inc.   1st Theme — D191

2nd Theme — D192

Concerto, Vn. & Orch.
By permission of Augener,
Ltd., London   1st Theme — C193

2nd Theme — D194

3rd Theme — D195

4th Theme — D196

5th Theme — D197

6th Theme — D198

Eventyr
"Once Upon a Time", Orch.
By permission of Augener,
Ltd., London

1st Theme   D199

2nd Theme   D200

3rd Theme   D201

Hassan,
Suite for Orch.
By permission of the
copyright owner,
Boosey and Hawkes, Inc.

Intermezzo   D202

Serenade   D203

In a Summer Garden, Orch.
By permission of Associated
Music Publishers, Inc.

1st Theme, A   D204

1st Theme, B   D205

2nd Theme   D206

3rd Theme   D207

4th Theme   D208

Irmelin–Prelude, Orch.
By permission of the copyright
owner, Boosey and Hawkes, Inc.

D209

Paris, Nocturne, Orch.
By permission of Associated
Music Publishers, Inc.

1st Theme   D210

2nd Theme   D211

3rd Theme   D212

4th Theme   D213

Sonata No. 2, Vn. & Pft.
By permission of the
copyright owner,
Boosey and Hawkes, Inc.

1st Theme   D214

2nd Theme   D215

3rd Theme   D216

4th Theme   D217

**Two Pieces
for Small
Orchestra**
Copyright by the
Oxford University Press
Reproduced by permission.

No. 1, On Hearing the
First Cuckoo in Spring   D218

No.II Summer Night on the River — D219

The Walk to the Paradise Garden, from A Village Romeo & Juliet, Orch.
By permission of the copyright owner, Boosey and Hawkes, Inc.
1st Theme — D220
2nd Theme — D221

DETT, Robert Nathaniel (1882-1943)

Juba Dance, Pft. from In the Bottoms
By permission of Clayton F. Summy Co., owners of the copyright.
1st Theme — D222
2nd Theme — D223

DIAMOND, David (1915-   )

Rounds, Str. Orch.
Permission granted by Elkan-Vogel Co., Inc. Philadelphia, Pa. Copyright 1946
1st Movement 1st Theme — D223a
1st Movement 2nd Theme — D223b
1st Movement 3rd Theme — D223c
2nd Movement — D223d
3rd Movement 1st Theme — D223e
3rd Movement 2nd Theme — D223f

DINICU, ARR. BY HEIFETZ

Hora Staccato, Vn. & Pft.
Copyright 1930 by Carl Fischer, Inc., N. Y.
1st Theme — D224
2nd Theme — D225

DITTERSDORF, Carl Ditters von (1739-1799)

Quartet, No. 5, in E Flat, Str.
1st Movement — D226
2nd Movement 1st Theme — D227
2nd Movement 2nd Theme — D228

3rd Movement  D229

Quartet, No. 6,
in A, Str.

1st Movement D230

2nd Movement D231

3rd Movement D232

DOHNÁNYI, Ernö von (1877-1960)

Capriccio, Op. 28, Pft. D233

Rhapsody, Op. 11, No. 3,
Pft.   1st Theme D234
By permission of Associated
Music Publishers, Inc.

              2nd Theme D235

Ruralia Hungarica, Op. 32a, No. 1 D236

Ruralia Hungarica, Op. 32a,   1st Theme D237
No. 2

              2nd Theme D238

Ruralia Hungarica, Op. 32a,
No. 7   D239

Suite, Op. 19, Orch.   Andante con
By permission of Associated Variazioni D240
Music Publishers, Inc.

              Scherzo
              1st Theme D241

              2nd Theme D242

              Romance
              1st Theme D243

              2nd Theme D244

              Rondo
              1st Theme D245

              2nd Theme D246

DONIZETTI, Gaetano (1797-1848)

Daughter of the Regiment Overture — 1st Theme — D24

2nd Theme — D24

3rd Theme — D24

4th Theme — D25

La Favorita Overture — 1st Theme — D25

2nd Theme — D252

Don Pasquale Overture — 1st Theme — D253

2nd Theme — D254

DOWLAND, John (1563-1626)

M. George Whitehead, His Almand
Lute & Strings — D255

Mrs. Nichols' Almand
Lute & Strings — D256

M. Henry Nöel, His Galliard
Lute & Strings — D257

M. Thomas Collier, His Galliard
Lute & Strings — D258

M. John Langton's Pavan
Lute & Strings — D259

The King of Denmark's Galliard
Lute & Strings — D260

The Earl of Essex Galliard
Lute & Strings — D261

DRDLA, Franz (1868-1944)

Souvenir, Vn. & Pft. — 1st Theme — D261a

2nd Theme — D261b

DRIGO, Riccardo (1846-1930)

es Millions
'Arlequin, Serenade
n. & Pft.
1st Theme — D261c

2nd Theme — D261d

alse Bluette, Vn. & Pft.
— D261e

DUKAS, Paul (1865-1935)

pprenti Sorcier
he Sorcerer's Apprentice)
cherzo for Orch.
rmission for reprint granted
Durand & Cie, Paris.
an-Vogel Co., Inc.
iladelphia, Copyright Owners.
Intro. — D262

1st Theme — D263

2nd Theme — D264

Péri
nce Poem for Orch.
rmission for reprint granted
Durand & Cie, Paris.
an-Vogel Co., Inc.
iladelphia, Copyright Owners.
1st Theme — D265

2nd Theme — D266

3rd Theme — D267

4th Theme — D268

DVORÁK, Antonin (1841-1904)

agatelles, Op. 47,
t. & Str.
permission of Associated
usic Publishers, Inc.
1st Movement — D269

2nd Movement — D270

4th Movement — D271

5th Movement
1st Theme — D272

5th Movement
2nd Theme — D273

arnaval Overture, Op. 92
permission of Associated
Music Publishers, Inc.
1st Theme — D274

2nd Theme — D275

3rd Theme — D276
4th Theme — D277

Concerto in B Minor, Op.104, Cello & Orch.
Copyright 1930 by G. Schirmer, Inc.

1st Movement 1st Theme — D278
1st Movement 2nd Theme — D279
2nd Movement 1st Theme — D280
2nd Movement 2nd Theme — D281
3rd Movement 1st Theme — D282
3rd Movement 2nd Theme — D283

Concerto in A Minor, Op. 53, Vn. & Orch.
By permission of Associated Music Publishers, Inc.

1st Movement 1st Theme, A — D284
1st Movement 1st Theme, B — D285
1st Movement 2nd Theme — D286
2nd Movement 1st Theme — D287
2nd Movement 2nd Theme — D288
3rd Movement 1st Theme — D289
3rd Movement 2nd Theme — D290
3rd Movement 3rd Theme — D291

Humoresque, Op. 101, No. 7, Pft.
By permission of Associated Music Publishers, Inc.

1st Theme — D292
2nd Theme — D293
3rd Theme — D294

Quartet in D, Op. 23, Pft. & Str.
By permission of Associated Music Publishers, Inc.

1st Movement 1st Theme — D295

Quartet in E Flat,
Op. 87, Pft. & Str.
By permission of
Associated Music
Publishers, Inc.

Quart., in F, Op. 96
Str."American"
By permission of
Associated Music
Publishers, Inc.

1st Movement
2nd Theme   D296

2nd Movement   D297

3rd Movement
1st Theme   D298

3rd Movement
2nd Theme   D299

1st Movement
1st Theme   D300

1st Movement
2nd Theme   D301

2nd Movement   D302

3rd Movement
1st Theme   D303

3rd Movement
2nd Theme   D304

4th Movement
1st Theme   D305

4th Movement
2nd Theme   D306

1st Movement
1st Theme   D307

1st Movement
2nd Theme   D308

2nd Movement   D309

3rd Movement
1st Theme   D310

3rd Movement
2nd Theme
A   D311

3rd Movement
2nd Theme
B   D312

4th Movement
Intro.   D313

4th Movement
1st Theme   D314

4th Movement
2nd Theme   D315

DVORAK

D316—D332c

Quartet in A Flat, Op. 105, Str.
By permission of Associated Music Publishers, Inc.

1st Movement 1st Theme

D316

1st Movement 2nd Theme

D317

2nd Movement 1st Theme

D318

2nd Movement 2nd Theme

D319

3rd Movement

D320

4th Movement 1st Theme

D321

4th Movement 2nd Theme

D322

4th Movement 3rd Theme

D323

Quartet in G, Op. 106, Str.
By permission of Associated Music Publishers, Inc.

1st Movement 1st Theme

D324

1st Movement 2nd Theme

D325

2nd Movement

D326

3rd Movement 1st Theme

D327

3rd Movement 2nd Theme

D328

3rd Movement 3rd Theme

D329

4th Movement 1st Theme

D330

4th Movement 2nd Theme

D331

4th Movement 3rd Theme

D332

Quintet, Op. 81 Pft. & Str.

1st Movement 1st Theme

D332a

1st Movement 2nd Theme

D332b

2nd Movement Dumka 1st Theme, A

D332c

2nd Movement 1st Theme, B — D332d

2nd Movement 1st Theme, C — D332e

2nd Movement 2nd Theme — D332f

3rd Movement — D332g

4th Movement 1st Theme — D332h

4th Movement 2nd Theme — D332i

Quintet in E Flat, Op. 97, Str.
By permission of Associated Music Publishers, Inc.

1st Movement 1st Theme — D333

1st Movement 2nd Theme — D334

2nd Movement 1st Theme — D335

2nd Movement 2nd Theme — D336

3rd Movement — D337

4th Movement — D338

Scherzo Capriccioso, Op. 66, Orch.
By permission of Associated Music Publishers, Inc.

1st Theme — D339

2nd Theme — D340

3rd Theme — D341

4th Theme — D342

Serenade for Strings, in E, Op. 22
By permission of Associated Music Publishers, Inc.

1st Movement 1st Theme — D343

1st Movement 2nd Theme — D344

2nd Movement 1st Theme — D345

2nd Movement 2nd Theme — D346

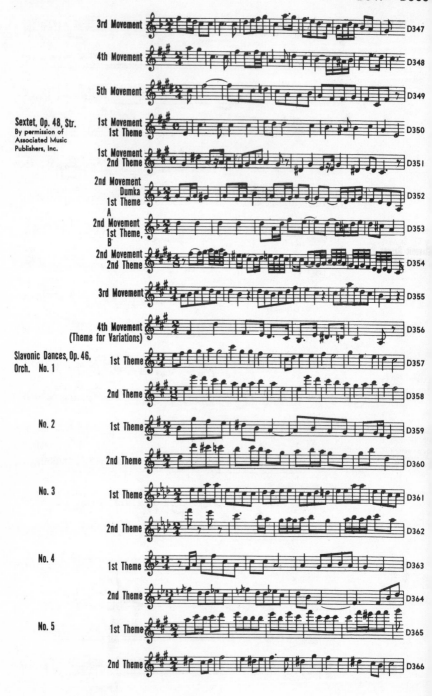

3rd Movement — D347
4th Movement — D348
5th Movement — D349

Sextet, Op. 48, Str.
By permission of
Associated Music
Publishers, Inc.

1st Movement 1st Theme — D350
1st Movement 2nd Theme — D351
2nd Movement Dumka 1st Theme A — D352
2nd Movement 1st Theme, B — D353
2nd Movement 2nd Theme — D354
3rd Movement — D355
4th Movement (Theme for Variations) — D356

Slavonic Dances, Op. 46, Orch. No. 1

1st Theme — D357
2nd Theme — D358

No. 2

1st Theme — D359
2nd Theme — D360

No. 3

1st Theme — D361
2nd Theme — D362

No. 4

1st Theme — D363
2nd Theme — D364

No. 5

1st Theme — D365
2nd Theme — D366

2nd Theme — D387

No. 6   1st Theme — D388

2nd Theme — D389

No. 7   1st Theme — D390

2nd Theme — D391

3rd Theme — D392

4th Theme — D393

No. 8   1st Theme — D394

2nd Theme — D395

3rd Theme — D396

4th Theme — D397

5th Theme — D398

Slavonic Rhapsody, Op. 45,
No. 3, Orch.
By permission of
Associated Music
Publishers, Inc.
  1st Theme — D399

2nd Theme — D400

3rd Theme — D401

Sonatina in G, Op. 100,
Vn. & Pft.
By permission of
Associated Music
Publishers, Inc.
  1st Movement 1st Theme — D402

1st Movement 2nd Theme — D403

(Arr. by Kreisler
as "Indian Lament")
  2nd Movement 1st Theme — D404

2nd Movement 2nd Theme — D405

3rd Movement — D406

DVORAK

4th Movement 1st Theme — D407

4th Movement 2nd Theme — D408

4th Movement 3rd Theme — D409

Symphony No. 1, in D. Op. 60
By permission of Associated Music Publishers, Inc.

1st Movement 1st Theme — D410

1st Movement 2nd Theme — D411

2nd Movement — D412

3rd Movement 1st Theme A — D413

3rd Movement 1st Theme B — D414

3rd Movement 2nd Theme — D415

4th Movement 1st Theme — D416

4th Movement 2nd Theme — D417

Symphony No. 2 in D Minor, Op. 70
By permission of Associated Music Publishers, Inc.

1st Movement 1st Theme — D418

1st Movement 2nd Theme — D419

2nd Movement — D420

3rd Movement 1st Theme — D421

3rd Movement 2nd Theme — D422

4th Movement 1st Theme — D423

4th Movement 2nd Theme — D424

4th Movement 3rd Theme — D425

Symphony No. 4 in G, Op. 88
By permission of Novello & Co., Ltd., London

1st Movement 1st Theme — D426

Symphony No. 5,
in E Minor, Op. 95
"From The New World"
Published and
Copyrighted 1928
by Oliver Ditson Co.

Trio in F Minor, Op. 65, 1st Movement
Vn., Pft. & Cello
By permission of Associated
Music Publishers, Inc.

1st Movement
2nd Theme — D447

2nd Movement — D448

3rd Movement — D449

4th Movement
1st Theme — D450

4th Movement
2nd Theme — D451

rio, Op. 90 Vn.
ft. & Cello, "Dumky"
y permission of
ssociated Music
ublishers, Inc.

1st Movement
Intro. — D452

1st Movement
1st Theme,
A — D453

1st Movement
1st Theme,
B — D454

1st Movement
2nd Theme — D455

1st Movement
3rd Theme — D456

2nd Movement — D457

3rd Movement
1st Theme — D458

3rd Movement
2nd Theme — D459

4th Movement
1st Theme — D460

4th Movement
2nd Theme — D461

5th Movement
Intro. — D462

5th Movement — D463

Wedding Dance From
Die Waldtaube, Op. 110,
Orch.
By permission of Associated
Music Publishers, Inc.

1st Theme — D464

2nd Theme — D465

Waltzes, Op. 54, Pft.
No. 1
By permission of Associated
Music Publishers, Inc.

D466

No. 3   1st Theme   D467

2nd Theme   D468

No. 6   D469

ELGAR, Sir Edward (1857-1934)

Chanson de Nuit, Op. 15, No. 1,
Orch.
By permission of Novello & Co., Ltd., London.   E1

Cockaigne, In London Town
Op. 40, Concert Overture,
Orch.   1st Theme   E2
By permission of the
copyright owner,
Boosey and Hawkes, Inc.   2nd Theme   E3

3rd Theme   E4

4th Theme   E5

Concerto in E Minor,
Op. 85, Cello & Orch.   1st Movement / Intro.   E6
By permission of
Novello & Co., Ltd.,
London.   1st Movement / 1st Theme   E7

1st Movement / 2nd Theme   E8

2nd Movement / 1st Theme   E9

2nd Movement / 2nd Theme   E10

3rd Movement   E11

4th Movement   E12

Concerto in B Minor,
Op. 61, Vn. & Orch.   1st Movement / 1st Theme, / A   E13
By permission of
Novello & Co., Ltd.,
London.   1st Movement / 1st Theme, / B   E14

1st Movement / 2nd Theme   E15

2nd Movement / 1st Theme   E16

2nd Movement 2nd Theme E17

3rd Movement 1st Theme E18

3rd Movement 2nd Theme E19

Contrasts, Op. 10, No. 3,
Orch.
By permission of
Novello & Co., Ltd., London.

1st Theme E20

2nd Theme E21

"Enigma" Variations, Op. 36,
Orch.
By permission of Novello & Co., Ltd., London.

Theme E22

Falstaff, Op. 68,
Symphonic Study
By Permission of
Novello & Co., Ltd., London

1st Theme E23

2nd Theme E24

3rd Theme E25

4th Theme E26

5th Theme E27

6th Theme E28

7th Theme E29

8th Theme E30

9th Theme E31

Introduction and Allegro,
Op. 47, Str. Quart. & Str. Orch.
By permission of
Novello & Co., Ltd., London.

Intro. E32

1st Theme E33

2nd Theme E34

3rd Theme E35

May Song, Orch.

1st Theme E36

Symphony No. 1,
in A Flat, Op. 55
By permission of
Novello & Co., Ltd.,
London.

The Wand of Youth
Suite No. 1, Op. 1a, Orch.
By permission of
Novello & Co., Ltd., London.

2nd Movement
2nd Theme — E57

3rd Movement
1st Theme — E58

3rd Movement
2nd Theme — E59

1st Movement
Intro. — E60

1st Movement
1st Theme — E61

1st Movement
2nd Theme — E62

2nd Movement
1st Theme — E63

2nd Movement
2nd Theme — E64

2nd Movement
3rd Theme — E65

2nd Movement
4th Theme — E66

3rd Movement
1st Theme — E67

3rd Movement
2nd Theme, A — E68

3rd Movement
2nd Theme, B — E69

3rd Movement
3rd Theme — E70

4th Movement
1st Theme — E71

4th Movement
2nd Theme — E72

4th Movement
3rd Theme — E73

Overture — E74

Serenade — E75

Minuet (Old Style) — E76

* For Symphony No. 2, E73a-E73k, see Page 526.

Sun Dance — E77

Fairy Pipers — E78

Slumber Scene — E79

ENESCO, Georges (1881-1955)

Poème Roumain, Op. 1
Symphonic Suite

By permission of
M M Enoch & Cie.,
Music Publishers,
27 Boulevard
des Italiens, Paris.

1st Movement / 1st Theme — E80

1st Movement / 2nd Theme — E81

1st Movement / 3rd Theme — E82

2nd Movement / 1st Theme — E83

2nd Movement / 2nd Theme — E84

2nd Movement / Roumanian Folk Song / 3rd Theme — E85

2nd Movement / 4th Theme — E86

2nd Movement / 5th Theme — E87

2nd Movement / Roumanian National Anthem — E88

Roumanian Rhapsody No. 1,
Op. 11, Orch.

By permission of
M M Enoch & Cie.,
Music Publishers,
27 Boulevard
des Italiens, Paris.

1st Theme, A — E89

1st Theme, B — E90

2nd Theme — E91

3rd Theme, A — E92

3rd Theme, B — E93

4th Theme — E94

5th Theme — E95

6th Theme — E96

7th Theme — E97

8th Theme — E98

Roumanian Rhapsody No. 2
Op. 11, Orch.
By permission of
M M Enoch & Cie.,
Music Publishers,
27 Boulevard
des Italiens, Paris.

1st Theme — E99

2nd Theme — E100

3rd Theme — E101

4th Theme — E102

5th Theme — E103

ERKEL, Franz (1810-1893)

Hunyadi László, Opera
Overture

1st Theme — E104

2nd Theme — E105

3rd Theme — E106

4th Theme — E107

FALLA, Manuel de (1876-1946)

El Amor Brujo,
Ballet
By permission of
the copyright holders,
J. & W. Chester, Ltd., 11
Great Marlborough
Street, London, W. 1.

Introduction & Scene — F1

En La Cueva — F2

Canción del Amor Dolido — F3

Dance of Terror
1st Theme — F4

2nd Theme — F5

Ritual Fire Dance
1st Theme — F6

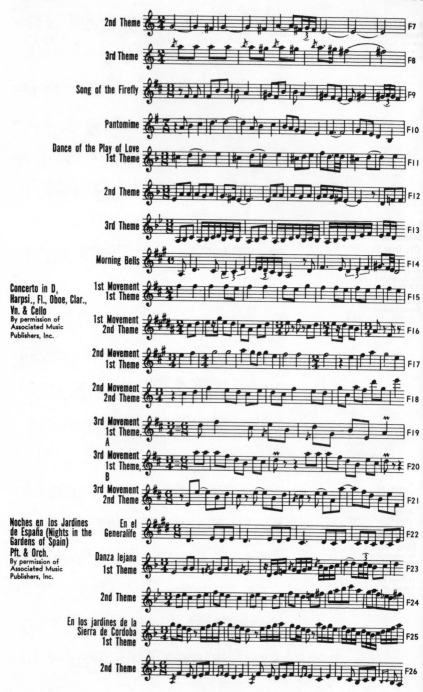

2nd Theme F7
3rd Theme F8
Song of the Firefly F9
Pantomime F10
Dance of the Play of Love
1st Theme F11
2nd Theme F12
3rd Theme F13
Morning Bells F14

Concerto in D,
Harpsi., Fl., Oboe, Clar.,
Vn. & Cello
By permission of
Associated Music
Publishers, Inc.

1st Movement
1st Theme F15
1st Movement
2nd Theme F16
2nd Movement
1st Theme F17
2nd Movement
2nd Theme F18
3rd Movement
1st Theme,
A F19
3rd Movement
1st Theme,
B F20
3rd Movement
2nd Theme F21

Noches en los Jardines
de España (Nights in the
Gardens of Spain)
Pft. & Orch.
By permission of
Associated Music
Publishers, Inc.

En el
Generalife F22
Danza lejana
1st Theme F23
2nd Theme F24
En los jardines de la
Sierra de Cordoba
1st Theme F25
2nd Theme F26

de FALLA

4 Pieces Espagñoles, Pft.
Permission for reprint granted by Durand & Cie, Paris. Elkan-Vogel Co., Inc. Philadelphia, Copyright Owners.

Aragonesa — F27

Cubana — F28

Montañesa 1st Theme — F29

2nd Theme — F30

Andaluza 1st Theme — F31

2nd Theme — F32

3 Dances from El Sombrero de Tres Picos (The Three Cornered Hat), Orch.
By permission of the copyright holders, J. & W. Chester, Ltd., 11 Great Marlborough Street, London, W. 1.

Dance of the Neighbors 1st Theme — F33

2nd Theme — F34

Danse du Corregidor (Mayor's Dance) 1st Theme — F35

2nd Theme — F36

Jota 1st Theme — F37

2nd Theme — F38

3rd Theme — F39

4th Theme — F40

Miller's Dance — F41

Suite Populaire Espagñole, Vn. & Pft.
By permission of the copyright holders, J. & W. Chester, Ltd., 11 Great Marlborough Street, London, W. 1.

El Pano Moruno — F42

Nana — F43

Canción — F44

Polo — F45

Asturiana — F46

Jota 1st Theme — F47

2nd Theme — F48

La Vida Breve
Orch.
By permission of Associated
Music Publishers, Inc.

Dance, No. 1 1st Theme — F49

2nd Theme — F50

Dance No. 2 1st Theme — F51

2nd Theme — F52

FARNABY, Giles (1560-1600)

His Conceit, Fitzwilliam Virginal
Book No. 273, Harpsi. — F53

His Dreame, Fitzwilliam Virginal
Book No. 260, Harpsi. — F54

His Humour, Fitzwilliam Virginal
Book No. 196, Harpsi. — F55

His Rest, Fitzwilliam Virginal
Book No. 195, Harpsi. — F56

Rosa Solis, Fitzwilliam Virginal
Book No. 143, Harpsi. — F57

Tower Hill, Fitzwilliam Virginal
Book No. 245, Harpsi. — F58

A Toye, Fitzwilliam Virginal
Book No. 270, Harpsi. — F59

FAURÉ, Gabriel (1845-1924)

Ballade, Op. 19, Pft. & Orch 1st Theme
By permission of
J. Hamelle Music
Publishers, Paris. — F60

2nd Theme — F61

3rd Theme — F62

4th Theme — F63

Barcarolle No. 5, Op. 66, Pft.
By permission of J. Hamelle
Music Publishers, Paris. — F64

Barcarolle No. 6, Op. 70, Pft.
By permission of
J. Hamelle Music
Publishers, Paris.

Dolly, Op. 56, Pft.,
4 Hands
By permission of
J. Hamelle Music
Publishers, Paris.

Berceuse

Mi-a-ou
1st Theme

2nd Theme

Le Jardin de Dolly

Kitty-Valse
1st Theme

2nd Theme

Tendresse

Le Pas Espagnol
1st Theme

2nd Theme

Elégie, Op. 24,
Cello & Orch.
By permission of
J. Hamelle Music
Publishers, Paris.

1st Theme

2nd Theme

Impromptu, No. 2,
Op. 34, Pft.
By permission of
International Music Co.

1st Theme

2nd Theme

Impromptu, No.3,
Op. 34, Pft.
By permission of
International Music Co.

1st Theme

2nd Theme

3rd Nocturne, Op. 33. No. 3, Pft.
By permission of
J. Hamelle Music
Publishers, Paris.

4th Nocturne, Op. 36, Pft.
By permission of
J. Hamelle Music
Publishers, Paris.

6th Nocturne, Op. 63, Pft.
By permission of
J. Hamelle Music
Publishers, Paris.

1st Theme

2nd Theme

F65
F66
F67
F68
F69
F70
F71
F72
F73
F74
F75
F76
F76a
F76b
F76c
F76d
F77
F78
F79
F80

Pelléas and Mélisande,
Op. 80, Orch.
By permission of
J. Hamelle Music
Publishers, Paris.

Prélude
1st Theme — F81

2nd Theme — F82

Fileuse — F83

Quartet in C Minor,
Op. 15, Pft. & Str.
By permission of
J. Hamelle Music
Publishers, Paris.

1st Movement
1st Theme — F84

1st Movement
2nd Theme — F85

2nd Movement
1st Theme — F86

2nd Movement
2nd Theme — F87

3rd Movement — F88

4th Movement
1st Theme — F89

4th Movement
2nd Theme — F90

4th Movement
3rd Theme — F91

Quartet in E Minor,
Op. 121, Str.
Permission for reprint
granted by Durand & Cie,
Paris. Elkan-Vogel Co.,Inc.
Philadelphia, Copyright
Owners,

1st Movement
1st Theme — F92

1st Movement
2nd Theme — F93

2nd Movement — F94

3rd Movement — F95

Sicilienne, Op. 78, Cello & Pft.
By permission of
J. Hamelle Music
Publishers, Paris. — F96

Sonata in A,
Op. 13, Vn. & Pft.
By permisssion of The
Boston Music Co.,
copyright owner.

1st Movement
1st Theme — F97

1st Movement
2nd Theme — F98

2nd Movement
1st Theme,
A — F99

2nd Movement
1st Theme,
B — F100

FIELD, John (1782-1837)

Nocturne No. 3, Pft.

Nocturne No. 4, Pft.

Nocturne No. 5, Pft.

Sonata in C Minor, Op. 1, No. 3, Pft.

FLOTOW, Friedrich von (1812-1883)

Alessandro Stradella Overture

Fatme (Zilda) Overture

2nd Theme — F119

3rd Theme — F120

Martha Overture

1st Theme — F121

2nd Theme — F122

3rd Theme — F123

FRANÇAIX, Jean (1912-   )

Sonatine, Vn. & Pft.
By permission of Associated Music Publishers, Inc.

1st Movement — F124

2nd Movement
1st Theme — F125

2nd Movement
2nd Theme — F126

3rd Movement — F127

FRANCK, César (1822-1890)

Three Chorals, Organ No. 1

1st Theme — F128

2nd Theme — F129

No. 2

1st Theme — F130

2nd Theme — F131

No. 3

1st Theme — F132

2nd Theme — F133

Les Djinns, Symphonic Poem, Pft. & Orch.
By permission of M M Enoch & Cie., Music Publishers, 27 Boulevard des Italiens, Paris.

1st Theme — F134

2nd Theme — F135

3rd Theme — F136

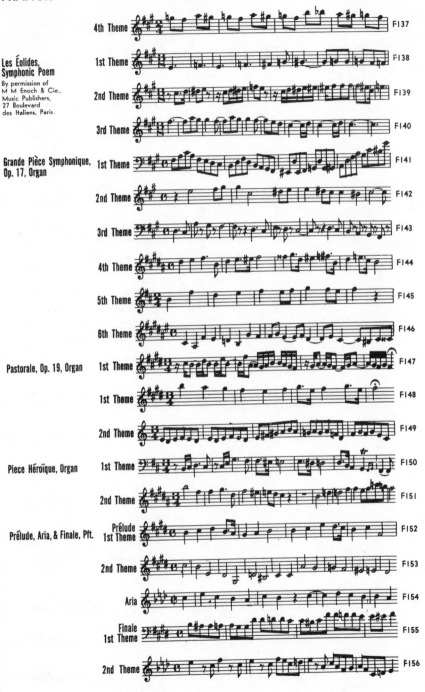

Les Éolides, Symphonic Poem
By permission of
M M Enoch & Cie.,
Music Publishers,
27 Boulevard
des Italiens, Paris.

Grande Pièce Symphonique, Op. 17, Organ

Pastorale, Op. 19, Organ

Piece Héroïque, Organ

Prélude, Aria, & Finale, Pft.

4th Theme   F137

1st Theme   F138

2nd Theme   F139

3rd Theme   F140

1st Theme   F141

2nd Theme   F142

3rd Theme   F143

4th Theme   F144

5th Theme   F145

6th Theme   F146

1st Theme   F147

1st Theme   F148

2nd Theme   F149

1st Theme   F150

2nd Theme   F151

Prélude 1st Theme   F152

2nd Theme   F153

Aria   F154

Finale 1st Theme   F155

2nd Theme   F156

FRANCK

188

F157—F176

Prélude, Chorale & Fugue, Pft.

By permission of
M M Enoch & Cie.,
Music Publishers,
27 Boulevard
des Italiens, Paris.

Prélude, Fugue & Variations, Op. 18 Organ or Pft.

Quartet in D, Str.

Quintet in F Minor, Pft. & Str.

1st Movement 2nd Theme — F177
1st Movement 3rd Theme — F178
2nd Movement 1st Theme — F179
2nd Movement 2nd Theme — F180
2nd Movement 3rd Theme — F181
3rd Movement 1st Theme — F182
3rd Movement 2nd Theme — F183

Sonata, Vn. & Pft.

1st Movement Theme — F184
1st Movement 2nd Theme — F185
2nd Movement 1st Theme — F186
2nd Movement 2nd Theme — F187
3rd Movement (Recitative-Fantasia) — F188
3rd Movement 2nd Theme A — F189
3rd Movement 2nd Theme B — F190
3rd Movement 3rd Theme — F191
4th Movement — F192

Symphonic Variations, Pft.
By permission of M M Enoch & Cie., Music Publishers, 27 Boulevard des Italiens, Paris.

Intro. — F193
1st Theme — F194
2nd Theme — F195

Symphony in D Minor
1st Movement Intro. — F196

1st Movement
1st Theme — F197

1st Movement
2nd Theme — F198

1st Movement
3rd Theme — F199

2nd Movement
1st Theme — F200

2nd Movement
2nd Theme — F201

2nd Movement
3rd Theme — F202

2nd Movement
4th Theme — F203

3rd Movement
1st Theme — F204

3rd Movement
2nd Theme — F205

FRANCOEUR, François (1698-1787)

Gavotte, Vn. & Pft. — F206

Sarabande, Vn. or Cello & Pft. — F207

Siciliano, Vn. & Pft. — F208

Sonata in D Minor,
Vn. & Pft. or Harpsi — 1st Movement Adagio — F209

2nd Movement
Courante — F210

3rd Movement
Allemande — F211

4th Movement
Sarabande — F212

5th Movement
Rondeau — F213

FRANCOEUR Arr. by KREISLER

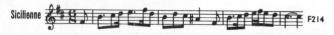

Sicilienne et Rigaudon,
Vn. & Pft.

Sicilienne — F214

Rigaudon  F215

FREDERICK II, King of Prussia (1712-1786)

Concerto No. 2, in
G, Flute & Str.

1st Movement
1st Theme  F216

1st Movement
2nd Theme F217

2nd Movement F218

3rd Movement F219

FRESCOBALDI, Girolamo (1583-1643)

Capriccio on the Cuckoo,
Harpsi.  F220

Capriccio on La Girolometa
Harpsi. F221

Capriccio on L'Aria di Ruggiero
Harpsi. F222

Capriccio: La Spagnoletta
Harpsi. F223

Fugue in G Minor, Organ & Str. F224

Ricercar Cromatico Post. Il Credo
Organ F225

Toccata, Spinet or Lute F226

FUCÎK, Julius (1872-1916)

Entry of the Gladiators,
March

1st Theme 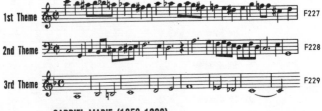 F227

2nd Theme F228

3rd Theme F229

GABRIEL-MARIE (1852-1928)

La Cinquantaine, Air Dans
Le Style Ancien, Pft.

1st Theme G1

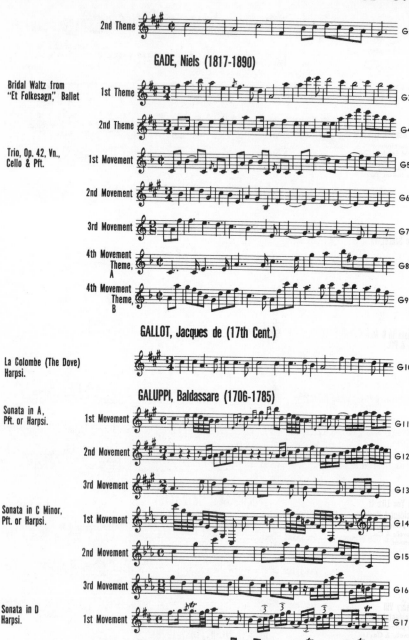

2nd Theme ... G2

GADE, Niels (1817-1890)

Bridal Waltz from
"Et Folkesagn," Ballet   1st Theme ... G3

2nd Theme ... G4

Trio, Op. 42, Vn.,
Cello & Pft.   1st Movement ... G5

2nd Movement ... G6

3rd Movement ... G7

4th Movement
Theme,
A ... G8

4th Movement
Theme,
B ... G9

GALLOT, Jacques de (17th Cent.)

La Colombe (The Dove)
Harpsi. ... G10

GALUPPI, Baldassare (1706-1785)

Sonata in A,
Pft. or Harpsi.   1st Movement ... G11

2nd Movement ... G12

3rd Movement ... G13

Sonata in C Minor,
Pft. or Harpsi.   1st Movement ... G14

2nd Movement ... G15

3rd Movement ... G16

Sonata in D
Harpsi.   1st Movement ... G17

2nd Movement ... G18

3rd Movement  G19

4th Movement G20

GANNÉ, Louis (1862-1923)

La Czarina, Mazurka
By permission of
M M Enoch & Cie.,
Music Publishers,
27 Boulevard
des Italiens, Paris.

1st Theme  G20a

2nd Theme G20b

GAUTIER, Jean (1822-1878)

The Secret, Vn. & Pft.

1st Theme 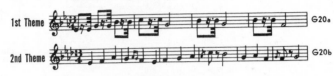 G20c

2nd Theme G20d

GEMINIANI, Francesco (1687-1762)

Sonata in C Minor,
Vn. & Pft.

1st Movement  G21

2nd Movement G22

3rd Movement
Siciliano G23

4th Movement G24

GERMAN, Sir Edward (1862-1936)

As You Like It
Incidental Music
By permission of
Novello & Co., Ltd.,
London.

1st Movement
Woodland Dance  G25

2nd Movement
Children's Dance G26

3rd Movement
Rustic Dance 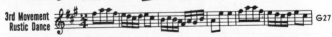 G27

Henry VIII
Incidental Music
By permission of
Novello & Co., Ltd., London

Morris Dance
1st Theme  G28

2nd Theme G29

Shepherd's Dance  G30

Torch Dance — G31

Romeo and Juliet
Incidental Music, Orch.
By permission of Novello & Co., Ltd., London.
Pavane — G32

Welsh Rhapsody, Orch.
By permission of
Novello & Co., Ltd., London.
1st Theme
Loudly Proclaim — G33

2nd Theme — G34

3rd Theme
Hunting the Hare — G35

4th Theme
Bells of Aberdovy — G36

5th Theme
David of the White Rock — G37

6th Theme
Men of Harlech — G38

GERSHWIN, George (1898-1937)

An American in Paris,
Orch.
Copyright 1930 by
New World Music Corp.
Reprinted by
special permission.
1st Theme — G39

2nd Theme — G40

3rd Theme
Blues Theme — G41

4th Theme — G42

Concerto in F,
Pft. & Orch.
Copyright 1927
by Harms, Inc.
Reprinted by
special permission.
1st Movement
1st Theme — G43

1st Movement
2nd Theme — G44

1st Movement
3rd Theme — G45

2nd Movement
1st Theme,
A — G46

2nd Movement
1st Theme,
B — G47

2nd Movement
2nd Theme — G48

2nd Movement
3rd Theme — G49

3rd Movement / 1st Theme — G50
3rd Movement / 2nd Theme — G51

Prelude No. 1, Pft.
Copyright 1927 by New
World Music Corp.
Reprinted by special permission.

Prelude No. 2, Pft.
Copyright 1927 by New
World Music Corp.
Reprinted by special permission.

Prelude No. 3, Pft.
Copyright 1927 by New
World Music Corp.
Reprinted by special permission.

Rhapsody in Blue,
Pft. & Orch.
Copyright 1924 by
Harms, Inc.
Reprinted by special permission

G52
1st Theme — G53
2nd Theme — G54
G55
1st Theme — G56
2nd Theme — G57
3rd Theme — G58
4th Theme — G59
5th Theme — G60

GIBBONS, Orlando (1583-1625)

The Lord of Salisbury, His Pavane,
Harpsi.   G61

The Queen's Command, Harpsi.   G62

GLAZUNOFF, Alexander (1865-1936)

Carnaval, Overture,
Op. 45, Orch.
By permission of Associated
Music Publishers, Inc.

1st Theme — G63
2nd Theme — G64
3rd Theme — G65
4th Theme — G66
5th Theme — G67

Concerto in A Minor, Op. 82, Vn. & Orch.
By permission of Associated Music Publishers, Inc.

1st Theme — G68
2nd Theme — G69
3rd Theme — G70
4th Theme — G71
5th Theme — G72

Une Fête Slave, from Slav Str. Quartet Op. 26, No. 4, Orch.
By permission of Associated Music Publishers, Inc.

1st Theme — G73
2nd Theme — G74
3rd Theme — G75

Méditation, Op. 32, Vn. & Pft.
By permission of Associated Music Publishers, Inc. — G76

Mélodie Arabe, Op. 20, No. 1, Cello & Pft.
By permission of Associated Music Publishers, Inc.

1st Theme — G77
2nd Theme — G78

Novelettes, Op. 15, Str. Quart.
By permission of Associated Music Publishers, Inc.

1st Movement Alla Spagnuola 1st Theme — G78a
1st Movement 2nd Theme — G78b
2nd Movement Orientale 1st Theme — G78c
2nd Movement 2nd Theme — G78d
3rd Movement Interludium in Modo Antico — G78e
4th Movement Waltz 1st Theme — G78f
4th Movement 2nd Theme — G78g
5th Movement All 'Ungherese — G78h

Ouverture Solennelle
By permission of Associated Music Publishers, Inc.

1st Theme — G79

2nd Theme — G80

3rd Theme — G81

4th Theme — G82

Rêverie, Op. 24
Fr. Horn & Pft.
By permission of Associated
Music Publishers, Inc.
— G83

The Seasons (Ballet), Bacchanal
Op. 67
By permission of Associated
Music Publishers, Inc.
— G84

Stenka Razin, Op. 13,
Symphonic Poem,
Orch.
By permission of Associated
Music Publishers, Inc.
1st Theme   Volga Boat Song — G85

2nd Theme — G86

Valsa de Concert,
Op. 47, Orch.
By permission of Associated
Music Publishers, Inc.
1st Theme — G87

2nd Theme — G88

3rd Theme — G89

GLIÈRE, Reinhold (1875-1956)

Russian Sailors' Dance
from the Red Poppy, Ballet
— G90

Symphony No. 3, Op. 42
"Ilia Mourometz"
Scherzo
1st Theme — G91

2nd Theme — G92

GLINKA, Michael (1804-1857)

Capriccio Brilliant on the
Jota Aragonesa, Orch.
1st Theme — G92a

2nd Theme — G93

Kamarinskaya, Orch.
1st Theme — G94

2nd Theme, A — G95

2nd Theme, B — G96

The Lark, (Arr. by Balakirev), Pft. — G97

A Life for the Czar or Ivan Soussanine, Overture — Intro. — G98

1st Theme — G99

2nd Theme — G100

3rd Theme — G101

4th Theme — G102

Quartet in F, Str. — 1st Movement 1st Theme — G103

1st Movement 2nd Theme — G104

2nd Movement — G105

3rd Movement 1st Theme — G106

3rd Movement 2nd Theme — G107

4th Movement — G108

Romance, Pft., Vn. & Cello (Also as Song) — G109

Russlan and Ludmilla, Overture — 1st Theme — G110

2nd Theme — G111

Souvenir of a Night in Madrid, Orch. — 1st Theme Jota — G112

2nd Theme Punto Muruno — G113

3rd Theme Seguidillas Manchegas — G114

4th Theme Seguidillas Manchegas — G115

GLUCK, Christoph (1714-1787)

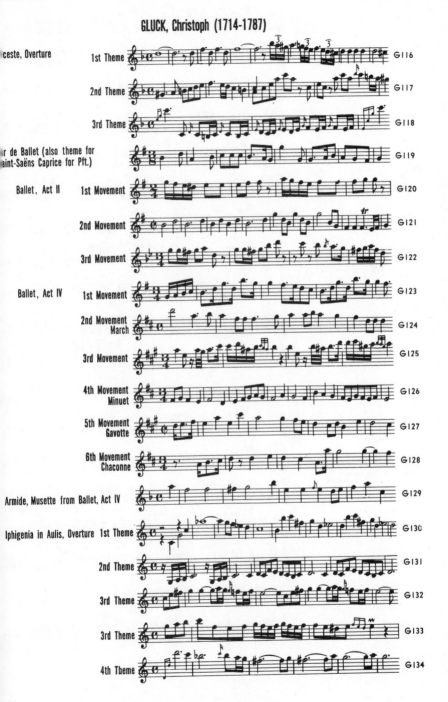

Alceste, Overture — 1st Theme — G116

2nd Theme — G117

3rd Theme — G118

Air de Ballet (also theme for Saint-Saëns Caprice for Pft.) — G119

Ballet, Act II — 1st Movement — G120

2nd Movement — G121

3rd Movement — G122

Ballet, Act IV — 1st Movement — G123

2nd Movement March — G124

3rd Movement — G125

4th Movement Minuet — G126

5th Movement Gavotte — G127

6th Movement Chaconne — G128

Armide, Musette from Ballet, Act IV — G129

Iphigenia in Aulis, Overture — 1st Theme — G130

2nd Theme — G131

3rd Theme — G132

3rd Theme — G133

4th Theme — G134

Act I — Air Gai — G135

Lento — G136

Act II — March — G137

(Theme used by Brahms) — Gavotte 1st Theme — G138

2nd Theme — G139

Act III — Danse des Esclaves — G140

(Also in Orpheus) — Chaconne — G141

Orpheus and Eurydice, Overture — G142

Dance of the Furies — G143

Dance of the Happy Spirits — G144

Melody — G145

GODARD, Benjamin (1849-1895)

Au Matin, Op. 83, Pft. — G146

Berceuse from Jocelyn — 1st Theme, A — G147

1st Theme, B — G148

2nd Theme — G149

2nd Mazurka, Pft. — G150

GODOWSKY, Leopold (1870-1938)

Alt-Wien, Pft. — G151

GOLDMARK, Karl (1830-1915)

Im Frühling, Op. 36, Overture
By permission of Associated Music Publishers, Inc.

1st Theme — G152

2nd Theme — G153

Sakuntala, Op. 13, Overture
By permission of Associated Music Publishers, Inc.

1st Theme — G154

2nd Theme — G155

3rd Theme — G156

4th Theme — G157

Symphony, Op. 26, "Rustic Wedding"
By permission of Associated Music Publishers, Inc.

1st Movement Wedding March — G158

2nd Movement Bridal Song — G159

3rd Movement Serenade 1st Theme — G160

3rd Movement 2nd Theme — G161

4th Movement In the Garden 1st Theme — G162

4th Movement 2nd Theme — G163

5th Movement Dance 1st Theme — G164

5th Movement 2nd Theme — G165

GOOSSENS, Eugene (1893-1962)

The Hurdy-Gurdy Man, Op. 18, No. 3, Pft.
By permission of the copyright holders, J. & W. Chester, Ltd., 11 Great Marlborough Street, London, W. 1.

G166

GOSSEC, François Joseph (1734-1829)

Gavotte in D, Vn. & Pft.

1st Theme — G167

2nd Theme — G168

Tambourin, Vn. & Pft. G169

GOTTSCHALK, Louis (1829-1869)

The Dying Poet, Pft. G169a

GOUNOD, Charles Francois (1818-1893)

Faust, Ballet Music, Act V 1st Theme G170

2nd Theme G171

3rd Theme G172

4th Theme G173

5th Theme G174

6th Theme G175

Funeral March of a Marionette, Orch. 1st Theme G176

2nd Theme G177

The Queen of Sheba Cortège G178

GRAENER, Paul (1872-1944)

Die Flöte von Sans-Souci, Op. 88, Orch.
Copyright by Eulenburg, Licensed by SESAC, Inc., N. Y. Intro. 1st Theme G179

Intro. 2nd Theme G180

1st Movement Sarabande G181

2nd Movement Gavotte G182

3rd Movement Air G183

4th Movement Rigaudon G184

GRAINGER, Percy (1882-1961)

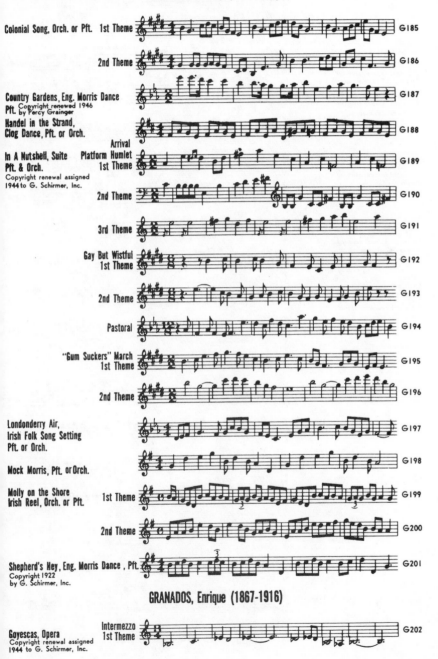

Colonial Song, Orch. or Pft. 1st Theme — G185

2nd Theme — G186

Country Gardens, Eng. Morris Dance
Pft. Copyright renewed 1946
by Percy Grainger — G187

Handel in the Strand,
Clog Dance, Pft. or Orch. — G188

In A Nutshell, Suite   Arrival
Pft. & Orch.   Platform Humlet
Copyright renewal assigned   1st Theme — G189
1944 to G. Schirmer, Inc.

2nd Theme — G190

3rd Theme — G191

Gay But Wistful
1st Theme — G192

2nd Theme — G193

Pastoral — G194

"Gum Suckers" March
1st Theme — G195

2nd Theme — G196

Londonderry Air,
Irish Folk Song Setting
Pft. or Orch. — G197

Mock Morris, Pft. or Orch. — G198

Molly on the Shore
Irish Reel, Orch. or Pft.   1st Theme — G199

2nd Theme — G200

Shepherd's Hey, Eng. Morris Dance , Pft. — G201
Copyright 1922
by G. Schirmer, Inc.

GRANADOS, Enrique (1867-1916)

Goyescas, Opera   Intermezzo
Copyright renewal assigned   1st Theme — G202
1944 to G. Schirmer, Inc.

2nd Theme   G203

3rd Theme   G204

The Maiden and the Nightingale,
Goyescas No. 4, Pft.
Copyright renewal assigned
1944 to G. Schirmer, Inc.   G205

Spanish Dance, No. 2, Pft.   1st Theme   G206
Copyright renewal assigned
1943 to G. Schirmer, Inc.

2nd Theme   G207

Spanish Dance, No. 4,
Villanesca, Pft.   1st Theme   G208
Copyright renewal assigned
1943 to G. Schirmer, Inc.

2nd Theme   G209

Spanish Dance, No. 5,
Playera-Andaluza, Pft.   1st Theme   G210
Copyright renewal assigned
1943 to G. Schirmer, Inc.

2nd Theme   G211

Spanish Dance, No. 6,
Rondalla Aragonesa   1st Theme   G212
Copyright renewal assigned
1943 to G. Schirmer, Inc.

2nd Theme   G213

GRETRY, André (1741-1813)

Ballet Suite from
Cephale et Procris   Gavotte   G214

Tambourin
1st Theme,
A   G215

1st Theme,
B   G216

2nd Theme   G217

Minuet
Nymphes de Diane   G218

Gigue   G219

Colinette à la Cour
Opera   Tambourin   G220

Gavotte   G221

GRIEG, Edvard (1843-1907)

Richard Coeur-de-Lion Opera — Rustic Dance — G222

La Rosière de Salency Opera — 1st Entr'acte 1st Theme — G223

2nd Theme — G224

2nd Entr'acte — G225

Ballet Suite from La Rosière Républicaine — Danse Legere — G226

Gavotte Gracieuse — G227

Contre Danse — G228

Romance — G229

Danse Generale — G230

Carmagnole — G231

Ballet Suite From Zémire et Azor — 1st Movement Air — G232

2nd Movement Pantomime — G233

3rd Movement Passepied — G234

Album Leaf, Op. 12, No. 7, Pft. — G235

Ballade, Op. 24, Pft. — G236

By Permission of C. F. Peters, Clayton F. Summy Co., Chicago, Agents in the U. S.

Concerto, Op. 16, Pft. & Orch. — 1st Movement Intro. — G237

1st Movement 1st Theme, A — G238

1st Movement 1st Theme, B — G239

1st Movement 2nd Theme — G240

The Lonely Wanderer, Op. 43, No. 2, Pft. — G261

Lyric Suite, Op. 54, Pft. Shepherd Boy
By Permission of C. F. Peters,
Clayton F. Summy Co., Chicago,
Agents in the U. S. — G262

Norwegian Rustic March — G263

March of the Dwarfs
1st Theme — G264

2nd Theme — G265

Nocturne — G266

Melancholy, Op. 65, No. 3, Pft.
By Permission of C. F. Peters,
Clayton F. Summy Co., Chicago,
Agents in the U. S. — G267

Mélodie, Op. 47, No. 3, Pft.
By Permission of C. F. Peters, Clayton F.
Summy Co., Chicago, Agents in the U. S. — G268

Norwegian Bridal Procession,
Op. 19, No. 2, Pft.
By Permission of C. F. Peters, Clayton F.
Summy Co., Chicago, Agents in the U. S. — G269

Norwegian Dances,   No. 1
Op. 35, Pft. or Str. Orch.   1st Theme
By Permission of C. F. Peters,
Clayton F. Summy Co., Chicago,
Agents in the U. S. — G270

2nd Theme — G271

No. 2
1st Theme — G272

2nd Theme — G273

No. 3 — G274

No. 4
1st Theme — G275

2nd Theme — G276

Norwegian Melody, Op. 12,   1st Theme
No. 7, Pft.
Copyright 1899
by G. Schirmer, Inc. — G277

2nd Theme — G278

Norwegian Melodies,   1st Movement
Op. 63, Str. Orch.   Popular Song
By Permission of C. F.
Peters, Clayton F. Summy   2nd Movement
Co., Chicago,   1st Theme
Agents in the U. S.   Cow Keeper's Tune — G279

— G280

Peasant Dance — 2nd Movement 2nd Theme — G281

Papillon (Butterfly), Op. 43, No. 1, Pft. — G282

Peer Gynt, Suite No. 1, Op. 46, Orch. — 1st Movement Morning Mood — G283

2nd Movement Ase's Death — G284

3rd Movement Anitra's Dance 1st Theme — G285

3rd Movement 2nd Theme — G286

4th Movement In the Hall of the Mountain King — G287

Peer Gynt, Suite No. 2, Op. 55 Orch. Copyright 1899 by G. Schirmer, Inc. — 1st Movement Ingrid's Complaint 1st Theme — G288

1st Movement 2nd Theme — G289

2nd Movement Arabian Dance 1st Theme — G290

2nd Movement 2nd Theme — G291

3rd Movement Peer Gynt's Return Home — G292

4th Movement Solvejg's Song Intro. — G293

4th Movement 1st Theme — G294

4th Movement 2nd Theme — G295

Puck, Op. 71, No. 3, Pft. By Permission of C. F. Peters, Clayton F. Summy Co., Chicago, Agents in the U.S. — G296

Quartet in G Minor, Op. 27, Str. By permission of International Music Co. — 1st Movement 1st Theme — G297

1st Movement 2nd Theme — G298

2nd Movement Romanze 1st Theme — G298a

2nd Movement 2nd Theme — G299

3rd Movement Intermezzo 1st Theme — G300

3rd Movement 2nd Theme — G301

4th Movement 1st Theme — G302

4th Movement 2nd Theme — G303

Scherzo-Impromptu, Op. 73, No. 2, Pft.
By Permission of C. F. Peters, Clayton
F. Summy Co., Chicago, Agents in the U.S. — G304

Sigurd Jorsalfar, Orch. 1st Movement
Op. 56, In the King's Hall (Prelude)
(Incidental Music), — G305

By Permission of C. F.
Peters, Clayton F. Summy 1st Movement
Co., Chicago, 2nd Theme
Agents in the U. S. — G306

2nd Movement
Borghild's Dream (Intermezzo) — G307

3rd Movement
Triumphal March
1st Theme — G308

3rd Movement
2nd Theme — G309

Sonata in A Minor, 1st Movement
Op. 36, Cello & Pft. 1st Theme — G310
By Permission of
C. F. Peters, Clayton 1st Movement
F. Summy Co., Chicago, 2nd Theme
Agents in the U. S. — G311

2nd Movement — G312

3rd Movement
1st Theme — G313

3rd Movement
2nd Theme — G314

3rd Movement
3rd Theme — G315

Sonata in E Minor, 1st Movement
Op. 7, Pft. 1st Theme — G316
Published and Copyrighted
(renewal 1936) 1st Movement
by Oliver Ditson Co. 2nd Theme — G317
Used by permission.

1st Movement
3rd Theme — G318

2nd Movement — G319

3rd Movement — G320

4th Movement — G321

Sonata in G, Op. 13,
No. 2, Vn. & Pft.
1st Movement
Intro. — G322

1st Movement
1st Theme — G323

1st Movement
2nd Theme — G324

1st Movement
3rd Theme — G325

2nd Movement — G326

3rd Movement
1st Theme — G327

3rd Movement
2nd Theme — G328

Sonata in C Minor,
Op. 45, No. 3, Vn. & Pft.
Copyright 1917 by
Carl Fischer, Inc., N. Y.
1st Movement
Intro. — G329

1st Movement
1st Theme — G330

1st Movement
2nd Theme — G331

2nd Movement
1st Theme — G332

2nd Movement
2nd Theme — G333

3rd Movement
1st Theme — G334

3rd Movement
2nd Theme — G335

Summer's Eve, Op. 71, No. 2, Pft.
By Permission of C. F. Peters, Clayton F.
Summy Co., Chicago, Agents in the U. S. — G336

Symphonic Dances,
Op. 64, Orch.
By Permission of C. F. Peters,
Clayton F. Summy Co., Chicago,
Agents in the U. S.
No. 1 — G337

No. 2
1st Theme,
A — G338

1st Theme,
B — G339

2nd Theme — G340

No. 3 — G341

No. 4
1st Theme — G342

2nd Theme — G343

To Spring, Op. 43, No. 6, Pft. — G344

Two Elegaic Melodies,
Op. 34, Str. Orch.
By Permission of C. F.
Peters, Clayton F. Summy Co.,
Chicago, Agents in the U. S.

No. 1
Heart Wounds — G345

No. 2
Springtime — G346

Two Melodies, Op. 53,
Str. Orch.
By Permission of C. F.
Peters, Clayton F. Summy Co.,
Chicago, Agents
in the U. S.

No. 1
Norwegian — G347

No. 2
The First Meeting — G348

Waltz, Op. 12, No. 2, Pft.
By Permission of C. F.
Peters, Clayton F. Summy Co.,
Chicago, Agents in the U. S.

1st Theme — G349

2nd Theme — G350

Wedding Day at Troldhaugen,
Op. 65, No. 6, Pft.
By Permission of C. F.
Peters, Clayton F. Summy Co.,
Chicago, Agents in the U. S. — G351

GRIFFES, Charles Tomlinson (1884-1920)

The Pleasure Dome of
Kubla Khan, Orch.
Copyright 1920
by G. Schirmer, Inc.

1st Theme — G352

2nd Theme — G353

3rd Theme — G354

4th Theme — G355

Two Sketches (Based on
Indian Themes),
Str. Quart.
Copyright 1922
by G. Schirmer, Inc.

1st Movement
Farewell Song of
Chippewa Indians — G356

2nd Movement
1st Theme — G357

2nd Movement
2nd Theme — G358

2nd Movement
3rd Theme — G359

The White Peacock, Op. 7, No. 1, Pft.
Copyright renewal assigned
1945 to G. Schirmer, Inc. — G362

GROFÉ, Ferde (1892   )

Grand Canyon Suite,
Orch.
Copyright 1932 Robbins
Music Corp.
Used by special
permission Copyright
Proprietor.

1st Movement
Sunrise — G361

2nd Movement
Painted Desert — G362

3rd Movement
On the Trail
1st Theme — G363

3rd Movement
2nd Theme — G364

Mississippi Suite,
Orch.
Copyright 1926
Leo Feist, Inc.
Used by Special
Permission Copyright
Proprietor.

1st Movement
Father of Waters — G365

2nd Movement
Huckleberry Finn — G366

3rd Movement
Old Creole Days — G367

4th Movement
Mardi Gras
1st Theme — G368

4th Movement
2nd Theme — G369

HALVORSEN, Johan (1864-1935)

Andante Religioso
Vn. & Orch.
By permission of Associated
Music Publishers, Inc.

1st Theme — H1

2nd Theme — H2

Triumphal Entry
of the Boyars
Orch.
By permission of Associated
Music Publishers, Inc.

1st Theme — H3

2nd Theme — H4

HANDEL, George Frideric (1685-1759)

Concerto No. 1 in B
Flat, Oboe & Orch.

1st Movement — H5

2nd Movement
Fugue — H6

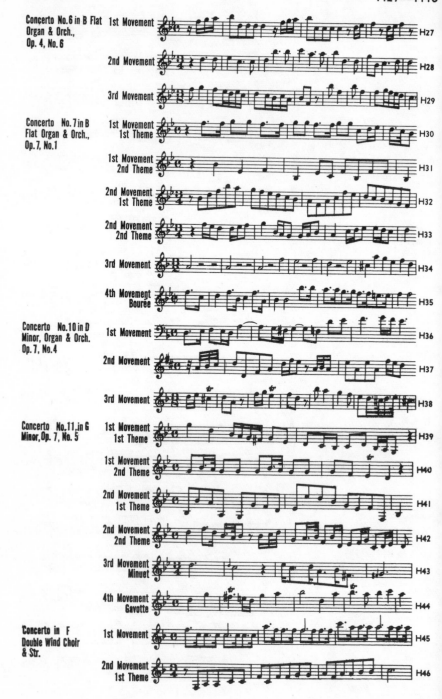

Concerto Grosso in A Minor, Op. 6, No. 4 Str. Orch.
1st Movement — H67
2nd Movement — H68
3rd Movement — H69
4th Movement 1st Theme — H70
4th Movement 2nd Theme — H71

Concerto Grosso in D, Op. 6, No. 5 Str. Orch.
1st Movement — H72
2nd Movement — H73
3rd Movement — H74
4th Movement — H75
5th Movement 1st Theme — H76
5th Movement 2nd Theme — H77
6th Movement — H78

Concerto Grosso in G Minor Op. 6, No. 6 Str. Orch.
1st Movement — H79
2nd Movement — H80
3rd Movement 1st Theme — H81
3rd Movement 2nd Theme — H82
4th Movement — H83
5th Movement — H84

Concerto Grosso in B flat Op. 6, No. 7 Str. Orch.
1st Movement — H85
2nd Movement — H86

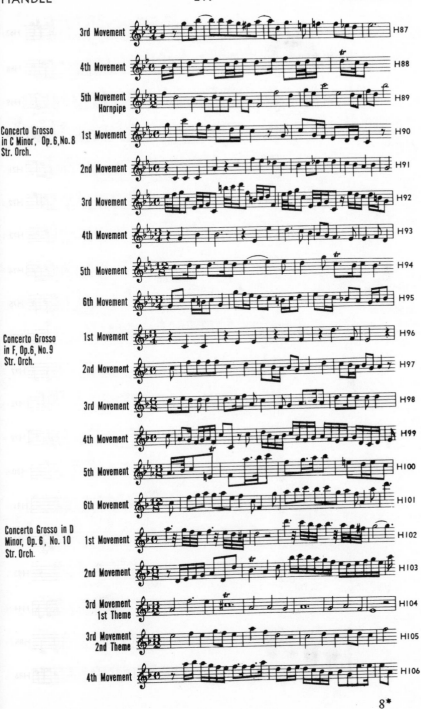

3rd Movement — H87

4th Movement — H88

5th Movement
Hornpipe — H89

Concerto Grosso
in C Minor, Op. 6, No. 8
Str. Orch.

1st Movement — H90

2nd Movement — H91

3rd Movement — H92

4th Movement — H93

5th Movement — H94

6th Movement — H95

Concerto Grosso
in F, Op. 6, No. 9
Str. Orch.

1st Movement — H96

2nd Movement — H97

3rd Movement — H98

4th Movement — H99

5th Movement — H100

6th Movement — H101

Concerto Grosso in D
Minor, Op. 6, No. 10
Str. Orch.

1st Movement — H102

2nd Movement — H103

3rd Movement
1st Theme — H104

3rd Movement
2nd Theme — H105

4th Movement — H106

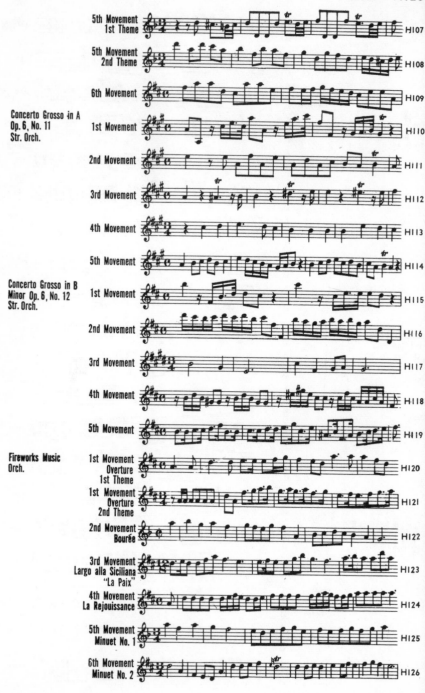

5th Movement 1st Theme — H107
5th Movement 2nd Theme — H108
6th Movement — H109

Concerto Grosso in A Op. 6, No. 11 Str. Orch.
1st Movement — H110
2nd Movement — H111
3rd Movement — H112
4th Movement — H113
5th Movement — H114

Concerto Grosso in B Minor Op. 6, No. 12 Str. Orch.
1st Movement — H115
2nd Movement — H116
3rd Movement — H117
4th Movement — H118
5th Movement — H119

Fireworks Music Orch.
1st Movement Overture 1st Theme — H120
1st Movement Overture 2nd Theme — H121
2nd Movement Bourée — H122
3rd Movement Largo alla Siciliana "La Paix" — H123
4th Movement La Rejouissance — H124
5th Movement Minuet No. 1 — H125
6th Movement Minuet No. 2 — H126

HANDEL

Alcina, Opera
- Overture 1st Theme — H127
- Overture 2nd Theme — H128
- Musette — H129
- Minuet — H130
- Gavotte From Ballet — H131
- Sarabande From Ballet — H132
- Minuet From Ballet — H133
- Gavotte No. 2 From Ballet — H134
- Tamburino — H135

Oratorios
- March from Joseph — H136
- March from Judas Maccabeus — H137
- Dead March from Saul — H138

Messiah
- Overture 1st Theme — H139
- 2nd Theme — H140
- Pt. 1 (Pastoral Symphony) — H141

Sonata in G, Flute & Fig. Bass Op. 1, No. 5
- 1st Movement — H142
- 2nd Movement — H143
- 3rd Movement — H144
- 4th Movement — H145
- 5th Movement — H146

Sonata in C,
Flute & Fig. Bass
Op. 1, No. 7

1st Movement — H147

2nd Movement — H148

3rd Movement — H149

4th Movement — H150

5th Movement — H151

Sonata in B Minor,
Flute & Fig. Bass
Op. 1, No. 9

1st Movement — H152

2nd Movement — H153

3rd Movement — H154

4th Movement — H155

5th Movement — H156

6th Movement — H157

7th Movement — H158

Sonata in F,
Flute & Fig. Bass
Op. 1, No. 11

1st Movement — H159

2nd Movement — H160

3rd Movement — H161

4th Movement — H162

Sonata in C Minor,
Fl., Vn., & Fig. Bass
Op. 2, No. 1

1st Movement — H163

2nd Movement — H164

3rd Movement — H165

4th Movement — H166

Sonata in F
Op. 1, No. 12
Vn. & Fig. Bass

1st Movement — H187

2nd Movement — H188

3rd Movement — H189

4th Movement — H190

Sonata in D
Op. 1, No. 13
Vn. & Fig. Bass

1st Movement — H191

2nd Movement — H192

3rd Movement — H193

4th Movement — H194

Sonata in A
Op. 1, No. 14
Vn. & Fig. Bass

1st Movement — H195

2nd Movement — H196

3rd Movement — H197

4th Movement — H198

Suite No. 1 in B Flat
Pft., 2nd Set.
Air and Variations — H199

Suite No. 2 in F
Pft.

1st Movement — H200

2nd Movement — H201

3rd Movement — H202

4th Movement — H203

Suite No. 3 in D Minor
Pft.

1st Movement
Allemande — H204

2nd Movement — H205

3rd Movement
Air — H206

4th Movement Gigue — H207

5th Movement Minuet — H208

Suite No. 4 in E Minor Pft.

1st Movement — H209

2nd Movement Allemande — H210

3rd Movement Courante — H211

4th Movement Sarabande — H212

5th Movement Gigue — H213

Suite No. 5 in E Pft.

1st Movement Prelude — H214

2nd Movement Allemande — H215

3rd Movement Courante — H216

Air (The Harmonious Blacksmith)

4th Movement 1st Theme, A — H217

4th Movement 1st Theme, B — H218

Suite No. 7 in G Minor Pft.

1st Movement Overture 1st Theme — H219

1st Movement Overture 2nd Theme — H220

2nd Movement — H221

3rd Movement — H222

4th Movement Sarabande — H223

5th Movement Gigue — H224

6th Movement — H225

Suite No. 8 in F Minor Pft.

1st Movement — H226

2nd Movement — H227

3rd Movement
Allemande — H228

4th Movement
Courante — H229

5th Movement
Gigue — H230

Suite in G
Pft., 2nd Set — Chaconne No. 2 — H231

Suite No. 4 in D Minor
Pft., 2nd Set — 1st Movement Allemande — H232

2nd Movement
Courante — H233

3rd Movement
Sarabande — H234

4th Movement
Gigue — H235

Suite No. 8 in G
Pft., 2nd Set — 1st Movement Allemande — H236

2nd Movement — H237

3rd Movement
Courante — H238

4th Movement
Aria — H239

5th Movement
Minuet — H240

6th Movement
Gavotte — H241

7th Movement — H242

Chaconne No.9 in G
from 2nd Set of Piano Suites — H243

Capriccio No. 3 in G Minor
from 3rd Collection of Piano Works — H244

Fantasia in C
No.4 from 3rd Collection of
Piano Works — H245

Water Music
Orch. — 1st Movement Overture — H246

2nd Movement — H247
3rd Movement — H248
4th Movement — H249
5th Movement Andante — H250
6th Movement — H251
7th Movement Air — H252
8th Movement — H253
9th Movement Bourrée — H254
10th Movement Hornpipe — H255
11th Movement — H256
12th Movement — H257
13th Movement 1st Theme — H258
13th Movement 2nd Theme — H259
14th Movement — H260
15th Movement Aria — H261
16th Movement — H262
17th Movement Air — H263
18th Movement Minuet 1st Theme — H264
18th Movement 2nd Theme — H265
19th Movement — H266

20th Movement
Coro H267

HANSON, Howard (1896-   )

Merry Mount Suite
Copyright 1933 by Harms, Inc.
Reprinted by special permission.
Overture H268

Children's Dance
1st Theme H269

2nd Theme H270

Prelude to Act II
& Maypole Dances
1st Theme H271

2nd Theme H272

3rd Theme H273

Symphony No. 2
"Romantic"
Copyright 1932 by
Eastman School of Music,
Rochester, N. Y.
1st Movement
Intro. H274

1st Movement
1st Theme H275

1st Movement
2nd Theme H276

1st Movement
3rd Theme,
A H277

1st Movement
3rd Theme,
B H278

2nd Movement H279

3rd Movement
1st Theme H280

3rd Movement
2nd Theme H281

HARRIS, Roy (1898-   )

Chorale for Strings, Op. 3
Copyright 1934 by
Harold Flammer, Inc.
Used by permission.
H282

Sonata Op. 1, Pft.
Copyright 1931
Cos Cob Press, Inc.
1st Movement
Prelude H283

2nd Movement
Andante Ostinato H284

Symphony No. 3 — 3rd Movement Scherzo — H285
1st Theme — H286
2nd Theme — H287
3rd Theme — H288
4th Theme — H289
5th Theme — H290
6th Theme, A — H291
6th Theme, B — H292

Three Variations on a Theme St. Quartet — H293

HAYDN, Franz Josef (1732-1809)

Andante & Variations, Pft. Op. 83, F. Minor — 1st Theme — H294
2nd Theme — H295

Arietta (Theme & Variations) E Flat Pft. — H296

Capriccio in G, Pft. — H297

Fantasia in C, Pft. — 1st Theme — H298
2nd Theme — H299

Concerto in D Cello & Orch. Op.101 — 1st Movement 1st Theme — H300
1st Movement 2nd Theme — H301
2nd Movement — H302
3rd Movement 1st Theme — H303

3rd Movement / 2nd Theme — H304
Concerto in D Pft. & Orch. / 1st Movement — H305
2nd Movement / 1st Theme — H306
2nd Movement / 2nd Theme — H307
3rd Movement / 1st Theme — H308
3rd Movement / 2nd Theme — H309
Concerto in E Flat Trumpet & Orch. / 1st Movement / 1st Theme — H310
1st Movement / 2nd Theme — H311
2nd Movement — H312
3rd Movement — H314
Quartet in B Flat Op. 1, No. 1, Str. "La Chasse" / 1st Movement — H315
2nd Movement — H316
3rd Movement — H317
4th Movement — H318
5th Movement — H319
Quartet in C Op. 1, No. 6 Str. / 1st Movement — H320
2nd Movement — H321
3rd Movement — H322
4th Movement / 1st Theme — H323
4th Movement / 2nd Theme — H324

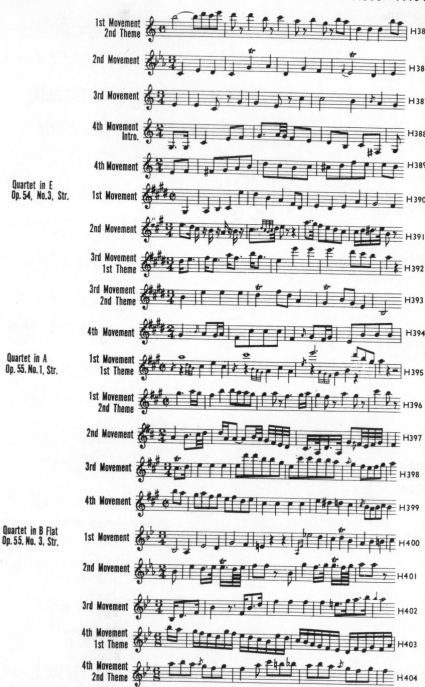

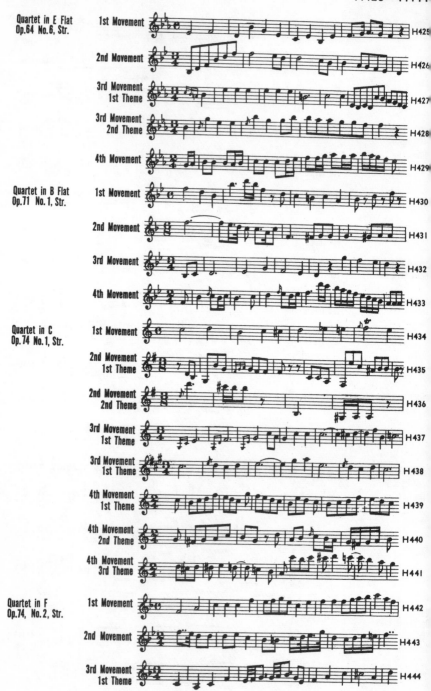

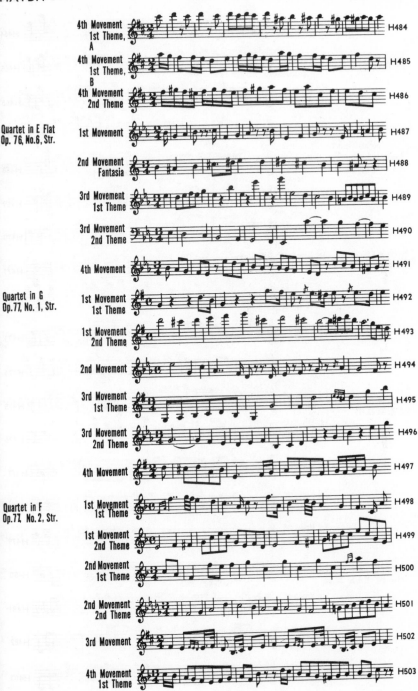

4th Movement 1st Theme, A — H484

4th Movement 1st Theme, B — H485

4th Movement 2nd Theme — H486

Quartet in E Flat Op. 76, No.6, Str.

1st Movement — H487

2nd Movement Fantasia — H488

3rd Movement 1st Theme — H489

3rd Movement 2nd Theme — H490

4th Movement — H491

Quartet in G Op. 77, No. 1, Str.

1st Movement 1st Theme — H492

1st Movement 2nd Theme — H493

2nd Movement — H494

3rd Movement 1st Theme — H495

3rd Movement 2nd Theme — H496

4th Movement — H497

Quartet in F Op. 77, No. 2, Str.

1st Movement 1st Theme — H498

1st Movement 2nd Theme — H499

2nd Movement 1st Theme — H500

2nd Movement 2nd Theme — H501

3rd Movement — H502

4th Movement 1st Theme — H503

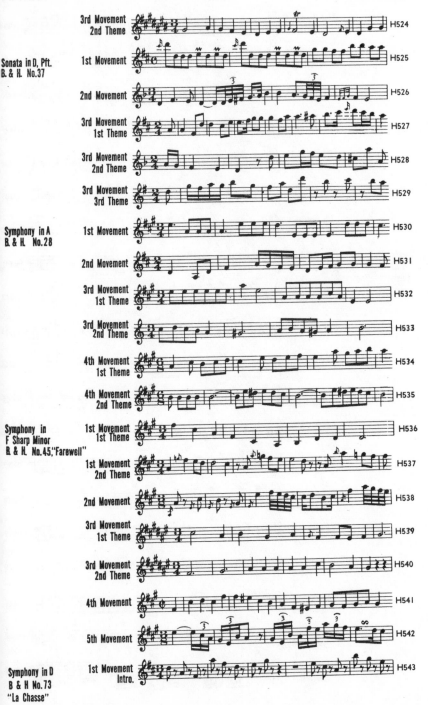

3rd Movement / 2nd Theme — H524

Sonata in D, Pft. B. & H. No.37 — 1st Movement — H525

2nd Movement — H526

3rd Movement / 1st Theme — H527

3rd Movement / 2nd Theme — H528

3rd Movement / 3rd Theme — H529

Symphony in A B. & H. No.28 — 1st Movement — H530

2nd Movement — H531

3rd Movement / 1st Theme — H532

3rd Movement / 2nd Theme — H533

4th Movement / 1st Theme — H534

4th Movement / 2nd Theme — H535

Symphony in F Sharp Minor B. & H. No.45,"Farewell" — 1st Movement / 1st Theme — H536

1st Movement / 2nd Theme — H537

2nd Movement — H538

3rd Movement / 1st Theme — H539

3rd Movement / 2nd Theme — H540

4th Movement — H541

5th Movement — H542

Symphony in D B. & H. No.73 "La Chasse" — 1st Movement Intro. — H543

1st Movement 1st Theme — H544
1st Movement 2nd Theme — H545
2nd Movement — H546
3rd Movement 1st Theme — H547
3rd Movement 2nd Theme — H548
4th Movement 1st Theme — H549
4th Movement 2nd Theme — H550

Symphony in C
B. & H. No.82
"L'Ours"

1st Movement 1st Theme — H551
1st Movement 2nd Theme — H552
2nd Movement — H553
3rd Movement 1st Theme — H554
3rd Movement 2nd Theme — H555
4th Movement 1st Theme, A — H556
4th Movement 1st Theme, B — H557
4th Movement 2nd Theme — H558

Symphony in D
B. & H. No. 86

1st Movement Intro. — H559
1st Movement 1st Theme — H560
1st Movement 2nd Theme — H561
2nd Movement 1st Theme — H562
2nd Movement 2nd Theme — H563

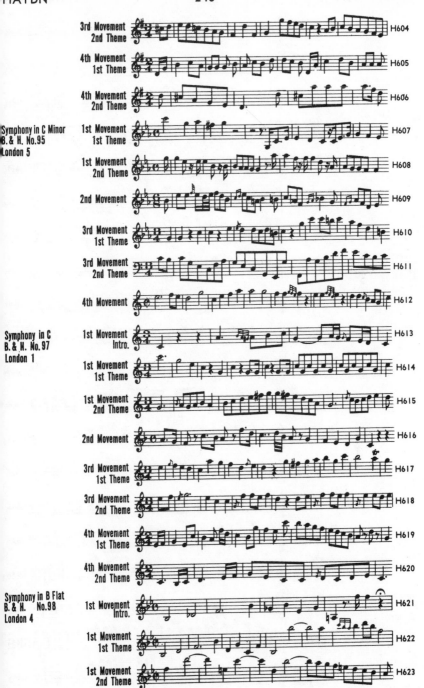

2nd Movement / 1st Theme — H624
2nd Movement / 2nd Theme — H625
3rd Movement / 1st Theme — H626
3rd Movement / 2nd Theme — H627
4th Movement / 1st Theme — H628
4th Movement / 2nd Theme — H629
4th Movement / 1st Theme — H630

Symphony in E Flat
B. & H. No.99
London 10
"Imperial"

1st Movement / Intro. — H631
1st Movement / 1st Theme — H632
1st Movement / 2nd Theme — H633
2nd Movement / 1st Theme — H634
2nd Movement / 2nd Theme — H635
3rd Movement / 1st Theme — H636
3rd Movement / 2nd Theme — H637
4th Movement / 1st Theme — H638
4th Movement / 2nd Theme — H639
4th Movement / 3rd Theme — H640

Symphony in G
B. & H. No.100
"Military"

1st Movement / Intro. — H641
1st Movement / 1st Theme — H642
1st Movement / 2nd Theme — H643

2nd Movement — H644

3rd Movement 1st Theme — H645

3rd Movement 2nd Theme — H646

4th Movement 1st Theme — H647

4th Movement 2nd Theme — H648

Symphony in D
B. & H. No. 101
"Clock"

1st Movement 1st Theme — H649

1st Movement 2nd Theme — H650

2nd Movement — H651

3rd Movement 1st Theme — H652

3rd Movement 2nd Theme — H653

4th Movement 1st Theme — H654

4th Movement 2nd Theme — H655

4th Movement 3rd Theme — H656

Symphony in B Flat
B. & H. No.102
London 9

1st Movement Intro. — H657

1st Movement 1st Theme — H658

1st Movement 2nd Theme — H659

1st Movement 3rd Theme — H660

2nd Movement — H661

3rd Movement 1st Theme — H662

3rd Movement 2nd Theme — H663

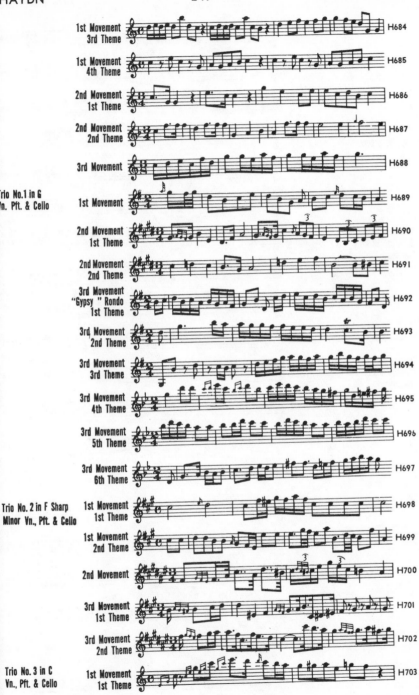

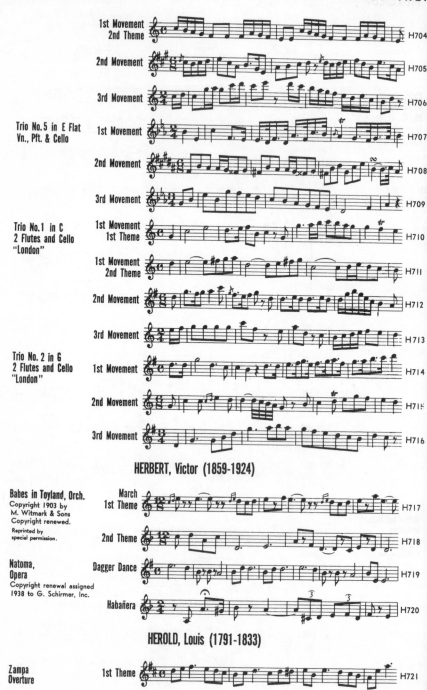

1st Movement 2nd Theme — H704

2nd Movement — H705

3rd Movement — H706

Trio No.5 in E Flat
Vn., Pft. & Cello — 1st Movement — H707

2nd Movement — H708

3rd Movement — H709

Trio No.1 in C
2 Flutes and Cello
"London" — 1st Movement 1st Theme — H710

1st Movement 2nd Theme — H711

2nd Movement — H712

3rd Movement — H713

Trio No. 2 in G
2 Flutes and Cello
"London" — 1st Movement — H714

2nd Movement — H715

3rd Movement — H716

HERBERT, Victor (1859-1924)

Babes in Toyland, Orch.
Copyright 1903 by
M. Witmark & Sons
Copyright renewed.
Reprinted by
special permission. — March 1st Theme — H717

2nd Theme — H718

Natoma,
Opera
Copyright renewal assigned
1938 to G. Schirmer, Inc. — Dagger Dance — H719

Habañera — H720

HEROLD, Louis (1791-1833)

Zampa
Overture — 1st Theme — H721

HINDEMITH, Paul (1895-1963)

Kleine Kammermusik
Op.24 No.2
Ob., Fl., Cl., Hn., Fag.
By permission of
Associated Music
Publishers, Inc.

Mathis der Mahler
Symphony
By permission of
Associated Music
Publishers, Inc.

2nd Theme   H722

1st Movement
1st Theme   H723

1st Movement
2nd Theme   H724

2nd Movement
Waltz
1st Theme   H725

2nd Movement
2nd Theme   H726

2nd Movement
3rd Theme   H727

3rd Movement
1st Theme   H728

3rd Movement
2nd Theme   H729

4th Movement   H730

5th Movement
1st Theme   H731

5th Movement
2nd Theme   H732

5th Movement
3rd Theme   H733

5th Movement
4th Theme   H734

1st Movement
Concert of Angels
Intro.   H735

1st Movement
1st Theme,
A   H736

1st Movement
1st Theme,
B   H737

1st Movement
2nd Theme   H738

1st Movement
3rd Theme   H739

1st Movement
4th Theme   H740

9*

2nd Movement
Entombment
1st Theme — H741

2nd Movement
2nd Theme — H742

3rd Movement
Temptation of St. Anthony
Intro. — H743

3rd Movement
1st Theme — H744

3rd Movement
2nd Theme — H745

3rd Movement
3rd Theme — H746

3rd Movement
4th Theme — H747

3rd Movement
5th Theme — H748

3rd Movement
6th Theme — H749

Quartet
Op. 22, No. 3, Str.
By permission of
Associated Music
Publishers, Inc.

1st Movement — H750

2nd Movement
1st Theme — H751

2nd Movement
2nd Theme — H752

3rd Movement
1st Theme — H753

3rd Movement
2nd Theme — H754

4th Movement — H755

5th Movement
1st Theme — H756

5th Movement
2nd Theme — H757

5th Movement
3rd Theme — H758

Der Schwanendreher
Concerto, Vla. & Orch.
On Old Folk Tunes
By permission
of Associated Music
Publishers, Inc.

1st Movement
"Zwischen Berg
und Tiefem Tal"
1st Theme — H759

1st Movement
2nd Theme — H760

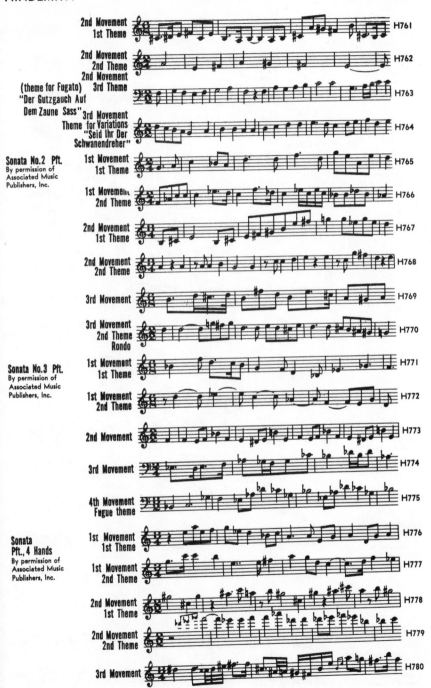

- 2nd Movement 1st Theme — H761
- 2nd Movement 2nd Theme — H762
- 2nd Movement 3rd Theme (theme for Fugato) "Der Gutzgauch Auf Dem Zaune Sass" — H763
- 3rd Movement Theme for Variations "Seid Ihr Der Schwanendreher" — H764

Sonata No.2 Pft.
By permission of Associated Music Publishers, Inc.

- 1st Movement 1st Theme — H765
- 1st Movement 2nd Theme — H766
- 2nd Movement 1st Theme — H767
- 2nd Movement 2nd Theme — H768
- 3rd Movement — H769
- 3rd Movement 2nd Theme Rondo — H770

Sonata No.3 Pft.
By permission of Associated Music Publishers, Inc.

- 1st Movement 1st Theme — H771
- 1st Movement 2nd Theme — H772
- 2nd Movement — H773
- 3rd Movement — H774
- 4th Movement Fugue theme — H775

Sonata Pft., 4 Hands
By permission of Associated Music Publishers, Inc.

- 1st Movement 1st Theme — H776
- 1st Movement 2nd Theme — H777
- 2nd Movement 1st Theme — H778
- 2nd Movement 2nd Theme — H779
- 3rd Movement — H780

Trauermusik, Orch.
(Funeral Music)
For George V of England
By permission of Associated
Music Publishers, Inc.

1st Movement   H781

2nd Movement   H782

3rd Movement   H783

4th Movement
Choral
Für deinen
Thron Tret'Ich Hiermit   H784

Trio No.2
Vn., Viola, Cello
By permission of
Associated Music Publishers, Inc.

1st Movement
1st Theme   H785

1st Movement
2nd Theme   H786

2nd Movement
1st Theme   H787

2nd Movement
2nd Theme   H788

3rd Movement
1st Theme   H789

3rd Movement
2nd Theme   H790

3rd Movement
3rd Theme   H791

HOLBROOKE, Josef (1878-1958)

Bronwen
Overture
Copyright by Lienau,
Licensed by
SESAC, Inc., N. Y.

1st Theme   H792

2nd Theme   H793

3rd Theme   H794

Quintet, Op. 27, No. 1
CL & Str.
By Permission of
Novello & Co., Ltd.,
London

1st Movement
Cavatina   H795

2nd Movement
Variations   H796

HOLST, Gustav Theodore (1874-1934)

The Planets, Op.32
Orch.

Mars, the Bringer
of War
Copyright 1921 by
Goodwin & Tabb,
Ltd., London.

1st Movement
1st Theme   H797

1st Movement
2nd Theme   H798

3rd Movement 2nd Theme — H819

4th Movement The Dargason Finale — H820

Two Songs without Words
Op. 22, Orch.
Copyright 1925
by E.C. Schirmer, Boston.

I Country Song 1st Theme — H821

2nd Theme — H822

II Marching Song 1st Theme — H823

2nd Theme — H824

3rd Theme — H825

HONEGGER, Arthur (1892-1955)

Chant de Nigamon
Orch.
Copyright by Editions Salabert
Editions Salabert,
22 Rue Chaucat, Paris
Salabert, Inc.,
I East 57 St., N.Y.

1st Theme — H826

2nd Theme — H827

3rd Theme — H828

4th Theme — H829

Concertino
Pft. & Orch.
Copyright by Editions
Salabert Editions Salabert,
22 Rue Chaucat, Paris
Salabert, Inc.,
I East 57 St., N.Y.

1st Movement 1st Theme — H830

1st Movement 2nd Theme — H831

1st Movement 3rd Theme — H832

2nd Movement — H833

3rd Movement 1st Theme — H834

3rd Movement 2nd Theme — H835

King David
Symphonic Psalm

1st Movement Intro. — H836

Cortège
By permission of
Novello & Co.,
Ltd., London.

1st Theme — H837

2nd Theme — H838

March of the Philistines — H839

March of the Israelites — H840

**Pastorale D'Été
Orch.**
Copyright by Editions Salabert
Editions Salabert,
22 Rue Chaucat, Paris
Salabert, Inc.,
I East 57 St., N. Y.

1st Theme — H841

2nd Theme — H842

3rd Theme — H843

4th Theme — H844

**Rugby,
Orch.**
Copyright by Editions Salabert
Editions Salabert,
22 Rue Chaucat, Paris
Salabert, Inc.,
I East 57 St., N. Y.

1st Theme — H845

2nd Theme — H846

HOWELLS, Herbert (1892-)

**Puck's Minuet, Op. 20,
No. 1, Orch.**
Copyright 1919 by
Goodwin & Tabb,
Ltd., London.

1st Theme — H847

2nd Theme — H848

HUBAY, Jeno (1858-1937)

**Hejre Kati, Op. 32, No. 4,
Vn. & Orch., from
Hungarian Czardas Scenes**
Copyright 1901
by Carl Fischer, Inc., N. Y.

1st Theme — H849

2nd Theme — H850

3rd Theme — H851

**Poème Hongrois, Op. 27, No. 1
Vn. & Orch.**

— H852

**Poème Hongrois, Op. 27,
No. 9 Vn. & Orch.**
By permission of J. Hamelle
Music Publishers, Paris

1st Theme — H853

2nd Theme — H854

HUMMEL, Johann (1778-1837)

Rondo in E Flat, Op.11

H855

HUMPERDINCK, Engelbert (1854-1921)

Hansel & Gretel, Opera
Prelude to Act 1
Copyright 1895
by B. Schott's Söhne

1st Theme

H856

2nd Theme

H857

Prelude to Act 2 "Witch's Ride"

H858

Pantomine

H859

Prelude "The Gingerbread House"
to Act 3   1st Theme

H860

2nd Theme

H861

"Gingerbread Waltz"

H862

Königskinder, Opera
Prelude

1st Theme,
A

H863

1st Theme,
B

H864

Prelude
to Act 2   "Children's Rounds"
1st Theme

H865

2nd Theme

H866

3rd Theme

H867

IBERT, Jacques (1890-1962)

Concerto, Alto Sax
& Small Orch.
Copyright by A. Leduc
Music Publishers, Paris

1st Movement
1st Theme

I1

1st Movement
2nd Theme

I2

2nd Movement

I3

3rd Movement
1st Theme

I4

Divertissement, Chamber Orch.
Permission for reprint granted by Durand & Cie, Paris. Elkan-Vogel Co., Inc. Philadelphia, Copyright Owners.

3rd Movement 2nd Theme — i5
1st Movement Intro. — i6
2nd Movement Cortege 1st Theme — i7
2nd Movement 2nd Theme — i8
3rd Movement Nocturne — i9
4th Movement Waltz 1st Theme — i10
4th Movement 2nd Theme — i11
5th Movement Parade 1st Theme — i12
5th Movement 2nd Theme — i13
6th Movement Finale — i14

Entr'Acte, Flute & Guitar
Copyright by A. Leduc Music Publishers, Paris

1st Theme — i15
2nd Theme — i16

Escales (Ports of Call) Orch.
Copyright by A. Leduc Music Publishers, Paris

1st Movement Rome—Palerme 1st Theme — i17
1st Movement 2nd Theme — i18
2nd Movement Tunis—Nefta — i19
3rd Movement Valencia 1st Theme — i20
3rd Movement 2nd Theme — i21

Histoires, Pft.
Copyright by A. Leduc Publishers, Paris

No. 1 La Meneuse de Tortues D'Or (The Keeper of the Golden Tortoises) — i22
No. 2 Le Petit Ane Blanc (The Little White Donkey) — i23
No. 3 Le Vieux Mendicant (The Old Beggar) — i24

No. 4
A Giddy Girl — 125

No. 8
Le Cage de Crystal
(The Crystal Cage) — 126

Pièce, flute alone
Copyright by A. Leduc
Music Publishers, Paris — 127

ILYINSKY, Alexander (1859-1919)

Berceuse, Pft. — 128

D'INDY, Vincent (1851-1931)

Le Camp de Wallenstein,
Op. 12, Orch.
Permission for reprint
granted by Durand & Cie,
Paris. Elkan-Vogel Co., Inc.
Philadelphia, Copyright
Owners.

1st Theme — 129
2nd Theme — 130
3rd Theme — 131
4th Theme — 132
5th Theme — 133

Istar, Op. 42,
Symphonic Variations
Permission for reprint granted
by Durand & Cie, Paris.
Elkan-Vogel Co., Philadelphia,
Inc. Copyright Owners.

1st Theme — 134
2nd Theme — 135
3rd Theme — 136
4th Theme — 137
5th Theme — 138
6th Theme — 139

Sonata in C,
Op. 59, Vn. &, Pft.
Permission for reprint
granted by Durand & Cie,
Paris. Elkan-Vogel Co., Inc.
Philadelphia, Copyright
Owners.

1st Movement
1st Theme — 140
1st Movement
2nd Theme — 141
1st Movement
3rd Theme — 142

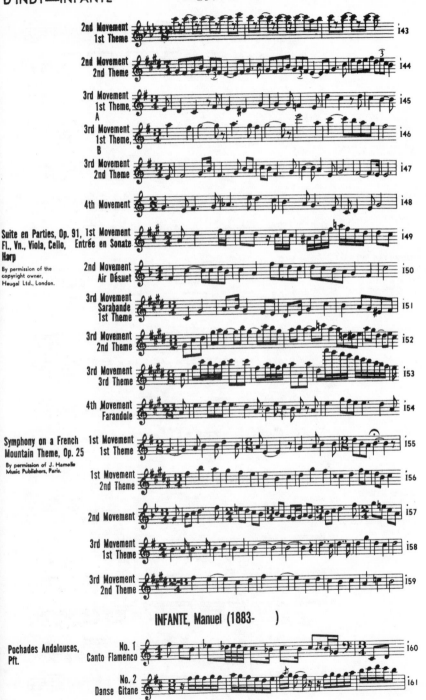

2nd Movement
1st Theme   143

2nd Movement
2nd Theme   144

3rd Movement
1st Theme,
A   145

3rd Movement
1st Theme,
B   146

3rd Movement
2nd Theme   147

4th Movement   148

Suite en Parties, Op. 91,
Fl., Vn., Viola, Cello,
Harp

By permission of the
copyright owner,
Heugal Ltd., London.

1st Movement
Entrée en Sonate   149

2nd Movement
Air Désuet   150

3rd Movement
Sarabande
1st Theme   151

3rd Movement
2nd Theme   152

3rd Movement
3rd Theme   153

4th Movement
Farandole   154

Symphony on a French
Mountain Theme, Op. 25

By permission of J. Hamelle
Music Publishers, Paris.

1st Movement
1st Theme   155

1st Movement
2nd Theme   156

2nd Movement   157

3rd Movement
1st Theme   158

3rd Movement
2nd Theme   159

INFANTE, Manuel (1883-   )

Pochades Andalouses,
Pft.

No. 1
Canto Flamenco   160

No. 2
Danse Gitane   161

No. 3
Aniers sur la Route de Seville

162

No. 4
Tientos

163

INGHELBRECHT, D. E. (1880-   )

Four Fanfares, Brass   No. 1
Pour une Fête
Copyright by Editions
Salabert Editions Salabert,
22 Rue Chaucat, Paris
Salabert, Inc.,
1 East 57 St., N. Y.

164

No. 2
Pour le Président

165

No. 3
Funèbre Pour des Mineurs Ensevelis

166

No. 4
Dédicatoire

167

Nurseries (3rd Set),   No. 1
Orch.   Nous N'irons Plus au Bois
Copyright by A. Leduc
Music Publishers, Paris

168

No. 2
Le Tour Prends Garde!

169

No. 3
Bon Voyage Monsieur Dumollet

170

No. 4
Sur le Pont d'Avignon

171

No. 5
Où est la Marguerite?

172

No. 6
Arlequin marie sa Fille

173

IPPOLITOFF-IVANOFF, Michael (1859-1935)

Caucasian Sketches,   1st Movement
Op. 10, Orch.   In the Mountain Pass
By permission of   1st Theme
International Music Co.

174

1st Movement
2nd Theme

175

1st Movement
3rd Theme

176

2nd Movement
In the Village
Intro.

177

2nd Movement
1st Theme

178

2nd Movement
2nd Theme

179

3rd Movement
In the Mosque   180

4th Movement
Procession of the Sardar
1st Theme   181

4th Movement
2nd Theme   182

Quartet, Op. 13, Str.   1st Movement
Intro.   183

1st Movement
1st Theme   184

1st Movement
2nd Theme   185

2nd Movement
(Humoresca—Scherzando)
1st Theme   186

2nd Movement
2nd Theme   187

3rd Movement
Intermezzo   188

4th Movement
1st Theme   189

4th Movement
2nd Theme   190

4th Movement
3rd Theme   191

IRELAND, John (1879-1962)

April, Pft.   192

Concertino Pastorale,
Str. Orch.
By permission of the
copyright owner, Boosey
and Hawkes, Inc.
                         1st Movement
                         Eclogue
                         1st Theme   193

                         1st Movement
                         2nd Theme   194

                         2nd Movement
                         Threnody   195

Concerto in E Flat
Pft. & Orch.
By permission of the
copyright holders,
J. & W. Chester, Ltd.,
11 Great Marlborough
Street, London, W. 1.
                         1st Movement
                         1st Theme   196

                         1st Movement
                         2nd Theme   197

                         2nd Movement
                         1st Theme   198

2nd Movement 2nd Theme
3rd Movement 1st Theme
3rd Movement 2nd Theme

The Holy Boy, Pft.

A London Overture, Orch. 1st Theme
By permission of the copyright owner, Boosey and Hawkes, Inc.
2nd Theme
3rd Theme

Phantasy in A Minor, Vn., Pft. & Cello 1st Theme
By permission of Augener, Ltd., London
2nd Theme
3rd Theme

Sonata in G Minor, Cello & Pft. 1st Movement 1st Theme
By permission of Augener, Ltd., London
1st Movement 2nd Theme
2nd Movement 1st Theme
2nd Movement 2nd Theme
3rd Movement 1st Theme
3rd Movement 2nd Theme

Trio No. 3 in E Minor & Major, Vn., Cello & Pft. 1st Movement 1st Theme
1st Movement 2nd Theme
2nd Movement 1st Theme
2nd Movement 2nd Theme, A

2nd Movement 2nd Theme, B — 1119

3rd Movement 1st Theme — 1120

3rd Movement 2nd Theme — 1121

4th Movement 1st Theme — 1122

4th Movement 2nd Theme — 1123

IVANOVICI, J. (-1902)

Waves of the Danube, Waltzes, Orch.

No. 1 1st Theme — 1124

No. 1 2nd Theme — 1125

No. 2 1st Theme — 1126

No. 2 2nd Theme — 1127

No. 3 — 1128

No. 4 — 1129

IVES, Charles (1874-1954)

New England Holidays, Orch. Washington's Birthday (Barn Dance) 1st Theme — 1130

Copyright 1937 by New Music Society of California, San Francisco, California.

2nd Theme — 1131

JACOBI, Frederick (1891-1952)

Indian Dances, Orch.

Buffalo Dance Intro. — J1

Theme — J2

Butterfly Dance — J3

War Dance 1st Theme — J4

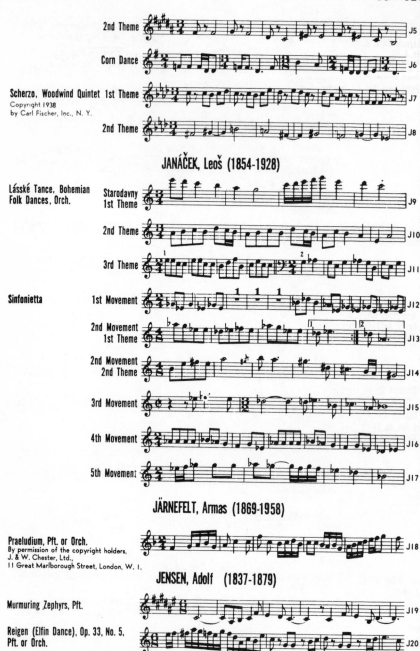

2nd Theme   J5

Corn Dance   J6

Scherzo, Woodwind Quintet 1st Theme   J7
Copyright 1938
by Carl Fischer, Inc., N. Y.

2nd Theme   J8

JANÁČEK, Leoš (1854-1928)

Lásské Tance, Bohemian
Folk Dances, Orch.   Starodavny 1st Theme   J9

2nd Theme   J10

3rd Theme   J11

Sinfonietta   1st Movement   J12

2nd Movement 1st Theme   J13

2nd Movement 2nd Theme   J14

3rd Movement   J15

4th Movement   J16

5th Movement   J17

JÄRNEFELT, Armas (1869-1958)

Praeludium, Pft. or Orch.
By permission of the copyright holders,
J. & W. Chester, Ltd.,
11 Great Marlborough Street, London, W. 1.   J18

JENSEN, Adolf (1837-1879)

Murmuring Zephyrs, Pft.   J19

Reigen (Elfin Dance), Op. 33, No. 5,
Pft. or Orch.   J20

JONGEN, Joseph (1873-1953)

Légende Naïve, Op. 59, No. 1,
Vn. & Pft.
By permission of the copyright holders,
J. & W. Chester, Ltd., 11 Great Marlborough
Street, London, W. 1.

Petite Suite, Pft.

1st Movement
Petite Marche
Militaire

2nd Movement
Conte Plaisant

3rd Movement
Nostalgie

4th Movement
Valse Gracieuse

5th Movement
Tambourin
1st Theme

5th Movement
2nd Theme

JUON, Paul (1872-1940)

Arva (Valse Mignonne),
Op. 52, No. 2, Vn. & Pft.
Copyright by Lienau, Licensed
by SESAC, Inc., N. Y.

1st Theme

2nd Theme

Berceuse, Op. 28, No. 3, Vn. & Pft.
Copyright by Lienau, Licensed
by SESAC, Inc., N. Y.

Chamber Symphony in
B Flat, Op. 27
Copyright by Lienau, Licensed
by SESAC, Inc., N. Y.

1st Movement
1st Theme

1st Movement
2nd Theme

2nd Movement

3rd Movement
1st Theme,
A

3rd Movement
1st Theme,
B

3rd Movement
2nd Theme

4th Movement

KABALEVSKY, Dmitri (1904-   )

Colas Breugnon, Op. 24,
Overture
Copyright 1946 by Leeds Music Corp., N. Y.
Reprinted here by permisssion
of the copyright owner.

1st Theme ... K1

2nd Theme ... K2

Symphony No. 2
in C Minor, Op. 19
Copyright 1945 by Leeds
Music Corp., N. Y.
Reprinted here by
permisssion of the
copyright owner.

1st Movement
1st Theme ... K3

1st Movement
2nd Theme ... K4

2nd Movement
Intro. ... K5

2nd Movement
1st Theme ... K6

2nd Movement
2nd Theme ... K7

3rd Movement
1st Theme ... K8

3rd Movement
2nd Theme ... K9

3rd Movement
3rd Theme ... K10

3rd Movement
4th Theme ... K11

KALINNIKOFF, Basil (1866-1901)

Symphony No. 1
in G Minor

1st Movement
1st Theme ... K12

1st Movement
2nd Theme ... K13

2nd Movement
1st Theme ... K14

2nd Movement
2nd Theme ... K15

3rd Movement
1st Theme ... K16

3rd Movement
2nd Theme ... K17

4th Movement
1st Theme ... K18

4th Movement
2nd Theme — K19

KETELBEY, Albert W. (1875-1959)

In a Chinese Temple Garden, Pft. or Orch.
By permission of Belwin, Inc., Sole Selling Agents for the copyright owner, Bosworth & Co.,Ltd., Copyright 1923.

1st Theme — K19a
2nd Theme — K19b
3rd Theme — K19c
4th Theme — K19d

In a Monastery Garden, Pft. or Orch.
Copyright 1915 by J.H. Larway.
Copyright renewed and assigned to Harms, Inc. N.Y.

1st Theme — K20
2nd Theme — K21
3rd Theme — K22

In a Persian Market, Pft. or Orch.
By permission of Belwin, Inc., Sole Selling Agents for the copyright owner, Bosworth & Co., Ltd., Copyright 1920 renewal copyright secured.

1st Theme — K22a
2nd Theme — K22b
3rd Theme — K22c
4th Theme — K22d
5th Theme — K22e
6th Theme — K22f

KHACHATURIAN, Aram (1903-   )

Concerto, Pft. & Orch.
Copyright 1945 by Leeds Music Corp., N.Y. Reprinted here by permission of the copyright owner.

1st Movement 1st Theme — K23
1st Movement 2nd Theme — K24
2nd Movement Intro. — K25
2nd Movement Theme — K26

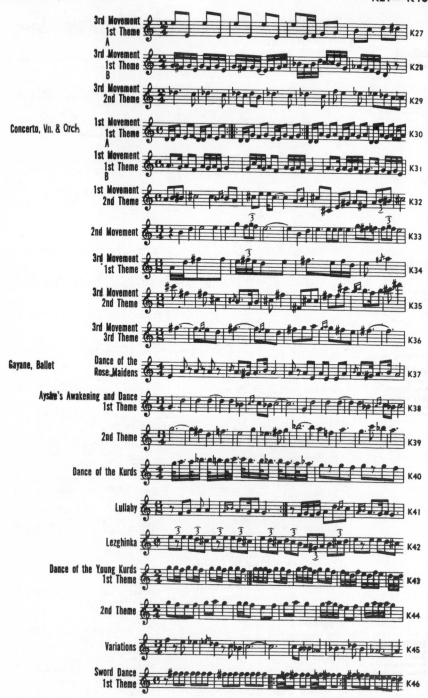

2nd Theme — K47

Masquerade
Suite for Orch.

1st Movement
Waltz
1st Theme — K48

1st Movement
2nd Theme — K49

2nd Movement
Nocturne — K50

3rd Movement
Mazurka — K51

4th Movement
Romance — K52

5th Movement
Galop — K53

Toccata, Pft.

1st Theme — K54

2nd Theme — K55

KHRENNIKOFF, Tikhon (1913-   )

Symphony No. 1, Op. 4
Copyright 1945 by Leeds
Music Corp., N. Y.
Reprinted here by
permission of the
copyright owner.

1st Movement
1st Theme — K56

1st Movement
2nd Theme — K57

1st Movement
3rd Theme — K58

2nd Movement
1st Theme — K59

2nd Movement
2nd Theme — K60

3rd Movement
1st Theme — K61

3rd Movement
2nd Theme — K62

KODÁLY, Zoltán (1882-1967)

Galanta Dances
Orch.
By permission of the copyright owner,
Boosey and Hawkes, Inc.

Intro. — K63

1st Movement — K64

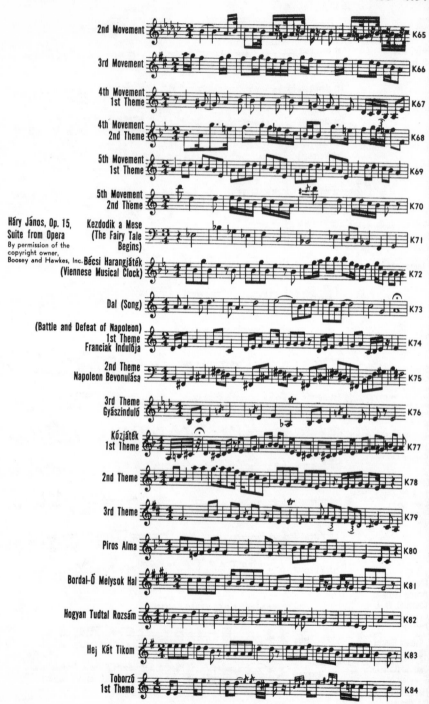

2nd Movement — K65

3rd Movement — K66

4th Movement
1st Theme — K67

4th Movement
2nd Theme — K68

5th Movement
1st Theme — K69

5th Movement
2nd Theme — K70

Háry János, Op. 15,
Suite from Opera
By permission of the
copyright owner,
Boosey and Hawkes, Inc.

Kezdodik a Mese
(The Fairy Tale
Begins) — K71

Bécsi Harangjáték
(Viennese Musical Clock) — K72

Dal (Song) — K73

(Battle and Defeat of Napoleon)
1st Theme
Franciak Indulója — K74

2nd Theme
Napoleon Bevonulása — K75

3rd Theme
Gyászinduló — K76

Közjáték
1st Theme — K77

2nd Theme — K78

3rd Theme — K79

Piros Alma — K80

Bordal-Ő Melysok Hal — K81

Hogyan Tudtal Rozsám — K82

Hej Két Tikom — K83

Toborzó
1st Theme — K84

2nd Theme — K85

A Császári Udvar Bevonulása
1st Theme — K86

2nd Theme — K87

Szegény Vagyok — K88

Felszántóm A Császár Udvarát — K89

KORNGOLD, Erich Wolfgang (1897-1957)

Much Ado About Nothing,
Suite, Op. 11
Vn. & Pft.
By permission of
Associated Music
Publishers, Inc.

1st Movement
Mädchen im
Brautgemach
1st Theme — K90

1st Movement
2nd Theme — K91

2nd Movement
Holzapfel und Schlehwein
1st Theme — K92

2nd Movement
2nd Theme — K93

3rd Movement
Mummenschantz — K94

KREISLER, Fritz (1875-1962)

Andantino, (Style of Padre Martini)
Vn. & Pft.
Copyright by Charles Foley, New York — K95

Caprice Viennois, Op. 2,
Vn. & Pft.
Copyright by
Charles Foley, New York

1st Theme,
A — K96

1st Theme,
B — K97

2nd Theme — K98

Chanson Louis XIII et
Pavane, (Style of
Couperin), Vn. & Pft.
Copyright by Charles Foley,
New York

1st Theme
Chanson — K99

2nd Theme
Pavane — K100

La Chasse, Caprice (Style of
Jean-Baptiste Cartier), Vn. & Pft.
Copyright by Charles Foley, New York — K101

Liebesfreud,
Old Viennese Song
Vn. & Pft.
Copyright by Charles Foley, New York

1st Theme — K102

2nd Theme · K103

3rd Theme · K104

Liebesleid,
Old Viennese Song
Vn. & Pft
Copyright by Charles Foley,
New York

1st Theme · K105

2nd Theme · K106

The Old Refrain
Viennese Popular Song
Vn. & Pft.
Copyright by Charles Foley, New York · K107

Polichinelle, Serenade
Vn. & Pft.
Copyright by Charles Foley, New York · K108

Praeludium and Allegro
(Style of Pugnani) Praeludium
Vn. & Pft.
Copyright by Charles Foley, New York · K109

Allegro · K110

La Précieuse
(Style of Couperin) 1st Theme · K111
Vn. & Pft.
Copyright by Charles Foley, 2nd Theme · K112
New York

Rondino on a Theme by Beethoven
Vn. & Pft.
Copyright by Charles Foley, New York · K113

Schön Rosmarin 1st Theme · K114
Vn. & Pft.
Copyright by Charles Foley, New York

2nd Theme · K115

Tambourin Chinois, Op. 3 1st Theme · K116
Vn. & Pft.
Copyright by Charles Foley, New York

2nd Theme · K117

Tempo di Minuetto
(Style of Pugnani), Vn. & Pft.
Copyright by Charles Foley, New York · K118

KREUTZER, Conradin (1780-1849)

Das Nachtlager in Granada, 1st Theme · K119
Overture

2nd Theme · K120

3rd Theme · K121

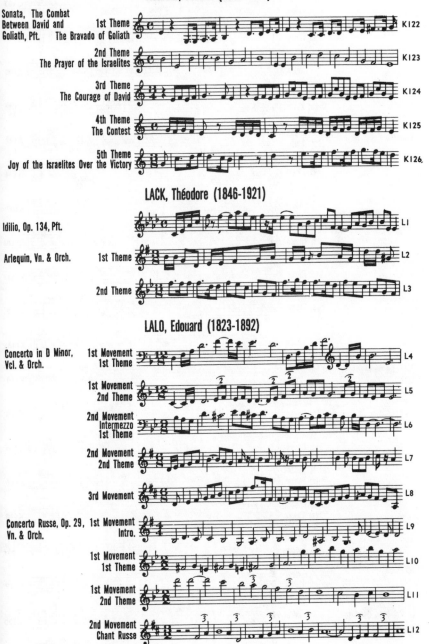

KUHNAU, Johann (1660-1722)

Sonata, The Combat Between David and Goliath, Pft. — 1st Theme — The Bravado of Goliath — K122

2nd Theme — The Prayer of the Israelites — K123

3rd Theme — The Courage of David — K124

4th Theme — The Contest — K125

5th Theme — Joy of the Israelites Over the Victory — K126

LACK, Théodore (1846-1921)

Idilio, Op. 134, Pft. — L1

Arlequin, Vn. & Orch. — 1st Theme — L2

2nd Theme — L3

LALO, Edouard (1823-1892)

Concerto in D Minor, Vcl. & Orch. — 1st Movement 1st Theme — L4

1st Movement 2nd Theme — L5

2nd Movement Intermezzo 1st Theme — L6

2nd Movement 2nd Theme — L7

3rd Movement — L8

Concerto Russe, Op. 29, Vn. & Orch. — 1st Movement Intro. — L9

1st Movement 1st Theme — L10

1st Movement 2nd Theme — L11

2nd Movement Chant Russe — L12

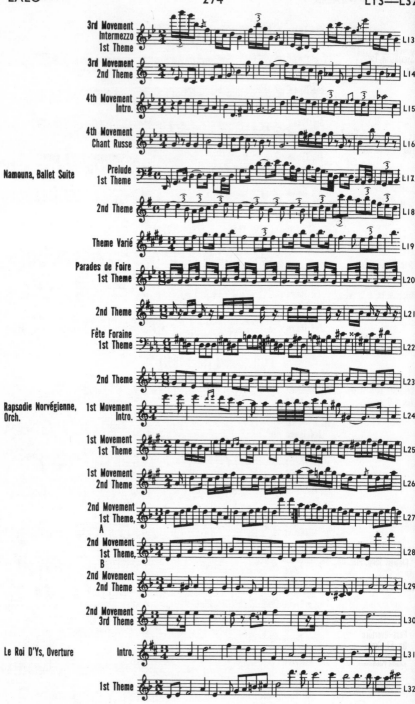

2nd Theme — L33

Symphonie Espagnole, Op. 21, Vn. & Orch.

1st Movement 1st Theme, A — L34

1st Movement 1st Theme, B — L35

1st Movement 2nd Theme — L36

2nd Movement 1st Theme — L37

2nd Movement 2nd Theme — L38

3rd Movement Intermezzo Intro. — L39

3rd Movement Intermezzo 1st Theme — L40

3rd Movement 2nd Theme — L41

4th Movement Intro. — L42

4th Movement — L43

5th Movement Intro. — L44

5th Movement 1st Theme — L45

5th Movement 2nd Theme — L46

LANGE, Gustav (1830-1889)

Flower Song, Pft. — L47

LASSEN, Eduard (1830-1904)

Fest-Overtüre Op. 51, Orch.
By permission of Associated Music Publishers, Inc.

Intro. — L48

1st Theme — L49

2nd Theme — L50

LECLAIR, Jean-Marie (1697-1764)

Sonata in D,
Op. 8, No. 3,
Vn. & Pft.

Trio-Sonata in D,
Op. 2, No. 8,
Fl., Viola di Gamba & Harpsi.

LECUONA, Ernesto (1900-   )

Suite Andalucia, Pft.
Copyright 1929 by
Ernesto Lecuono
Copyright assigned 1931
to Edward B. Marks Co.
Copyright Assigned 1932
to Edward B. Marks Corp.
Used by Permission

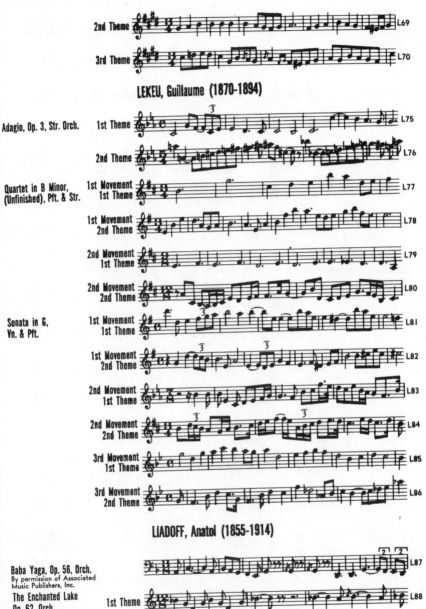

2nd Theme — L69

3rd Theme — L70

LEKEU, Guillaume (1870-1894)

Adagio, Op. 3, Str. Orch. — 1st Theme — L75

2nd Theme — L76

Quartet in B Minor, (Unfinished), Pft. & Str. — 1st Movement 1st Theme — L77

1st Movement 2nd Theme — L78

2nd Movement 1st Theme — L79

2nd Movement 2nd Theme — L80

Sonata in G, Vn. & Pft. — 1st Movement 1st Theme — L81

1st Movement 2nd Theme — L82

2nd Movement 1st Theme — L83

2nd Movement 2nd Theme — L84

3rd Movement 1st Theme — L85

3rd Movement 2nd Theme — L86

LIADOFF, Anatol (1855-1914)

Baba Yaga, Op. 56, Orch.
By permission of Associated
Music Publishers, Inc. — L87

The Enchanted Lake
Op. 62, Orch.
By permission of Associated
Music Publishers, Inc. — 1st Theme — L88

2nd Theme — L89

Kikimora, Op. 63, Orch.
By permission of Associated
Music Publishers, Inc.

1st Theme, A — L90

1st Theme, B — L91

2nd Theme — L92

3rd Theme — L93

The Music Box, Op. 32, Pft.
(or The Musical Snuff Box)
By permission of Associated
Music Publishers, Inc.

1st Theme — L94

2nd Theme — L95

3rd Theme — L96

Russian Folk Dances, Op. 58, Orch.
By permission of
Associated Music
Publishers, Inc.

Legend of the Birds — L97

I Danced With a Mosquito — L98

Cradle Song — L99

Village Dance — L100

LISZT, Franz (1811-1886)

Ballade No. 2,
in B Minor, Pft.

1st Theme — L101

2nd Theme — L102

Bénédiction de Dieu Dans la Solitude
Pft. — L103

Berceuse, Pft. — L104

Concerto No. 1 in E Flat
Pft. & Orch.

1st Theme — L105

2nd Theme — L106

3rd Theme — L107

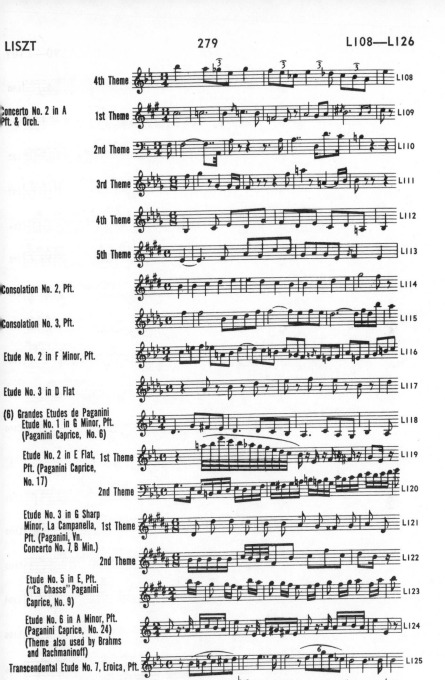

4th Theme — L108

Concerto No. 2 in A
Pft. & Orch.

1st Theme — L109

2nd Theme — L110

3rd Theme — L111

4th Theme — L112

5th Theme — L113

Consolation No. 2, Pft. — L114

Consolation No. 3, Pft. — L115

Etude No. 2 in F Minor, Pft. — L116

Etude No. 3 in D Flat — L117

(6) Grandes Etudes de Paganini
Etude No. 1 in G Minor, Pft.
(Paganini Caprice, No. 6) — L118

Etude No. 2 in E Flat, 1st Theme — L119
Pft. (Paganini Caprice,
No. 17)
2nd Theme — L120

Etude No. 3 in G Sharp
Minor, La Campanella, 1st Theme — L121
Pft. (Paganini, Vn.
Concerto No. 7, B Min.)
2nd Theme — L122

Etude No. 5 in E, Pft.
("La Chasse" Paganini
Caprice, No. 9) — L123

Etude No. 6 in A Minor, Pft.
(Paganini Caprice, No. 24)
(Theme also used by Brahms
and Rachmaninoff) — L124

Transcendental Etude No. 7, Eroica, Pft. — L125

Faust Symphony
1st Movement
Faust
1st Theme — L126

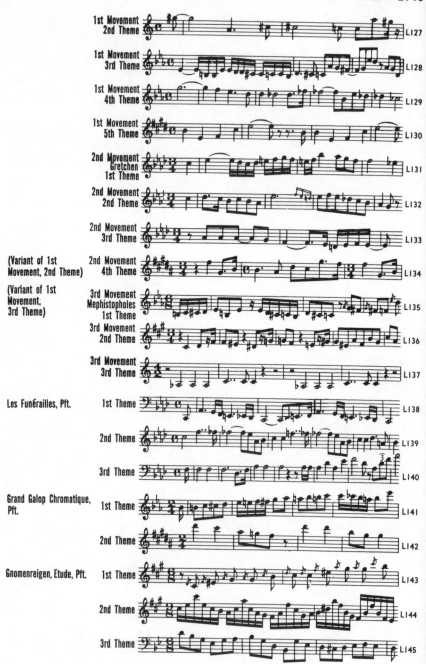

1st Movement
2nd Theme — LI27

1st Movement
3rd Theme — LI28

1st Movement
4th Theme — LI29

1st Movement
5th Theme — LI30

2nd Movement
Gretchen
1st Theme — LI31

2nd Movement
2nd Theme — LI32

2nd Movement
3rd Theme — LI33

(Variant of 1st
Movement, 2nd Theme)
2nd Movement
4th Theme — LI34

(Variant of 1st
Movement,
3rd Theme)
3rd Movement
Mephistopheles
1st Theme — LI35

3rd Movement
2nd Theme — LI36

3rd Movement
3rd Theme — LI37

Les Funérailles, Pft.
1st Theme — LI38

2nd Theme — LI39

3rd Theme — LI40

Grand Galop Chromatique,
Pft.
1st Theme — LI41

2nd Theme — LI42

Gnomenreigen, Etude, Pft.
1st Theme — LI43

2nd Theme — LI44

3rd Theme — LI45

Hungarian Rhapsody No. 8
in F Sharp Minor, Pft.   L165

Hungarian Rhapsody No. 9
in E Flat, Pft.   1st Theme   L166
"Carnival in Pesth"

                                   2nd Theme   L167

                                   3rd Theme   L168

                                   4th Theme   L169

Hungarian Rhapsody No. 10
in E, Pft.   1st Theme   L170

                                   2nd Theme   L171

Hungarian Rhapsody No. 12
in C Sharp Minor, Pft.   1st Theme   L172

                                   2nd Theme   L173

                                   3rd Theme   L174

                                   4th Theme   L175

                                   5th Theme   L176

Hungarian Rhapsody No. 13
in A Minor, Pft.   1st Theme   L177

                                   2nd Theme   L178

                                   3rd Theme   L179

Hungarian Rhapsody No. 14
in F Minor (same material   1st Theme   L180
as for Hungarian Fantasie,
Pft. & Orch.)

                                   2nd Theme   L181

                                   3rd Theme   L182

                                   4th Theme   L183

Hungarian Rhapsody No. 15
in A Minor, Pft.   1st Theme   L184
"Rakóczy March"

LISZT

2nd Theme — L185

3rd Theme — L186

Liebestraum No. 1, Pft. — L187

Liebestraum No. 2, Pft. — L188

Liebestraum No. 3, Pft. — L189

Mazeppa, Transcendental Etude No. 4, Pft. or Orch. — 1st Theme — L190

2nd Theme — L191

Mephisto Waltz, Pft. — 1st Theme — L192

2nd Theme — L193

3rd Theme — L194

Polonaise No. 1 in C Minor, Pft. — 1st Theme — L195

2nd Theme — L196

Polonaise No. 2 in E, Pft. — 1st Theme — L197

2nd Theme — L198

3rd Theme — L199

Rapsodie Espagnole, Pft. & Orch. — 1st Theme — Folies d'Espagne — L200

2nd Theme — Jota Aragonesa — L201

3rd Theme — L202

4th Theme — L203

Sonata in B Minor, Pft. — 1st Theme — L204

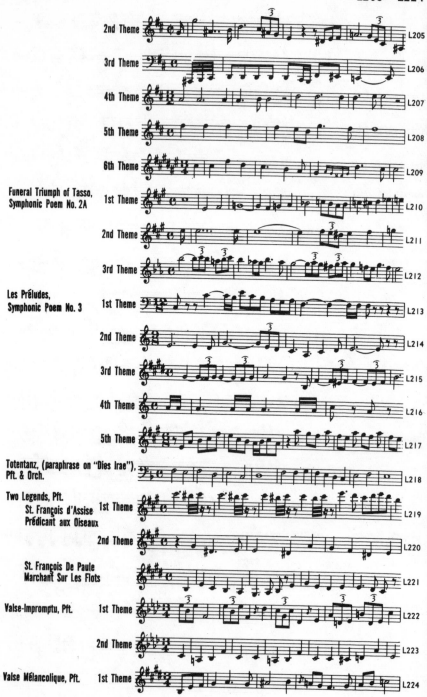

2nd Theme — L205
3rd Theme — L206
4th Theme — L207
5th Theme — L208
6th Theme — L209

Funeral Triumph of Tasso, Symphonic Poem No. 2A
1st Theme — L210
2nd Theme — L211
3rd Theme — L212

Les Préludes, Symphonic Poem No. 3
1st Theme — L213
2nd Theme — L214
3rd Theme — L215
4th Theme — L216
5th Theme — L217

Totentanz, (paraphrase on "Dies Irae"), Pft. & Orch. — L218

Two Legends, Pft.
St. François d'Assise Prédicant aux Oiseaux
1st Theme — L219
2nd Theme — L220

St. François De Paule Marchant Sur Les Flots — L221

Valse-Impromptu, Pft.
1st Theme — L222
2nd Theme — L223

Valse Mélancolique, Pft.
1st Theme — L224

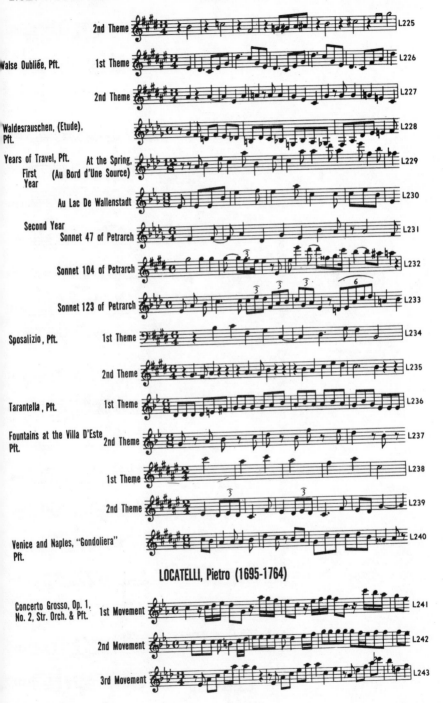

2nd Theme L225

Walse Oubliée, Pft. 1st Theme L226

2nd Theme L227

Waldesrauschen, (Etude), Pft. L228

Years of Travel, Pft.
First Year At the Spring, (Au Bord d'Une Source) L229

Au Lac De Wallenstadt L230

Second Year
Sonnet 47 of Petrarch L231

Sonnet 104 of Petrarch L232

Sonnet 123 of Petrarch L233

Sposalizio, Pft. 1st Theme L234

2nd Theme L235

Tarantella, Pft. 1st Theme L236

Fountains at the Villa D'Este Pft. 2nd Theme L237

1st Theme L238

2nd Theme L239

Venice and Naples, "Gondoliera" Pft. L240

LOCATELLI, Pietro (1695-1764)

Concerto Grosso, Op. 1, No. 2, Str. Orch. & Pft. 1st Movement L241

2nd Movement L242

3rd Movement L243

4th Movement  L244

5th Movement L245

LOEFFLER, Charles Martin (1861-1935)

La Mort de Tintagiles, Op. 6, Orch.
Copyright renewal assigned 1933 to G. Schirmer, Inc.

1st Theme, A L246

1st Theme, B L247

2nd Theme L248

3rd Theme L249

4th Theme L250

5th Theme L251

A Pagan Poem (after Virgil), Op. 14, Pft. & Orch.
Copyright renewal assigned 1937 to G. Schirmer, Inc.

Intro. L252

1st Theme L253

2nd Theme L254

3rd Theme L255

4th Theme L256

5th Theme L257

Quintet, Str. (In One Movement)
Copyright 1938 by G. Schirmer, Inc.

1st Theme L258

2nd Theme L259

3rd Theme L260

4th Theme L261

5th Theme L262

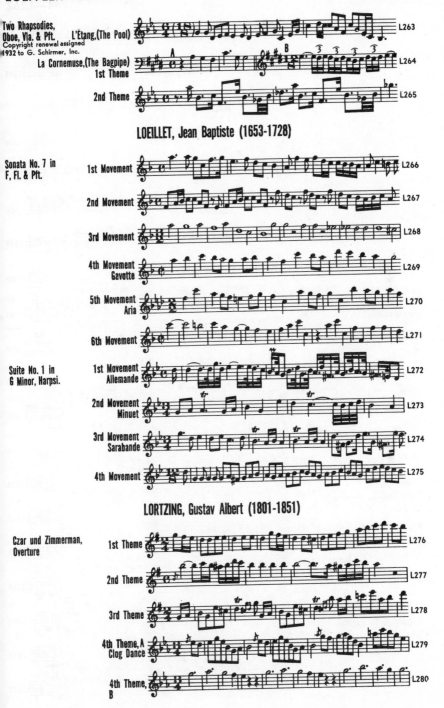

Two Rhapsodies, Oboe, Vla. & Pft.
Copyright renewal assigned 1932 to G. Schirmer, Inc.

L'Etang,(The Pool) — L263

La Cornemuse,(The Bagpipe) 1st Theme — L264

2nd Theme — L265

LOEILLET, Jean Baptiste (1653-1728)

Sonata No. 7 in F, Fl. & Pft.

1st Movement — L266

2nd Movement — L267

3rd Movement — L268

4th Movement Gavotte — L269

5th Movement Aria — L270

6th Movement — L271

Suite No. 1 in G Minor, Harpsi.

1st Movement Allemande — L272

2nd Movement Minuet — L273

3rd Movement Sarabande — L274

4th Movement — L275

LORTZING, Gustav Albert (1801-1851)

Czar und Zimmerman, Overture

1st Theme — L276

2nd Theme — L277

3rd Theme — L278

4th Theme, A Clog Dance — L279

4th Theme, B — L280

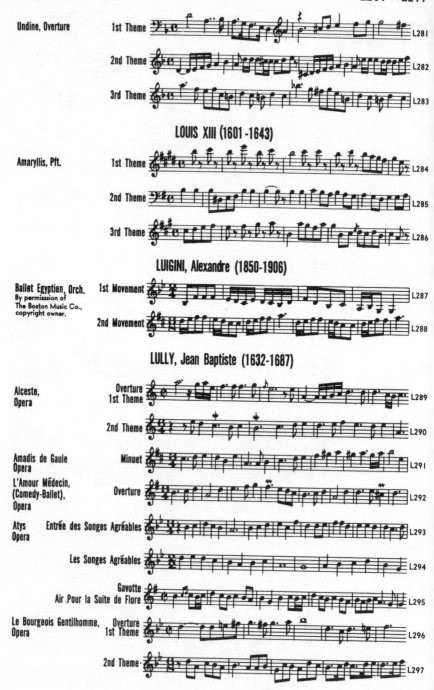

Undine, Overture — 1st Theme — L281

2nd Theme — L282

3rd Theme — L283

LOUIS XIII (1601-1643)

Amaryllis, Pft. — 1st Theme — L284

2nd Theme — L285

3rd Theme — L286

LUIGINI, Alexandre (1850-1906)

Ballet Egyptien, Orch. — 1st Movement — L287
By permisssion of
The Boston Music Co.,
copyright owner.

2nd Movement — L288

LULLY, Jean Baptiste (1632-1687)

Alceste, Opera — Overture 1st Theme — L289

2nd Theme — L290

Amadis de Gaule Opera — Minuet — L291

L'Amour Médecin, (Comedy-Ballet), Opera — Overture — L292

Atys Opera — Entrée des Songes Agréables — L293

Les Songes Agréables — L294

Gavotte Air Pour la Suite de Flore — L295

Le Bourgeois Gentilhomme, Opera — Overture 1st Theme — L296

2nd Theme — L297

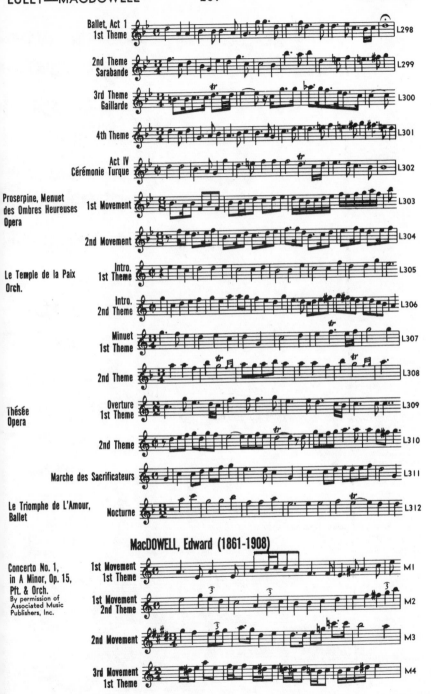

MacDOWELL, Edward (1861-1908)

3rd Movement 2nd Theme — M5

3rd Movement 3rd Theme — M6

3rd Movement 4th Theme — M7

Concerto No. 2.
in D Minor, Op. 23,
Pft. & Orch.
Copyright 1922 by
G. Schirmer, Inc.

1st Movement 1st Theme — M8

1st Movement 2nd Theme — M9

2nd Movement 1st Theme — M10

2nd Movement 2nd Theme — M11

2nd Movement 3rd Theme — M12

3rd Movement 1st Theme — M13

3rd Movement 2nd Theme — M14

Marionettes, Pft. Witch, Op. 38, No. 4
Revised and Augmented Edition,
Copyright 1929 by The Arthur P. Schmidt
Co. Used by Permission. — M15

Clown, Op. 38, No. 5
Revised and Augmented Edition,
Copyright 1929 by The Arthur P. Schmidt
Co. Used by Permission. — M16

Villain, Op. 38, No. 6.
Revised and Augmented Edition,
Copyright 1929 by The Arthur P. Schmidt Co.
Used by Permission — M17

Of Br'er Rabbit, Op. 61, No. 2, Pft.
Copyright 1930 by The Arthur
P. Schmidt Co. Used by Permission — M18

Of a Tailor and a Bear, Pft.
Copyright 1925 and 1942 by The
Arthur P. Schmidt Co. Used by Permission. — M19

An Old Garden. Op. 62. No. 1. Pft.,
Copyright 1930 by The Arthur P.
Schmidt Co. Used by Permission. — M20

Polonaise,
Op. 46, No. 12, Pft. — M21

Scotch Poem, Op. 31, No. 2, Pft.
Revised Edition, Copyright 1923 by The
Arthur P. Schmidt Co. Used by Permission — M22

Sea Pieces, Pft.
To the Sea, Op. 55, No. 1
Copyright 1926 by The Arthur P. Schmidt
Co. Used by Permission. — M23

A. D. 1620, Op. 55, No. 3
Copyright 1926 by The Arthur P. Schmidt
Co. Used by Permission. — M24

Starlight, Op. 55, No. 4   M25

Nautilus, Op. 55, No. 7   M26

Suite No. 2, (Indian) Orch.   **I. Legend, Intro.**   M27

1st Theme   M28

2nd Theme   M29

II. Love Song 1st Theme   M30

2nd Theme   M31

III. In War-Time   M32

IV. Elegy   M33

V. Village Festival 1st Theme   M34

2nd Theme   M35

Witches' Dance, Op. 17, No. 2, Pft.   M36

Woodland Sketches, Pft. To a Wild Rose, Op. 51, No. 1   M37

Will O'the Wisp, Op. 51, No. 2   M38

In Autumn, Op. 51, No. 4   M39

From an Indian Lodge, Op. 51, No. 5   **1st Theme**   M40

2nd Theme   M41

To a Water Lily, Op. 51, No. 6   **1st Theme**   M42

2nd Theme   M43

From Uncle Remus, Op. 51, No. 7   M44

A Deserted Farm,
Copyright 1924 by
The Arthur P. Schmid·
Used by Permission.

Op. 51, No. 8

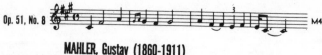

M45

MAHLER, Gustav (1860-1911)

Symphony No. 1
in D

1st Movement
Intro.

1st Movement
1st Theme

1st Movement
2nd Theme

1st Movement
3rd Theme

2nd Movement
1st Theme

2nd Movement
2nd Theme

3rd Movement
1st Theme

3rd Movement
2nd Theme

4th Movement
1st Theme,
A

4th Movement
1st Theme,
B

4th Movement
2nd Theme

Symphony No. 2
in C Minor
"Resurrection"

1st Movement
1st Theme,
A

1st Movement
1st Theme,
B

1st Movement
2nd Theme

1st Movement
3rd Theme

2nd Movement
1st Theme

2nd Movement
2nd Theme

2nd Movement
3rd Theme

M46
M47
M48
M49
M50
M51
M52
M53
M54
M55
M56
M57
M58
M59
M60
M61
M62
M63

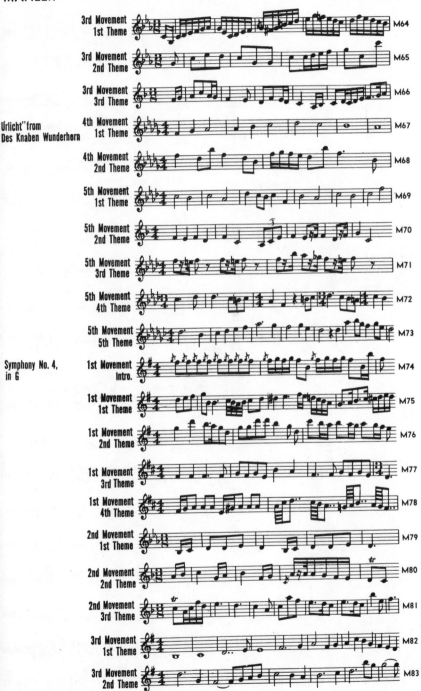

Urlicht" from
Des Knaben Wunderhorn

Symphony No. 4,
in G

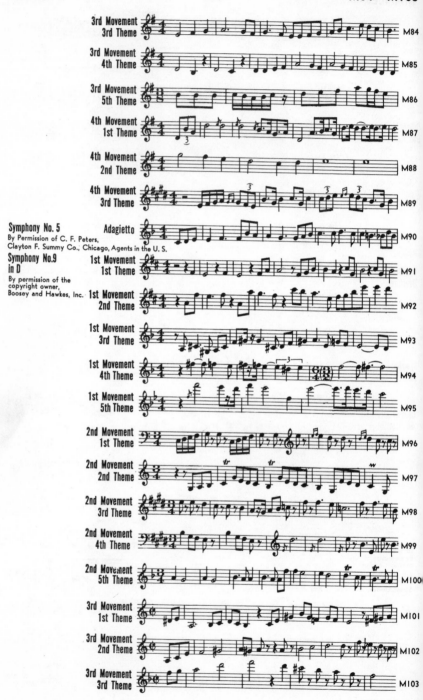

3rd Movement 3rd Theme — M84
3rd Movement 4th Theme — M85
3rd Movement 5th Theme — M86
4th Movement 1st Theme — M87
4th Movement 2nd Theme — M88
4th Movement 3rd Theme — M89

Symphony No. 5
By Permission of C. F. Peters,
Clayton F. Summy Co., Chicago, Agents in the U. S.

Adagietto — M90

Symphony No.9
in D
By permission of the
copyright owner,
Boosey and Hawkes, Inc.

1st Movement 1st Theme — M91
1st Movement 2nd Theme — M92
1st Movement 3rd Theme — M93
1st Movement 4th Theme — M94
1st Movement 5th Theme — M95
2nd Movement 1st Theme — M96
2nd Movement 2nd Theme — M97
2nd Movement 3rd Theme — M98
2nd Movement 4th Theme — M99
2nd Movement 5th Theme — M100
3rd Movement 1st Theme — M101
3rd Movement 2nd Theme — M102
3rd Movement 3rd Theme — M103

MAILLART, Louis (1817-1871)

Les Dragons De Villars Overture

MALIPIERO, Francesco (1882-)

Cantari Alla Madrigalesca, Str. Quartet

La Cimarosiana, Orch.
By permission of the copyright holders, J. & W. Chester, Ltd., 11 Great Marlborough Street, London, W. 1.

4th Movement 2nd Theme — M122

5th Movement — M123

Impressioni Dal Vero Orch.
By permission of the copyright holders, J. & W. Chester, Ltd., 11 Great Marlborough Street, London, W. 1.

Il Capinero 1st Theme — M124

2nd Theme — M125

Il Picchio 1st Theme — M126

2nd Theme — M127

Il Chiù — M128

Rispetti E Strambotti Quartet, Str.
By permission of the copyright holders, J. & W. Chester, Ltd., 11 Great Marlborough Street, London, W. 1.

1st Theme — M129

2nd Theme — M130

3rd Theme — M131

MARGIS, Alfred (1874-   )

Valse Bleue, Vn. & Pft.

1st Theme — M13

2nd Theme — M13

MARSHNER, Heinrich August (1795-1861)

Hans Heiling Overture

1st Theme — M132

2nd Theme — M133

3rd Theme — M134

MARTUCCI, Giuseppe (1856-1909)

Notturno, Orch.
Copyright 1922 by G. Ricordi & Co., Inc.

M135

MASCAGNI, Pietro (1863-1945)

Cavalleria Rusticana, Opera

Prelude 1st Theme — M136

2nd Theme — M137

Intermezzo 1st Theme — M138

2nd Theme — M139

MASSENET, Jules (1842-1912)

1st Movement Castillane — M140

2nd Movement Andalouse — M141

3rd Movement Aragonaise — M142

4th Movement Aubade — M143

5th Movement Catalane 1st Theme — M144

5th Movement 2nd Theme — M145

6th Movement Madrilène 1st Theme — M146

6th Movement 2nd Theme — M147

7th Movement Navarraise — M148

Prelude — M149

Danse Grecque 1st Theme — M150

2nd Theme — M151

Entr'acte — M152

Scène Religieuse — M153

Invocation, Elegy — M154

Finale, Saturnales 1st Theme — M155

2nd Theme — M156

Meditation from Opera Thais
By permission of the copyright owner, Heugel Ltd., London.

1st Theme — M157

2nd Theme — M158

Phedre Overture
By permission of the copyright owner, Heugel Ltd., London.

1st Theme — M159

2nd Theme — M160

3rd Theme — M161

Le Roi De Lahore Overture
By permission of the copyright owner, Heugel Ltd., London.

1st Theme — M162

2nd Theme — M163

Scènes Alsaciennes, Suite No. 7,
By permission of the copyright owner, Heugel Ltd., London.

I--Sunday Morning 1st Theme — M164

2nd Theme — M165

II--Cabaret 1st Theme — M166

2nd Theme — M167

3rd Theme — M168

III--Under the Lindens — M169

IV--Sunday Evening 1st Theme — M170

2nd Theme Alsatian Folk Tune — M171

3rd Theme Alsatian Tune — M172

Scènes Pittoresques, Suite No. 4,
By permission of the copyright owner, Heugel Ltd., London.

I--March 1st Theme — M173

2nd Theme — M174

3rd Theme — M175

4th Theme — M176

H--Air De Ballet 1st Theme — M177

2nd Theme — M178

HI--Angelus 1st Theme — M179

2nd Theme — M180

IV--Fête Bohême 1st Theme — M181

2nd Theme — M182

McDONALD, Harl (1899-1955)

Rhumba, from
Symphony No. 2
Permission granted by
Elkan-Vogel Co., Inc.,
Philadelphia, Pa.
Copyright 1936

1st Theme — M183

2nd Theme — M184

3rd Theme — M185

4th Theme — M186

MEDTNER, Nicolas (1880-1951)

Arabesque, "Tragedie-Fragment"
Op. 7, No. 3, Pft.
By permission of International Music Co.

— M187

Fairy Tales, Pft.
Op. 14, No. 2
By permission of International Music Co.

1st Theme — M188

2nd Theme — M189

Op. 20, No. 1 — M190

Op. 26, No. 3 — M191

Op. 34, No. 2 — M192

Op. 51, No. 1 — M193

Op. 51, No. 2   M194

Novelette, Op. 17, No. 1, Pft.
By permission of International Music Co.   M195

MENDELSSOHN, Felix (1809-1847)

Capriccio Brilliant,   1st Theme
Op. 22, Pft. & Orch.   Intro.   M196

2nd Theme   M197

3rd Theme   M198

4th Theme   M199

Concerto No. 1,   1st Movement
in G Minor, Op. 25,   Intro.   M200
Pft. & Orch.

1st Movement
1st Theme   M201

1st Movement
2nd Theme   M202

1st Movement
3rd Theme   M203

2nd Movement   M204

3rd Movement   M205

Concerto No. 2,   1st Movement
in D Minor, Op. 40,   Intro.   M206
Pft. & Orch.

1st Movement
1st Theme   M207

1st Movement
2nd Theme   M208

2nd Movement   M209

3rd Movement   M210

Concerto in E Minor,   1st Movement
Op. 64, Vn. & Orch.   1st Theme   M211

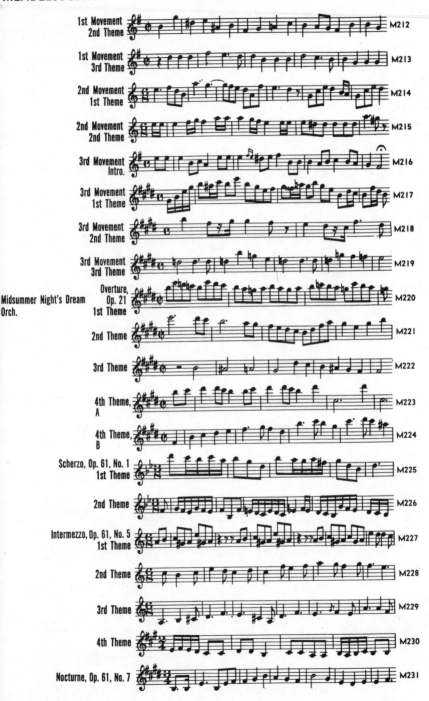

1st Movement / 2nd Theme — M212
1st Movement / 3rd Theme — M213
2nd Movement / 1st Theme — M214
2nd Movement / 2nd Theme — M215
3rd Movement / Intro. — M216
3rd Movement / 1st Theme — M217
3rd Movement / 2nd Theme — M218
3rd Movement / 3rd Theme — M219
Midsummer Night's Dream Orch. — Overture, Op. 21 / 1st Theme — M220
2nd Theme — M221
3rd Theme — M222
4th Theme, A — M223
4th Theme, B — M224
Scherzo, Op. 61, No. 1 / 1st Theme — M225
2nd Theme — M226
Intermezzo, Op. 61, No. 5 / 1st Theme — M227
2nd Theme — M228
3rd Theme — M229
4th Theme — M230
Nocturne, Op. 61, No. 7 — M231

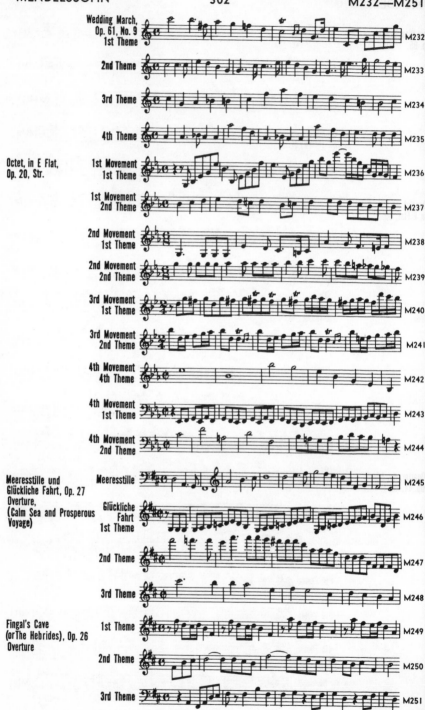

Ruy Blas, Overture, Op. 95

Intro.	M252
1st Theme	M253
2nd Theme A	M254
2nd Theme B	M255
3rd Theme	M256

Quartet No. 1, in E Flat, Op. 12, Str.

1st Movement Intro.	M257
1st Movement 1st Theme	M258
1st Movement 2nd Theme	M259
1st Movement 3rd Theme	M260
2nd Movement	M261
3rd Movement	M262
4th Movement 1st Theme	M263
4th Movement 2nd Theme	M264

Quartet, No. 3 in D, Op. 44, No. 1, Str.

1st Movement 1st Theme	M265
1st Movement 2nd Theme	M266
1st Movement 3rd Theme	M267
2nd Movement 1st Theme	M268
2nd Movement 2nd Theme	M269
3rd Movement 1st Theme, A	M270
3rd Movement 1st Theme, B	M271

3rd Movement 2nd Theme — M272

4th Movement 1st Theme — M273

4th Movement 1st Theme — M274

4th Movement 2nd Theme — M275

Quartet, No. 4, in E Minor, Op. 44, No. 2, Str.

1st Movement 1st Theme — M276

1st Movement 2nd Theme — M277

2nd Movement — M278

3rd Movement 1st Theme — M279

3rd Movement 2nd Theme — M280

4th Movement 1st Theme — M281

4th Movement 2nd Theme — M282

Andante and Rondo Capriccioso, Op. 14, Pft.

Andante — M283

Rondo 1st Theme — M284

2nd Theme — M285

Songs Without Words, Pft.

No. 1 in E, Op. 19, No. 1 — M286

No. 3 in A, Op. 19, No. 3, "Hunting Song" — M287

No. 6 in G Minor, Op. 19, No. 6 "Venetian Boat Song" No. 1 — M288

No. 9 in E, Op. 30, No. 3 "Consolation" — M289

No. 10 in B Minor, Op. 30, No. 4 — M290

No. 12 in F Sharp Minor, Op. 30 No. 6 "Venetian Boat Song", No. 2 — M291

No.14 in C Minor, Op. 38, No. 2, "Lost Happiness" — M292

No.18 in A Flat, Op. 38, No. 6, "Duet" — M293

No.20 in E Flat, Op. 53, No. 2, "The Fleecy Cloud" — M294

No.22 in F, Op. 53, No. 4, "Sadness of Soul" — M295

No.23 in A, Op. 53, No. 5, "Folk Song" — 1st Theme — M296

2nd Theme — M297

No.25 in G, Op. 62, No. 1. "May Breezes" — M298

No.27, in E Minor Op. 62, No. 3, "Funeral March" — M299

No.28, in G Op. 62, No. 4, "Morning Song" — M300

No.29, in A Minor, Op. 62, No. 5 "Venetian Boat Song", No. 3 — M301

No. 30, in A, Op. 62, No. 6 "Spring Song" — M302

No.34, in C, Op.67, No.4 "Spinning Song" — M303

No.35, in B Minor, Op. 67, No. 5 "Song of the Heather" — M304

No.45, in C, "Tarantella" — M305

No.47, in A, Op.102 No. 5 "The Joyous Peasant" — M306

No.48, in C, Op. 102, No. 6 "Faith" — M307

No. 49, in A, Op.102, No. 7 "Boat-Song" — M308

Scherzo, Op. 16, No. 2, Pft. — 1st Theme — M309

2nd Theme — M310

Symphony No. 3, in A Minor, Op.56 "Scotch" — 1st Movement Intro. — M311

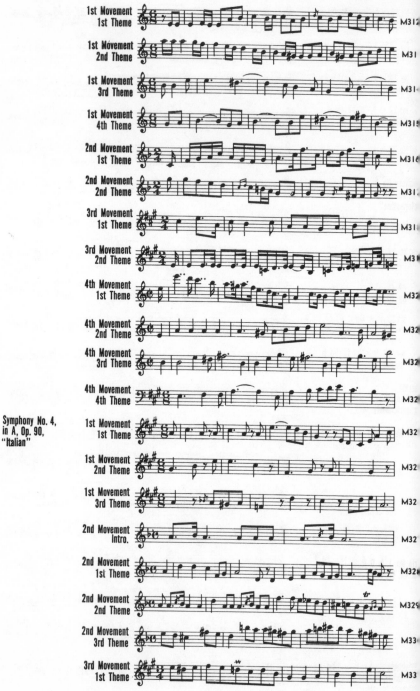

1st Movement 1st Theme — M312
1st Movement 2nd Theme — M31
1st Movement 3rd Theme — M31
1st Movement 4th Theme — M315
2nd Movement 1st Theme — M316
2nd Movement 2nd Theme — M31
3rd Movement 1st Theme — M31
3rd Movement 2nd Theme — M3
4th Movement 1st Theme — M32
4th Movement 2nd Theme — M32
4th Movement 3rd Theme — M32
4th Movement 4th Theme — M32

Symphony No. 4, in A, Op. 90, "Italian"

1st Movement 1st Theme — M32
1st Movement 2nd Theme — M32
1st Movement 3rd Theme — M32
2nd Movement Intro. — M32
2nd Movement 1st Theme — M32
2nd Movement 2nd Theme — M329
2nd Movement 3rd Theme — M33
3rd Movement 1st Theme — M33

3rd Movement 2nd Theme   M332

4th Movement 1st Theme   M333

4th Movement 2nd Theme   M334

4th Movement 3rd Theme   M335

4th Movement 4th Theme   M336

Symphony No. 5, D, Op. 107, "Reformation"

1st Movement Intro.   M337

1st Movement 1st Theme   M338

1st Movement 2nd Theme   M339

2nd Movement 1st Theme   M340

2nd Movement 2nd Theme   M341

3rd Movement 1st Theme   M342

Chorale, Ein Feste Burg ist unser Gott!

3rd Movement 2nd Theme   M343

3rd Movement 3rd Theme   M344

3rd Movement 4th Theme   M345

3rd Movement 5th Theme   M346

3rd Movement 6th Theme   M347

Trio No. 1, in D Minor, Op. 49, Vn, Cello, Pft.

1st Movement 1st Theme A   M348

1st Movement 1st Theme B   M349

2nd Movement 1st Theme   M350

2nd Movement 2nd Theme   M351

3rd Movement — M352

4th Movement / 1st Theme — M353

4th Movement / 2nd Theme — M354

Trio No. 2, in C Minor, Op. 66, Vn, Cello, Pft.

1st Movement / 1st Theme — M355

1st Movement / 2nd Theme — M356

1st Movement / 3rd Theme — M357

2nd Movement / 1st Theme — M358

2nd Movement / 2nd Theme — M359

3rd Movement / 1st Theme — M360

3rd Movement / 2nd Theme — M361

4th Movement / 1st Theme — M362

4th Movement / 2nd Theme — M363

Variations Serieuses, Op. 54, Pft. / Theme — M364

MEYERBEER, Giacomo (1791-1864)

Le Prophète Opera

Coronation March / 1st Theme — M365

2nd Theme — M366

MIASKOVSKY, Nicolas (1881-1950)

Sinfonietta in B Minor, Op. 32, No. 2, Str. Orch.

1st Movement / 1st Theme — M367

1st Movement / 2nd Theme — M368

2nd Movement / Theme for Variations — M369

3rd Movement / 1st Theme — M370

3rd Movement / 2nd Theme — M371

3rd Movement / 3rd Theme — M372

Symphony No. 21, / F Sharp Minor, Op. 51

1st Theme — M372a

2nd Theme — M372b

3rd Theme — M372c

4th Theme — M372d

5th Theme — M372e

6th Theme / (Variant of 4th Theme / Used as Fugue Theme) — M372 f

MILHAUD, Darius (1892-   )

Le Boeuf Sur Le Toit,(The Nothing Doing Bar), Ballet Based on South American Tunes

1st Theme / Barman Theme — M373

2nd Theme / Entry of the Negroes — M374

3rd Theme / Entry of the Women, A — M375

3rd Theme, B — M376

4th Theme / Entry of the Men — M377

5th Theme / Dance of the Bookmakers — M378

6th Theme / Tango — M379

7th Theme / Dance of the Policemen — M380

8th Theme / Dance of the Negro — M381

Concerto, Pft. & Orch.

1st Movement / 1st Theme — M382

1st Movement
2nd Theme — M383

1st Movement
3rd Theme — M384

2nd Movement — M385

3rd Movement
1st Theme — M386

3rd Movement
2nd Theme — M387

Création Du Monde, Ballet
By permission of Associated Music Publishers, Inc.

Prelude — M388

1st Movement — M389

2nd Movement — M390

3rd Movement — M391

4th Movement
1st Theme — M392

4th Movement
2nd Theme — M393

Pastorale for Oboe, Cl., Bassoon
By permission of Associated Music Publishers, Inc.

1st Theme — M394

2nd Theme — M395

Saudades Do Brazil, Pft.
Copyright by Editions Salabert Editions Salabert, 22 Rue Chaucat. Paris Salabert, Inc., 1 East 57 St., N. Y.

I Sorocaba — M396

VII Corcovado — M397

VIII Tijuca — M398

IX Sumare — M399

XII Paysandu — M400

MONIUSZKO, Stanislaw (1819-1872)

Halka Overture

Intro. — M401

1st Theme — M402

2nd Theme — M403

3rd Theme — M404

4th Theme — M405

MORGENSTERN, Sam (1907-   )

Toccata Guatemala, Pft.
Copyright 1947 by Carl
Fischer, Inc., N. Y.
Reprinted by permisssion.

1st Theme — M405 a

2nd Theme — M405 b

MOSZKOWSKI, Moritz (1854-1925)

Caprice Espagnol,
Op. 37, Pft.

1st Theme — M406

2nd Theme — M407

3rd Theme — M408

Etincelles (Sparks),
Op. 36, No. 6, Pft.

M409

Guitarre, Op. 45, No. 2,
Pft.
Copyright 1920 by Carl
Fischer, Inc., N. Y.

1st Theme — M410

2nd Theme — M411

Malaguena, from opera Boabdil,
Op. 49

M412

By Permission of C. F. Peters, Clayton F. Summy Co.,
Chicago, Agents in the U. S.
Serenata, Op. 15, No. 1, Pft.

M413

Spanish Dances, Pft.
Op. 12, No. 1

1st Theme — M414

2nd Theme — M415

3rd Theme — M416

Op. 12, No. 2

1st Theme — M417

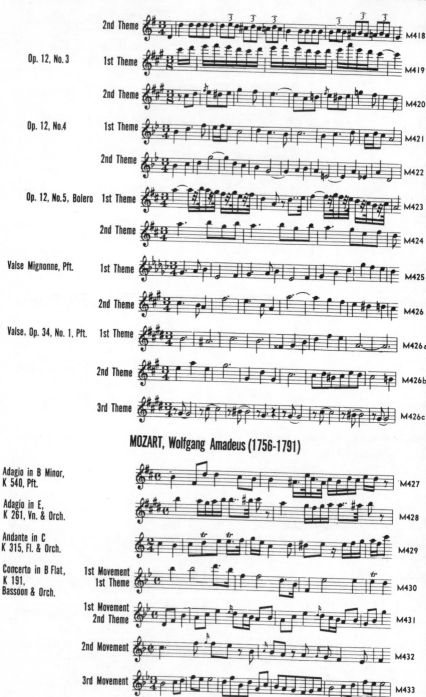

MOZART, Wolfgang Amadeus (1756-1791)

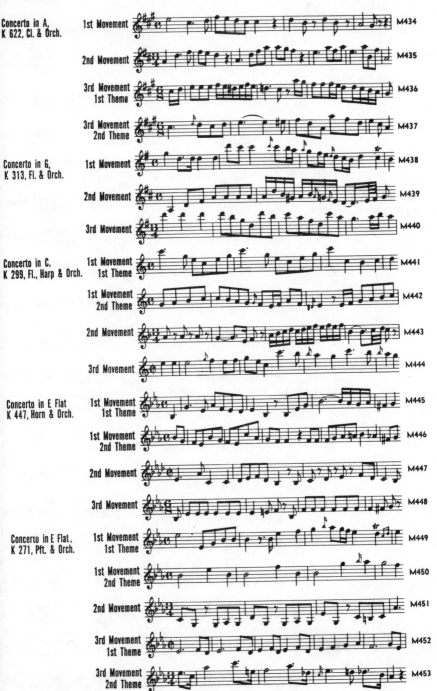

Concerto in A,
K 622, Cl. & Orch.   1st Movement   M434

2nd Movement   M435

3rd Movement
1st Theme   M436

3rd Movement
2nd Theme   M437

Concerto in G,
K 313, Fl. & Orch.   1st Movement   M438

2nd Movement   M439

3rd Movement   M440

Concerto in C,
K 299, Fl., Harp & Orch.   1st Movement
1st Theme   M441

1st Movement
2nd Theme   M442

2nd Movement   M443

3rd Movement   M444

Concerto in E Flat,
K 447, Horn & Orch.   1st Movement
1st Theme   M445

1st Movement
2nd Theme   M446

2nd Movement   M447

3rd Movement   M448

Concerto in E Flat,
K 271, Pft. & Orch.   1st Movement
1st Theme   M449

1st Movement
2nd Theme   M450

2nd Movement   M451

3rd Movement
1st Theme   M452

3rd Movement
2nd Theme   M453

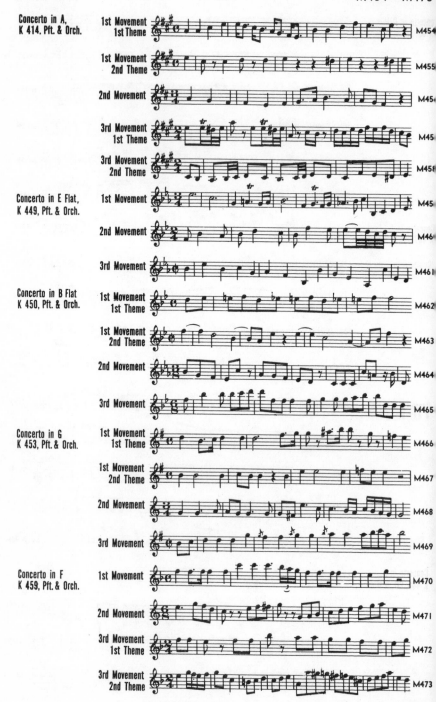

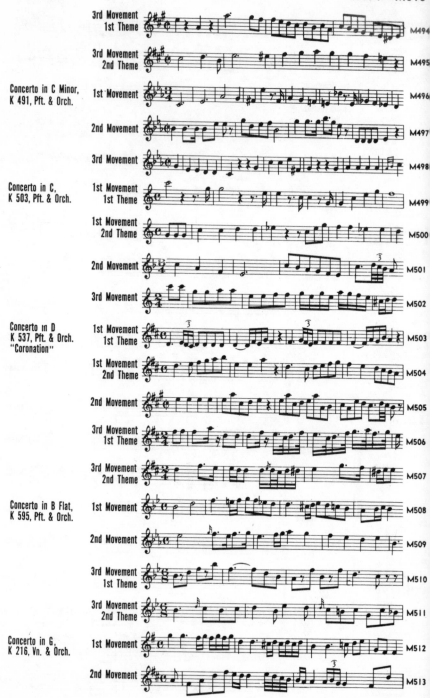

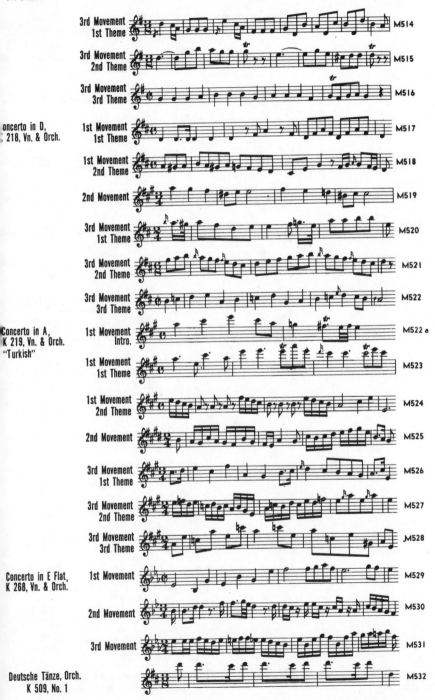

3rd Movement 1st Theme — M514
3rd Movement 2nd Theme — M515
3rd Movement 3rd Theme — M516

Concerto in D, K 218, Vn. & Orch.

1st Movement 1st Theme — M517
1st Movement 2nd Theme — M518
2nd Movement — M519
3rd Movement 1st Theme — M520
3rd Movement 2nd Theme — M521
3rd Movement 3rd Theme — M522

Concerto in A, K 219, Vn. & Orch. "Turkish"

1st Movement Intro. — M522 a
1st Movement 1st Theme — M523
1st Movement 2nd Theme — M524
2nd Movement — M525
3rd Movement 1st Theme — M526
3rd Movement 2nd Theme — M527
3rd Movement 3rd Theme — M528

Concerto in E Flat, K 268, Vn. & Orch.

1st Movement — M529
2nd Movement — M530
3rd Movement — M531

Deutsche Tänze, Orch. K 509, No. 1 — M532

K 509, No. 2 — M533
K 509, No. 4 — M534
K 509, No. 5 — M535
K 509, No. 6 — M536
K 571, No. 4 — M537
K 571, No. 6 — M538
K 600, No. 1 — M539
K 600, No. 2 — M540
K 600, No. 3 — M541
K 600, No. 4 — M542
K 600, No. 5 1st Theme — M543
2nd Theme (Der Kanarienvogel) — M544
K 600, No. 6 — M545
K 602, No. 3 1st Theme — M546
2nd Theme (Der Leiermann) — M547
K 605, No. 1 — M548
K 605, No. 2 — M549
K 605, No. 3 1st Theme — M550
2nd Theme (Die Schlitten Fahrt) — M551
Divertimento in D, K 136 2 Vns., Viola & Bass 1st Movement — M552

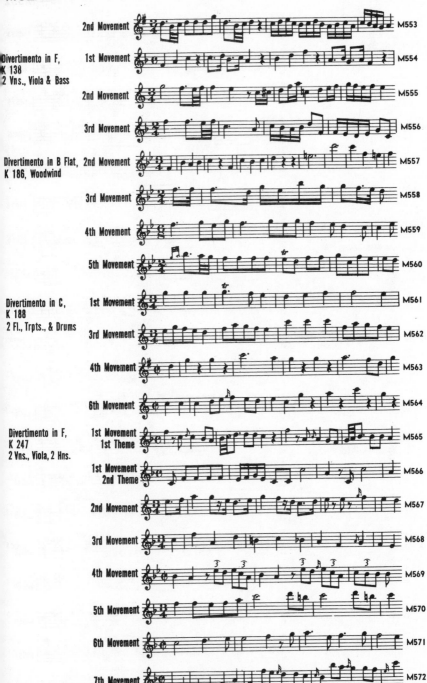

Divertimento in B Flat, K 287 — 2 Vns., Viola, Bass, 2 Horns
- 1st Movement — M573
- 2nd Movement — M574
- 3rd Movement — M575
- 4th Movement — M576
- 5th Movement — M577
- 6th Movement — M578

Divertimento in D, K 334 — 2 Vns., Viola, Bass, 2 Horns
- 1st Movement — M579
- 2nd Movement — M580
- 3rd Movement — M581
- 4th Movement — M582
- 5th Movement — M583
- 6th Movement — M584

Fantasia in F Minor, K 608, Mechanical Organ
- 1st Theme — M585
- 2nd Theme — M586
- 3rd Theme — M587

Fantasia in D Minor, K 397, Pft.
- 1st Theme — M588
- 2nd Theme — M589

Minuet, K 1, Pft. — M590

Minuet in F, K 2, Pft. — M591

Minuet in D, K 355, Pft. — M592

The Abduction From The Seraglio, Overture, K 384 — 1st Theme — M593

2nd Theme — M594

Bastien et Bastienne, Opera — Intro. — M594a

Cosi Fan Tutte, Overture K 588 — 1st Theme — M595

2nd Theme — M596

3rd Theme — M597

Don Giovanni, Overture K 527 — 1st Theme — M598

2nd Theme — M599

Idomeneo, Overture, K 366 — M600

The Magic Flute, Overture, K 620 — Intro. — M601

Theme — M602

Marriage of Figaro, Overture, K 492 — 1st Theme — M603

2nd Theme — M604

3rd Theme — M605

4th Theme — M606

5th Theme — M607

Il Re Pastore, Overture, K 208 — 1st Theme — M608

2nd Theme — M609

Der Schauspieldirektor, Overture, K 486 — 1st Theme — M610

2nd Theme — M611

Quartet in D,
K 285, Fl. & Str.
1st Movement — M612
2nd Movement — M613
3rd Movement — M614

Quartet in A,
K 298, Fl. & Str.
1st Movement — M615
2nd Movement 1st Theme — M616
2nd Movement 2nd Theme — M617
3rd Movement — M618

Quartet in F,
K 370, Oboe & Str.
1st Movement — M619
2nd Movement — M620
3rd Movement — M621

Quartet in G Minor
K 4, Pft. & Str.
1st Movement 1st Theme — M622
1st Movement 2nd Theme — M623
2nd Movement — M624
3rd Movement 1st Theme — M625
3rd Movement 2nd Theme — M626

Quartet in E Flat
K 493, Pft. & Str.
1st Movement 1st Theme — M627
1st Movement 2nd Theme — M628
2nd Movement — M629
3rd Movement — M630

Quartet in G
K 80, Str.
1st Movement — M631

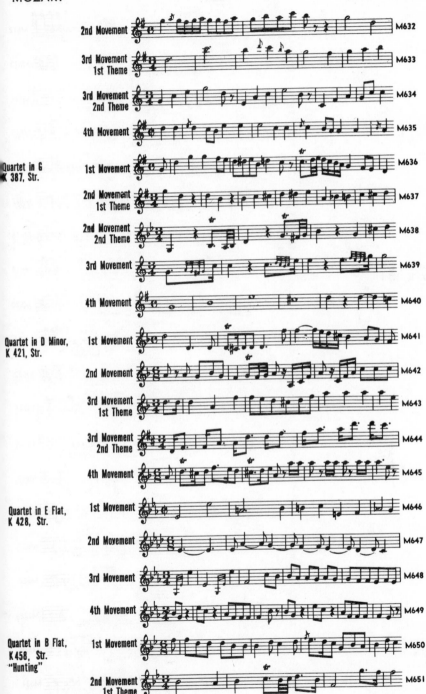

Quartet in G
K 387, Str.

Quartet in D Minor,
K 421, Str.

Quartet in E Flat,
K 428, Str.

Quartet in B Flat,
K 458, Str.
"Hunting"

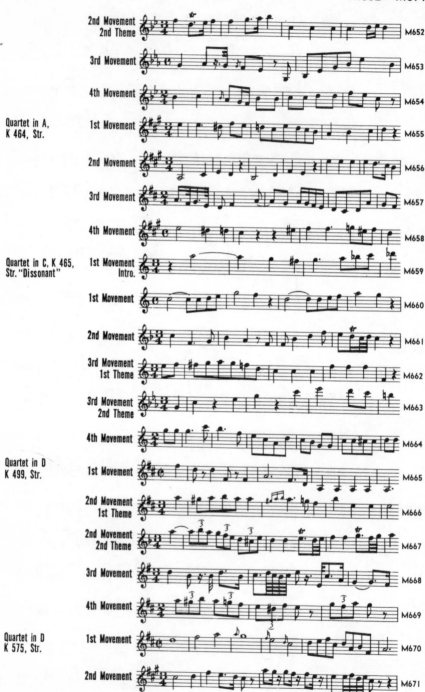

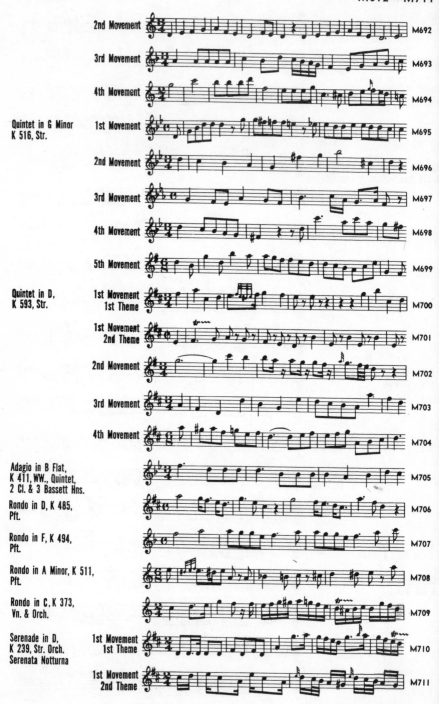

2nd Movement — M692

3rd Movement — M693

4th Movement — M694

Quintet in G Minor
K 516, Str. — 1st Movement — M695

2nd Movement — M696

3rd Movement — M697

4th Movement — M698

5th Movement — M699

Quintet in D,
K 593, Str. — 1st Movement 1st Theme — M700

1st Movement 2nd Theme — M701

2nd Movement — M702

3rd Movement — M703

4th Movement — M704

Adagio in B Flat,
K 411, WW., Quintet,
2 Cl. & 3 Bassett Hns. — M705

Rondo in D, K 485,
Pft. — M706

Rondo in F, K 494,
Pft. — M707

Rondo in A Minor, K 511,
Pft. — M708

Rondo in C, K 373,
Vn. & Orch. — M709

Serenade in D,
K 239, Str. Orch.
Serenata Notturna — 1st Movement 1st Theme — M710

1st Movement 2nd Theme — M711

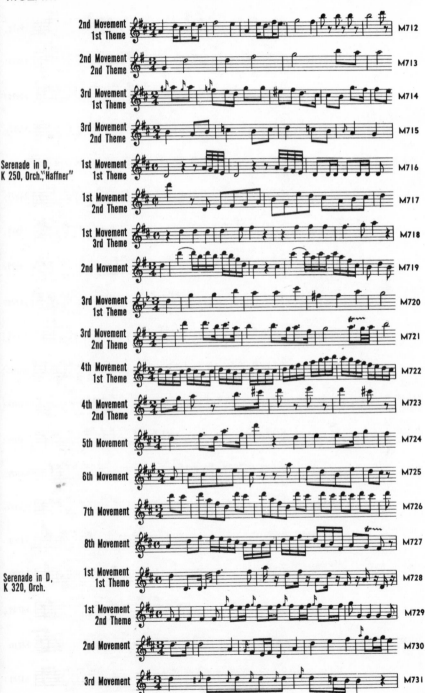

4th Movement — M732

5th Movement — M733

6th Movement
Minuet — M734

7th Movement — M735

Serenade in B Flat,
K 361, Woodw. &
Bass

1st Movement — M736

2nd Movement — M737

4th Movement — M738

5th Movement
1st Theme — M739

5th Movement
2nd Theme — M740

6th Movement
Theme & Variations — M741

7th Movement — M742

Serenade in E Flat,
K 375, Woodw.

1st Movement
1st Theme — M743

1st Movement
2nd Theme — M744

2nd Movement — M745

3rd Movement — M746

4th Movement
1st Theme — M747

4th Movement
2nd Theme — M748

5th Movement — M749

Serenade in C Minor,
K 388, Woodw.

1st Movement — M750

2nd Movement — M751

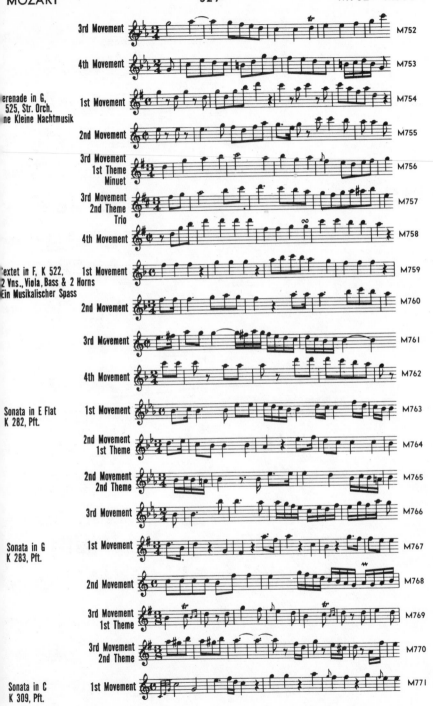

3rd Movement — M752

4th Movement — M753

Serenade in G,
525, Str. Orch.
ne Kleine Nachtmusik

1st Movement — M754

2nd Movement — M755

**3rd Movement
1st Theme
Minuet** — M756

**3rd Movement
2nd Theme
Trio** — M757

4th Movement — M758

extet in F, K 522,
2 Vns., Viola, Bass & 2 Horns
Ein Musikalischer Spass

1st Movement — M759

2nd Movement — M760

3rd Movement — M761

4th Movement — M762

Sonata in E Flat
K 282, Pft.

1st Movement — M763

**2nd Movement
1st Theme** — M764

**2nd Movement
2nd Theme** — M765

3rd Movement — M766

Sonata in G
K 283, Pft.

1st Movement — M767

2nd Movement — M768

**3rd Movement
1st Theme** — M769

**3rd Movement
2nd Theme** — M770

Sonata in C
K 309, Pft.

1st Movement — M771

2nd Movement — M772
3rd Movement — M773
Sonata in A Minor K 310, Pft. — 1st Movement M774
2nd Movement — M775
3rd Movement — M776
Sonata in D K 311, Pft. — 1st Movement 1st Theme M777
1st Movement 2nd Theme — M778
2nd Movement — M779
3rd Movement — M780
Sonata in C K 330, Pft. — 1st Movement M781
2nd Movement 1st Theme — M782
2nd Movement 2nd Theme — M783
3rd Movement — M784
Sonata in A K 331, Pft. — 1st Movement M785
2nd Movement — M786
3rd Movement 1st Theme — M787
3rd Movement 2nd Theme — M788
Sonata in F K 332, Pft. — 1st Movement 1st Theme M789
1st Movement 2nd Theme — M790
1st Movement 3rd Theme — M791

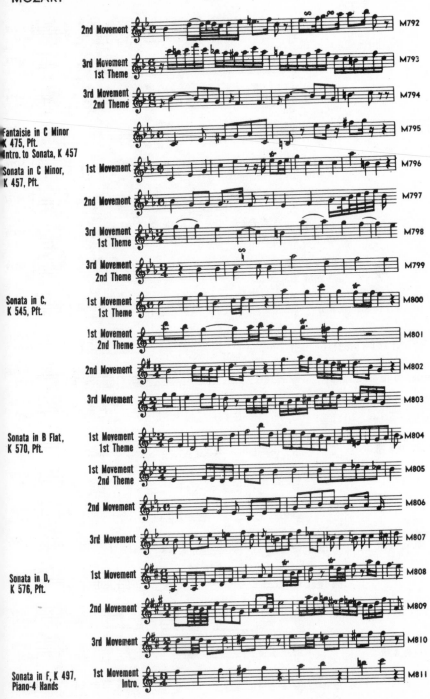

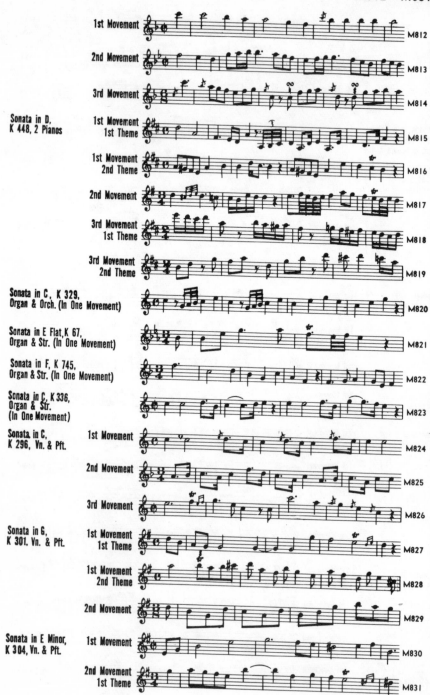

Sonata in F,
K 376, Vn. & Pft.

Sonata in F,
K 377, Vn. & Pft.

Sonata in B Flat,
K 378, Vn. & Pft.

Sonata in G
K 379, Vn. & Pft.

Sonata in E Flat,
K 380, Vn. & Pft.

Sonata in C,
K 404, Vn. & Pft.

Sonata in E Flat,
K 481, Vn. & Pft.

2nd Movement
2nd Theme — M832

1st Movement
1st Theme — M833

1st Movement
2nd Theme — M834

2nd Movement — M835

3rd Movement — M836

1st Movement — M837

2nd Movement — M838

3rd Movement — M839

1st Movement — M840

2nd Movement — M841

3rd Movement — M842

1st Movement
1st Theme — M843

1st Movement
2nd Theme — M844

2nd Movement — M845

1st Movement — M846

2nd Movement — M847

3rd Movement — M848

1st Movement — M849

2nd Movement — M850

1st Movement
1st Theme — M851

Sonata in A,
K 526, Vn. & Pft.

Symphony No. 1,
in E Flat, K 16

Symphony No. 12
in G, K 110

Symphony No. 13
in F, K 112

1st Movement
2nd Theme — M852

2nd Movement — M853

3rd Movement — M854

1st Movement
1st Theme — M855

1st Movement
2nd Theme — M856

3rd Movement — M857

1st Movement
1st Theme — M858

1st Movement
2nd Theme — M859

2nd Movement — M860

3rd Movement
1st Theme — M861

3rd Movement
2nd Theme — M862

1st Movement
1st Theme — M863

1st Movement
2nd Theme — M864

2nd Movement
1st Theme — M865

2nd Movement
2nd Theme — M866

3rd Movement
1st Theme — M867

3rd Movement
2nd Theme — M868

4th Movement
1st Theme — M869

4th Movement
2nd Theme — M870

1st Movement
1st Theme — M871

1st Movement 2nd Theme — M872
2nd Movement — M873
3rd Movement 1st Theme — M874
3rd Movement 2nd Theme — M875
4th Movement 1st Theme — M876
4th Movement 2nd Theme — M877

Symphony No. 25 in G Minor, K 183

1st Movement 1st Theme — M878
1st Movement 2nd Theme — M879
1st Movement 3rd Theme — M880
2nd Movement — M881
3rd Movement 1st Theme — M882
3rd Movement 2nd Theme — M883
4th Movement 1st Theme — M884
4th Movement 2nd Theme — M885

Symphony No. 28 in C, K 200

1st Movement 1st Theme — M886
1st Movement 2nd Theme — M887
2nd Movement 1st Theme — M888
2nd Movement 2nd Theme — M889
3rd Movement 1st Theme — M890
3rd Movement 2nd Theme — M891

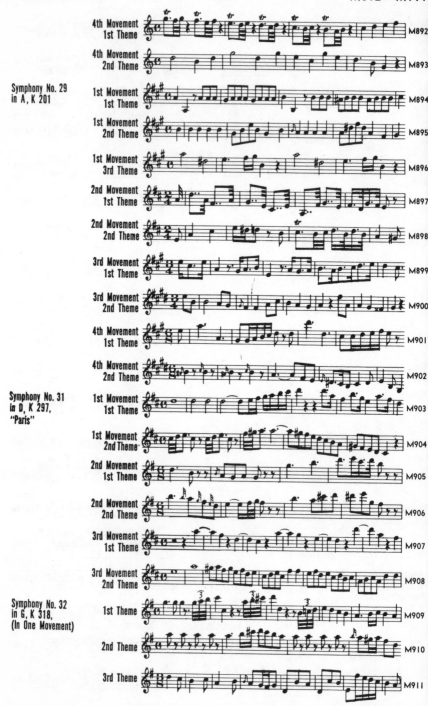

4th Movement 1st Theme — M892
4th Movement 2nd Theme — M893

Symphony No. 29 in A, K 201

1st Movement 1st Theme — M894
1st Movement 2nd Theme — M895
1st Movement 3rd Theme — M896
2nd Movement 1st Theme — M897
2nd Movement 2nd Theme — M898
3rd Movement 1st Theme — M899
3rd Movement 2nd Theme — M900
4th Movement 1st Theme — M901
4th Movement 2nd Theme — M902

Symphony No. 31 in D, K 297, "Paris"

1st Movement 1st Theme — M903
1st Movement 2nd Theme — M904
2nd Movement 1st Theme — M905
2nd Movement 2nd Theme — M906
3rd Movement 1st Theme — M907
3rd Movement 2nd Theme — M908

Symphony No. 32 in G, K 318, (In One Movement)

1st Theme — M909
2nd Theme — M910
3rd Theme — M911

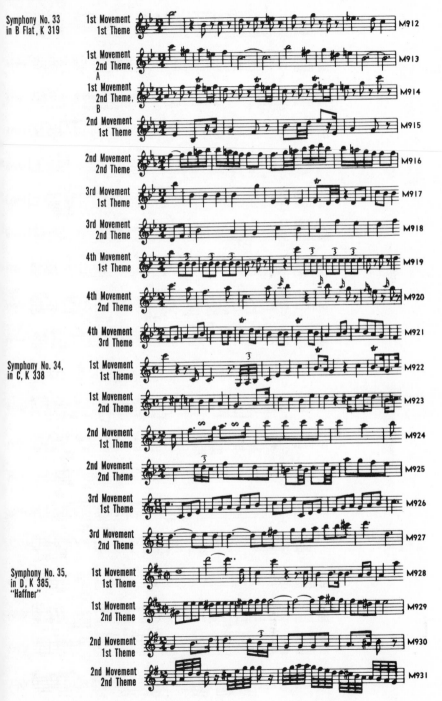

Symphony No. 33 in B Flat, K 319 — 1st Movement 1st Theme — M912
1st Movement 2nd Theme, A — M913
1st Movement 2nd Theme, B — M914
2nd Movement 1st Theme — M915
2nd Movement 2nd Theme — M916
3rd Movement 1st Theme — M917
3rd Movement 2nd Theme — M918
4th Movement 1st Theme — M919
4th Movement 2nd Theme — M920
4th Movement 3rd Theme — M921

Symphony No. 34, in C, K 338 — 1st Movement 1st Theme — M922
1st Movement 2nd Theme — M923
2nd Movement 1st Theme — M924
2nd Movement 2nd Theme — M925
3rd Movement 1st Theme — M926
3rd Movement 2nd Theme — M927

Symphony No. 35, in D, K 385, "Haffner" — 1st Movement 1st Theme — M928
1st Movement 2nd Theme — M929
2nd Movement 1st Theme — M930
2nd Movement 2nd Theme — M931

3rd Movement 1st Theme — M932

3rd Movement 2nd Theme — M933

4th Movement 1st Theme — M934

4th Movement 2nd Theme — M935

Symphony No. 36, in C, K 425 "Linz"

1st Movement Intro. — M936

1st Movement 1st Theme — M937

1st Movement 2nd Theme — M938

1st Movement 3rd Theme — M939

2nd Movement 1st Theme — M940

2nd Movement 2nd Theme — M941

3rd Movement 1st Theme — M942

3rd Movement 2nd Theme — M943

4th Movement 1st Theme — M944

4th Movement 2nd Theme — M945

4th Movement 3rd Theme — M946

Symphony No. 37 in G, K 444

1st Movement Intro. — M947

1st Movement 1st Theme — M948

1st Movement 2nd Theme — M949

2nd Movement 1st Theme — M950

2nd Movement 2nd Theme — M951

Symphony No. 40
in G Minor, K 550

1st Movement
1st Theme   M972

1st Movement
2nd Theme   M973

2nd Movement
1st Theme   M974

2nd Movement
2nd Theme   M975

2nd Movement
3rd Theme   M976

3rd Movement
1st Theme   M977

3rd Movement
2nd Theme   M978

4th Movement
1st Theme   M979

4th Movement
2nd Theme   M980

Symphony No. 41, in C
K 551, "Jupiter"

1st Movement
1st Theme   M981

1st Movement
2nd Theme   M982

1st Movement
3rd Theme   M983

2nd Movement
1st Theme   M984

2nd Movement
2nd Theme   M985

3rd Movement
1st Theme   M986

3rd Movement
2nd Theme   M987

4th Movement
1st Theme   M988

4th Movement
2nd Theme   M989

4th Movement
3rd Theme   M990

Symphonie Concertante
in E Flat, K 364,
Vn., Viola & Orch.

1st Movement
1st Theme   M991

1st Movement 2nd Theme — M992

2nd Movement — M993

3rd Movement 1st Theme — M994

3rd Movement 2nd Theme — M995

...o in B Flat, K 502, ...t., Vn. & Cello — 1st Movement — M996

2nd Movement — M997

3rd Movement — M998

...o in E, K 542, ...t., Vn. & Cello — 1st Movement — M999

2nd Movement — M1000

3rd Movement — M1001

...rio in C, ...548, Pft., Vn. & Cello — 1st Movement — M1002

2nd Movement — M1003

3rd Movement — M1004

...rio in G, ...564, Pft., Vn. & Cello — 1st Movement — M1005

2nd Movement — M1006

3rd Movement — M1007

...ariations in C, K 265, Pft. ...heme: "Ah, Vous Dirai-Je, Maman" — M1008

...ariations, K 455, Pft., ...Theme of Gluck) — M1009

...ariations on an Allegretto, ...n B Flat, K 500, Pft. — M1010

...ariations, K 573, Pft., ...Theme of Duport) — M1011

MUSSORGSKY, Modest Petrovich (1839-1881)

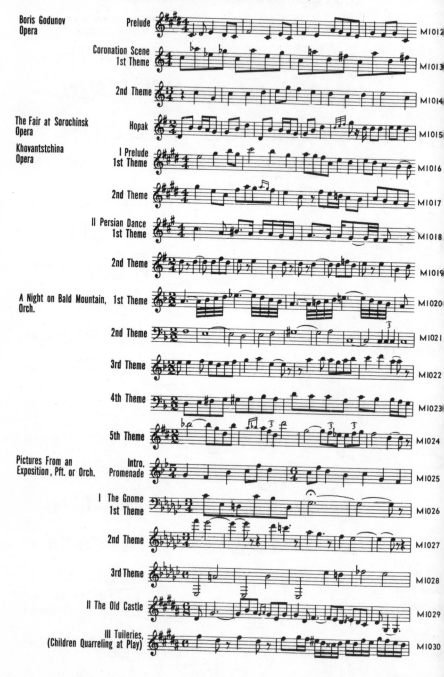

Boris Godunov Opera	Prelude	M1012
	Coronation Scene 1st Theme	M1013
	2nd Theme	M1014
The Fair at Sorochinsk Opera	Hopak	M1015
Khovantstchina Opera	I Prelude 1st Theme	M1016
	2nd Theme	M1017
	II Persian Dance 1st Theme	M1018
	2nd Theme	M1019
A Night on Bald Mountain, Orch.	1st Theme	M1020
	2nd Theme	M1021
	3rd Theme	M1022
	4th Theme	M1023
	5th Theme	M1024
Pictures From an Exposition, Pft. or Orch.	Intro. Promenade	M1025
	I The Gnome 1st Theme	M1026
	2nd Theme	M1027
	3rd Theme	M1028
	II The Old Castle	M1029
	III Tuileries, (Children Quarreling at Play)	M1030

IV Bydlo — M1031

V Ballet of Unhatched Chickens — M1032

VI Samuel Goldenberg and Schmuyle 1st Theme — M1033

2nd Theme — M1034

VII The Market Place at Limoges — M1035

VIII Con mortuis in lingua mortua — M1036

IX The Hut of Baba Yaga — M1037

X The Great Gate at Kiev — M1038

NARDINI, Pietro (1722-1793)

Sonata No. 2 in D, & Pft.
1st Movement — N1

2nd Movement 1st Theme — N2

2nd Movement 2nd Theme — N3

3rd Movement (Larghetto from another Sonata) — N4

4th Movement — N5

Sonata No. 7 in B Flat, & Pft.
1st Movement — N6

2nd Movement — N7

3rd Movement — N8

NARVAEZ, Luis de (16th Century)

Tema y Variaciones, Guitar — N9

NEVIN, Ethelbert (1862-1901)

Barchetta, Op. 21, No. 3, Pft.
By permisssion of The Boston Music Co.,
copyright owner.

A Day in Venice,
Op. 25, Pft.
Published and copyrighted (1898)
by The John Church Co.
Used by permission.

1st Movement
Dawn
Intro.

Theme

2nd Movement
Gondolieri

3rd Movement
Venetian Love Song
1st Theme

2nd Theme

4th Movement
Good Night

Lullaby, Op. 16, No. 3, Pft.
By permisssion of The Boston Music Co.,
copyright owner.

Narcissus, Op. 13, No. 4, Pft. 1st Theme
By permisssion of The Boston Music Co.,
copyright owner.

2nd Theme

A Shepherd's Tale, Op. 16, No. 1, Pft.
By permisssion of The Boston Music Co.,
copyright owner.

NICOLAI, Otto (1810-1849)

The Merry Wives of Windsor,
Overture

Intro.

1st Theme

2nd Theme

3rd Theme,
A

3rd Theme,
B

4th Theme

NIN, Joaquín (1879-1949)

Vals-Serenata from
Chaine de Valses, Pft.
By permission of Associated
Music Publishers, Inc.

Danse Ibérienne, Pft.
By permission of Associated
Music Publishers, Inc.

                1st Theme

                2nd Theme

                3rd Theme

"1830" Variations sur un
Theme Frivole
By permission of Associated
Music Publishers, Inc.

Suite Espagnole,
Vcl. & Pft.
By permission of
Associated Music
Publishers, Inc.

                1st Movement
                Old Castile

                2nd Movement
                1st Theme
                Murciana A

                2nd Movement
                1st Theme
                B

                3rd Movement
                Asturiana

                4th Movement
                Andaluza

NIN-KOCHANSKI

Granadina, Vn. & Pft.
By permission of Associated
Music Publishers, Inc.

Saeta, Vn. & Pft.
By permission of Associated
Music Publishers, Inc.

OFFENBACH, Jacques (1819-1880)

La Belle Hélène,
Opera
                Overture
                1st Theme

                2nd Theme

                Act II Entr'acte

                Act III Entr'acte

La Grande Duchesse de
Gerolstein, Opera
                Overture
                1st Theme

N27
N28
N29
N30
N31
N32
N33
N34
N35
N36
N37
N38
O1
O2
O3
O4
O5

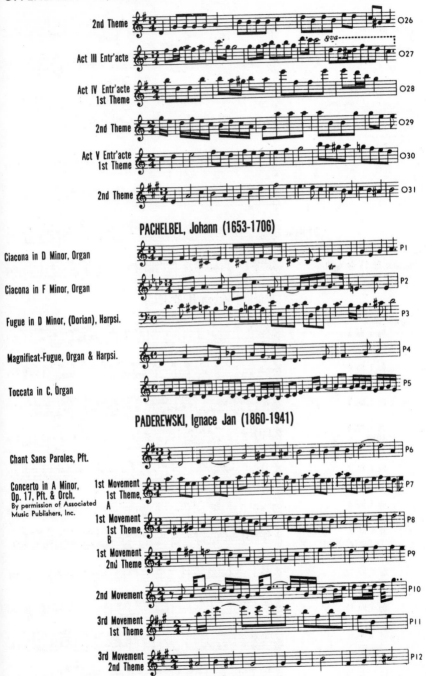

2nd Theme — O26

Act III Entr'acte — O27

Act IV Entr'acte
1st Theme — O28

2nd Theme — O29

Act V Entr'acte
1st Theme — O30

2nd Theme — O31

PACHELBEL, Johann (1653-1706)

Ciacona in D Minor, Organ — P1

Ciacona in F Minor, Organ — P2

Fugue in D Minor, (Dorian), Harpsi. — P3

Magnificat-Fugue, Organ & Harpsi. — P4

Toccata in C, Organ — P5

PADEREWSKI, Ignace Jan (1860-1941)

Chant Sans Paroles, Pft. — P6

Concerto in A Minor,
Op. 17, Pft. & Orch.
By permission of Associated
Music Publishers, Inc.

1st Movement
1st Theme,
A — P7

1st Movement
1st Theme,
B — P8

1st Movement
2nd Theme — P9

2nd Movement — P10

3rd Movement
1st Theme — P11

3rd Movement
2nd Theme — P12

Cracovienne Fantastique, Op. 14, No. 6, Pft. By permission of Associated Music Publishers, Inc.
1st Theme — P13
2nd Theme — P14

Mélodie, Op. 16, No. 2, Pft. By permission of Associated Music Publishers, Inc. — P15

Minuet, Op. 14, No. 1, Pft. Copyright 1899 by G. Schirmer, Inc.
1st Theme, A — P16
1st Theme, B — P17
2nd Theme — P18
3rd Theme — P19

Nocturne, Op. 16, No. 4, Pft. Copyright 1892 by G. Schirmer, Inc. — P20

PAGANINI, Niccolo (1782-1840)

Caprices, Vn.
Op. 1, No. 3 — P21
Op. 1, No. 4 — P22
Op. 1, No. 5 — P23
Op. 1, No. 6, (Liszt) — P24
Op. 1, No. 7 — P25
Op. 1, No. 8 — P26
Op. 1, No. 9, "La Chasse" (Liszt) — P27
Op. 1, No. 11 — P28
Op. 1, No. 13 — P29
Op. 1, No. 14 "Militaire" — P30
Op. 1, No. 15 — P31

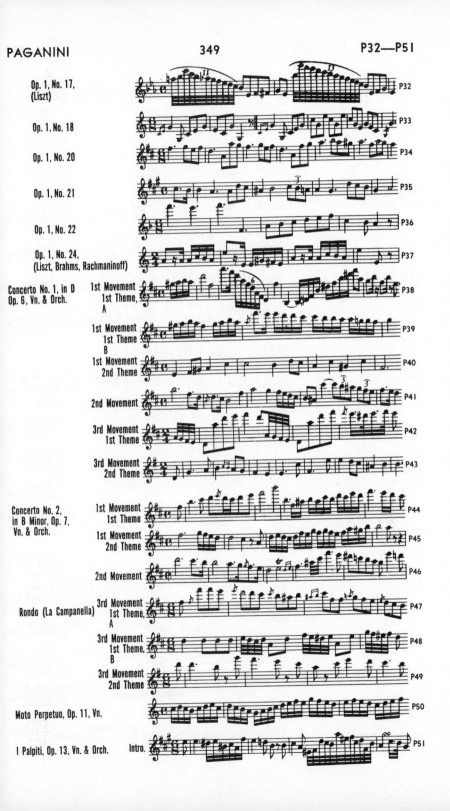

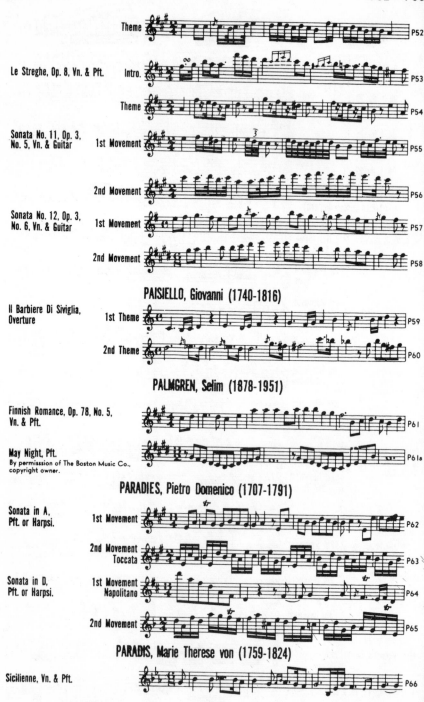

Theme — P52

Le Streghe, Op. 8, Vn. & Pft. — Intro. — P53

Theme — P54

Sonata No. 11, Op. 3, No. 5, Vn. & Guitar — 1st Movement — P55

2nd Movement — P56

Sonata No. 12, Op. 3, No. 6, Vn. & Guitar — 1st Movement — P57

2nd Movement — P58

PAISIELLO, Giovanni (1740-1816)

Il Barbiere Di Siviglia, Overture — 1st Theme — P59

2nd Theme — P60

PALMGREN, Selim (1878-1951)

Finnish Romance, Op. 78, No. 5, Vn. & Pft. — P61

May Night, Pft.
By permisssion of The Boston Music Co., copyright owner. — P61a

PARADIES, Pietro Domenico (1707-1791)

Sonata in A, Pft. or Harpsi. — 1st Movement — P62

2nd Movement Toccata — P63

Sonata in D, Pft. or Harpsi. — 1st Movement Napolitano — P64

2nd Movement — P65

PARADIS, Marie Therese von (1759-1824)

Sicilienne, Vn. & Pft. — P66

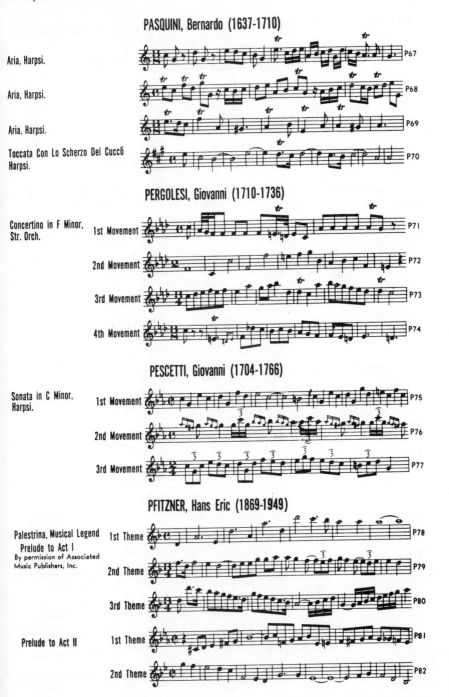

PASQUINI, Bernardo (1637-1710)

Aria, Harpsi. — P67

Aria, Harpsi. — P68

Aria, Harpsi. — P69

Toccata Con Lo Scherzo Del Cuccó Harpsi. — P70

PERGOLESI, Giovanni (1710-1736)

Concertino in F Minor, Str. Orch. — 1st Movement — P71

2nd Movement — P72

3rd Movement — P73

4th Movement — P74

PESCETTI, Giovanni (1704-1766)

Sonata in C Minor, Harpsi. — 1st Movement — P75

2nd Movement — P76

3rd Movement — P77

PFITZNER, Hans Eric (1869-1949)

Palestrina, Musical Legend Prelude to Act I
By permission of Associated Music Publishers, Inc. — 1st Theme — P78

2nd Theme — P79

3rd Theme — P80

Prelude to Act II — 1st Theme — P81

2nd Theme — P82

Prelude to Act III   1st Theme   P83

2nd Theme   P84

PHILIPS, Peter (1560-1633)

Galliardo, Harpsi.   P85

PICK-MANGIAGALLI, Riccardo (1882-1949)

Il Carillon Magico, (Ballet)
Copyright 1920 by
G. Ricordi & Co., Inc.   Intermezzo delle Rose   P86

La Danse d'Olaf,
Op. 33, No. 2
Orch. or Pft.
Copyright 1916 by
G. Ricordi & Co., Inc.   1st Theme   P87

2nd Theme   P88

Notturno, Op. 28, No. 1,
Orch.
Copyright 1923 by
G. Ricordi & Co., Inc.   1st Theme   P89

2nd Theme   P90

I Piccoli Soldati, Orch.
Copyright by G. Ricordi
& Co., Inc.   1st Theme   P91

2nd Theme   P92

Rondo Fantastico, Op. 28,
No. 2, Orch.
Copyright by G. Ricordi
& Co., Inc.   1st Theme   P93

2nd Theme   P94

3rd Theme   P95

PIERNÉ, Gabriel (1863-1937)

Cydalise et le Chèvre-pied,
Ballet Suite, Orch.
By permission of the
copyright owner,
Heugel Ltd., London.   March of the Little Fauns
1st Theme A   P96

1st Theme, B   P97

Dance Lesson in the
Hypo-Lydian Mode   P98

Finale   P99

2nd Theme P116
3rd Theme P117
4th Theme P118
5th Theme P119
6th Theme P120
7th Theme P121
8th Theme P122
9th Theme P123
10th Theme P124

Quartet No. 1, Str.
Copyright Cos Cob
Press, Inc.

1st Movement 1st Theme, A P125
1st Movement 1st Theme, B P126
1st Movement 2nd Theme, A P127
1st Movement 2nd Theme, B P128
2nd Movement 1st Theme, A P129
2nd Movement 1st Theme, B P130
3rd Movement 1st Theme P131
3rd Movement 2nd Theme P132

Suite for Oboe
and Pft.
Copyright 1934 by
E. C. Schirmer, Boston.

1st Movement Prelude P133
2nd Movement Sarabande P134
3rd Movement Minuet P135

PIZZETTI, Ildebrando (1880-1968)

PLATTI, Giovanni (1690-1762)

POLDINI, Eduard (1869-1957)

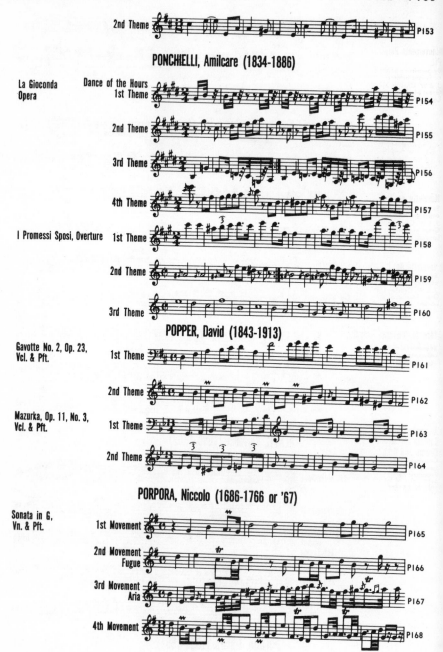

2nd Theme P153

PONCHIELLI, Amilcare (1834-1886)

La Gioconda
Opera

Dance of the Hours
1st Theme P154

2nd Theme P155

3rd Theme P156

4th Theme P157

I Promessi Sposi, Overture **1st Theme** P158

2nd Theme P159

3rd Theme P160

POPPER, David (1843-1913)

Gavotte No. 2, Op. 23,
Vcl. & Pft.
1st Theme P161

2nd Theme P162

Mazurka, Op. 11, No. 3,
Vcl. & Pft.
1st Theme P163

2nd Theme P164

PORPORA, Niccolo (1686-1766 or '67)

Sonata in G,
Vn. & Pft.
1st Movement P165

2nd Movement
Fugue P166

3rd Movement
Aria P167

4th Movement P168

POULENC, Francis (1899-1963)

Mouvements Perpétuels, Pft.
By permission of the
copyright holders,
J. & W. Chester, Ltd., 11
Great Marlborough Street,
London, W. 1.

No. 1 — P169

No. 2 — P170

No. 3
1st Theme — P171

2nd Theme — P172

Novelette No. 1, Pft.
By permission of the
copyright holders,
J. & W. Chester, Ltd., 11
Great Marlborough Street,
London, W. 1.

1st Theme — P173

2nd Theme — P174

Novelette No. 2, Pft.
By permission of the
copyright holders,
J. & W. Chester, Ltd., 11
Great Marlborough Street,
London, W. 1.

1st Theme — P175

2nd Theme — P176

Toccato, Pft.
By permission of the
copyright owner,
Heugel Ltd., London.

Intro. — P177

1st Theme — P178

PROKOFIEFF, Serge (1891-1953)

**Alexander Nevsky,
Cantata for Solo,
Chorus and Orch., Op. 78**
Copyright 1945 by
Leeds Music Corp., N. Y.
Reprinted here by
permisssion of the
copyright owner.

1st Movement — P179

2nd Movement
1st Theme — P180

2nd Movement
2nd Theme — P181

3rd Movement
1st Theme — P182

3rd Movement
2nd Theme — P183

4th Movement
1st Theme — P184

4th Movement
2nd Theme — P185

4th Movement
3rd Theme — P186

PROKOFIEFF
358
P187—P206

4th Movement
4th Theme — P187

5th Movement
1st Theme — P188

5th Movement
2nd Theme — P189

5th Movement
3rd Theme — P190

5th Movement
4th Theme — P191

5th Movement
5th Theme — P192

5th Movement
6th Theme — P193

6th Movement — P194

7th Movement — P195

Classical Symphony,
Op. 25
By permission of the
copyright owner,
Boosey and Hawkes, Inc.

1st Movement
1st Theme — P196

1st Movement
2nd Theme — P197

2nd Movement — P198

3rd Movement
Gavotte
1st Theme — P199

3rd Movement
2nd Theme — P200

4th Movement
1st Theme — P201

4th Movement
2nd Theme — P202

Concerto No. 3, Op. 26,
Pft. & Orch.
Copyright 1945 by
Leeds Music Corp., N. Y.
Reprinted here by
permisssion of the
copyright owner.

1st Movement
1st Theme,
A — P203

1st Movement
1st Theme,
B — P204

1st Movement
2nd Theme — P205

2nd Movement — P206

3rd Movement / 1st Theme — P207

3rd Movement / 2nd Theme — P208

Concerto No. 1, Op. 19, Vn. & Orch.
By permission of the copyright owner, Boosey and Hawkes, Inc.

1st Movement — P209

2nd Movement / 1st Theme — P210

2nd Movement / 2nd Theme — P211

3rd Movement / 1st Theme — P212

3rd Movement / 2nd Theme — P213

Concerto No. 2, Op. 63, Vn. & Orch.
By permission of International Music Co.

1st Movement / 1st Theme — P214

1st Movement / 2nd Theme — P215

2nd Movement / 1st Theme — P216

2nd Movement / 2nd Theme — P217

3rd Movement / 1st Theme — P218

3rd Movement / 2nd Theme — P219

3rd Movement / 3rd Theme — P220

Contes de la Vieille Grand'mère, Pft.
Op. 31, No. 2
By permission of the copyright owner, Boosey and Hawkes, Inc.

Op. 31, No. 3 — P221 / P222

Gavotte, Op. 12, No. 2, Pft. — P223

Gavotte, Op. 32, No. 3, Pft.
By permission of the copyright owner, Boosey and Hawkes, Inc.
— P224

Lieutenant Kije, Op. 60, Orch.
By permission of Broude Brothers

1st Movement / Birth of Kije / 1st Theme — P225

1st Movement / 2nd Theme — P226

1st Movement / 3rd Theme	P227
2nd Movement / Romance / 1st Theme	P228
2nd Movement / 2nd Theme	P229
2nd Movement / 3rd Theme	P230
3rd Movement / Kije's Wedding / 1st Theme	P231
3rd Movement / 2nd Theme	P232
4th Movement / Troika	P233

Love of Three Oranges, Op. 33 — March / P234
Opera
By permission of the copyright owner, Boosey and Hawkes, Inc.
Scherzo / P235

March, Op. 12, No. 1, Pft. / P236

Music for Children, Op. 65, Pft. — March / P237
Copyright 1946 by Leeds Music Corp., N. Y. Reprinted here by permission of the copyright owner.
Waltz / P238

Overture on Hebrew Themes, Op. 34, Cl., Pft. & Str. Quartet — 1st Theme / P239
By permission of the copyright owner, Boosey and Hawkes, Inc.
2nd Theme / P240

Peter and the Wolf, Op. 67, Orch. — 1st Theme / Peter / P241
Copyright 1946 by Leeds Music Corp., N. Y. Reprinted here by permisssion of the copyright owner.
2nd Theme / The Bird / P242
3rd Theme / The Duck / P243
4th Theme / The Cat / P244
5th Theme / The Grandfather / P245
6th Theme / The Wolf / P246

Quartet, Op. 50
Str.
by permission of
International Music Co.

Romeo and Juliet,
Op. 64, Suite No. 1,
Orch.
Copyright 1946 by
Leeds Music Corp., N. Y.
Reprinted here by
permisssion of the
copyright owner.

7th Movement
3rd Theme — P267

The Montagues and
the Capulets
1st Movement
1st Theme — P268

1st Movement
2nd Theme — P269

1st Movement
3rd Theme — P270

2nd Movement
Juliet—The Little Girl
1st Theme — P271

2nd Movement
2nd Theme — P272

2nd Movement
3rd Theme,
A — P273

2nd Movement
3rd Theme,
B — P274

3rd Movement
Friar Lawrence
1st Theme — P275

3rd Movement
2nd Theme — P276

4th Movement
Dance — P277

5th Movement
Romeo and Juliet Before Parting
1st Theme — P278

5th Movement
2nd Theme — P279

5th Movement
3rd Theme — P280

6th Movement
Dance of the Maids
From the Antilles — P281

7th Movement
Romeo at Juliet's
Grave — P282

1st Movement
1st Theme — P283

1st Movement
2nd Theme — P284

2nd Movement
1st Theme — P285

2nd Movement
2nd Theme — P286

3rd Movement 1st Theme — P287

3rd Movement 2nd Theme — P288

4th Movement 1st Theme — P289

4th Movement 2nd Theme — P290

4th Movement 3rd Theme — P291

Sonata No. 7, Op. 83
Pft.
Copyright 1945 by
Leeds Music Corp., N. Y.
Reprinted here by
permission of the
copyright owner.

1st Movement 1st Theme — P292

1st Movement 2nd Theme — P293

2nd Movement — P294

3rd Movement — P295

Sonata in D, Op. 94,
Vn. & Pft.
Copyright 1946 by
Leeds Music Corp., N. Y.
Reprinted here by
permission of the
copyright owner.

1st Movement 1st Theme — P296

1st Movement 2nd Theme — P297

2nd Movement 1st Theme — P298

2nd Movement 2nd Theme — P299

2nd Movement 3rd Theme — P300

3rd Movement — P301

4th Movement 1st Theme — P302

4th Movement 2nd Theme — P303

4th Movement 3rd Theme — P304

4th Movement 4th Theme — P305

Suggestion Diabolique, Op. 4, No. 4,
Pft. — P306

Symphony No. 5 in B Flat, Op. 100

1st Movement 1st Theme — P307
1st Movement 2nd Theme — P308
1st Movement 3rd Theme — P309
1st Movement 4th Theme — P310
2nd Movement 1st Theme — P311
2nd Movement 2nd Theme — P312
2nd Movement 3rd Theme — P313
3rd Movement 1st Theme — P314
3rd Movement 2nd Theme A — P315
3rd Movement 2nd Theme B — P316
3rd Movement — P317
4th Movement 1st Theme — P318
4th Movement 2nd Theme — P319
4th Movement 3rd Theme — P320

PUGNANI, Gaetano (1731-1798)

Sonata in E, No. 1, Vn. & Pft.

1st Movement — P321
2nd Movement — P322
3rd Movement — P323

PURCELL, Henry (c. 1659-1695)

Bonduca, or The British Heroine Opera

Air No. 1 — P324

Hornpipe — P325

Air No. 2 — P326

Dido and Aeneas Opera

Overture 1st Theme — P327

2nd Theme — P328

The Triumphing Dance — P329

Sailor's Dance — P330

Fairy Queen Opera

Hornpipe — P331

Rondeau — P332

Jig — P333

The Monkey's Dance — P334

Three-Part Fantasia, No. 3, Str. — P335

Four-Part Fantasia, No. 1, Str. — P336

Four-Part Fantasia, No. 4, Str. — P337

Four-Part Fantasia, No. 9, Str. — P338

A New Irish Tune (Lillibullero), Harpsi. — P339

Sonata No. 3, in A Minor, 2 Vns. & Harpsi. — 1st Movement — P340

2nd Movement — P341

3rd Movement — P342

4th Movement — P343

5th Movement — P344

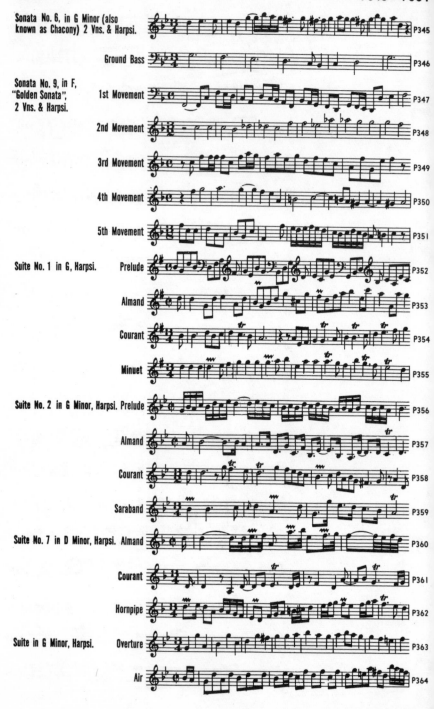

Sonata No. 6, in G Minor (also known as Chacony) 2 Vns. & Harpsi. P345

Ground Bass P346

Sonata No. 9, in F, "Golden Sonata", 2 Vns. & Harpsi. 1st Movement P347

2nd Movement P348

3rd Movement P349

4th Movement P350

5th Movement P351

Suite No. 1 in G, Harpsi. Prelude P352

Almand P353

Courant P354

Minuet P355

Suite No. 2 in G Minor, Harpsi. Prelude P356

Almand P357

Courant P358

Saraband P359

Suite No. 7 in D Minor, Harpsi. Almand P360

Courant P361

Hornpipe P362

Suite in G Minor, Harpsi. Overture P363

Air P364

Jig   P365

QUANTZ, Johann (1697-1773)

Concerto in G, Fl. & Str.

1st Movement 1st Theme, A   Q1

1st Movement 1st Theme, B   Q2

2nd Movement Arioso   Q3

3rd Movement   Q4

QUILTER, Roger (1877-1953)

A Children's Overture, Orch.

1st Theme Girls & Boys, Come Out to Play   Q5

2nd Theme Upon Paul's Steeple Stands a Tree   Q6

3rd Theme Dance, Get Up and Bake Your Pies   Q7

4th Theme I Saw Three Ships Go Sailing By   Q8

5th Theme Sing a Song of Sixpence   Q9

6th Theme There Was a Lady Loved a Swine   Q10

7th Theme Over the Hills and Far Away   Q11

8th Theme The Frog and the Crow   Q12

9th Theme A Frog He Would A-Wooing Go   Q13

10th Theme Baa, Baa, Black Sheep   Q14

11th Theme Here We Go Round the Mulberry Bush   Q15

12th Theme Oranges and Lemons   Q16

RACHMANINOFF, Sergei (1873-1943)

Concerto No. 1, in F Sharp Minor, Op. 1, Pft. & Orch.
By permission of the copyright owner, Boosey and Hawkes, Inc.

1st Movement 1st Theme

R1

1st Movement 2nd Theme

R2

2nd Movement

R3

3rd Movement 1st Theme

R4

3rd Movement 2nd Theme

R5

3rd Movement 3rd Theme

R6

Concerto No. 2, in C Minor, Op. 18, Pft. & Orch.

1st Movement 1st Theme

R7

1st Movement 2nd Theme

R8

2nd Movement 1st Theme, A

R9

2nd Movement 1st Theme, B

R10

3rd Movement 1st Theme

R11

3rd Movement 2nd Theme

R12

Concerto No. 3, Op. 30, Pft. & Orch.
By permission of the copyright owner, Boosey and Hawkes, Inc.

1st Movement 1st Theme

R13

1st Movement 2nd Theme

R14

2nd Movement 1st Theme

R15

2nd Movement 2nd Theme

R16

3rd Movement 1st Theme

R17

3rd Movement 2nd Theme

R18

3rd Movement 3rd Theme

R19

Elégie, Op. 3, No. 1, Pft. — 1st Theme — R20

2nd Theme — R21

Etude Tableau, Op. 33, No. 1, Pft.
By permission of
International Music Co. — R22

Etude Tableau, Op. 33, No. 2, Pft.
By permission of
International Music Co. — R23

Fantasy, Suite No. 1,
Op. 5, 2 Pfts., 4 Hands
By permission of the
copyright owner,
Boosey and Hawkes, Inc.
— 1st Movement Barcarolle 1st Theme — R24
— 1st Movement 2nd Theme — R25
— 2nd Movement A Night for Love — R26
— 3rd Movement Tears — R27
— 4th Movement A Russian Easter 1st Theme — R28
— 4th Movement 2nd Theme — R29

The Isle of the Dead,
Op. 29, Orch.
By permission of
International Music Co.
— 1st Theme — R30
— 2nd Theme — R31

Mélodie, Op. 3, No. 3, Pft.
Copyright by
Charles Foley,
New York — R32

Moment Musical, Op. 16, No. 2, Pft.
Copyright by
Charles Foley,
New York — R33

Polichinelle, Op. 3,
No. 4, Pft.
By permission of the
copyright owner,
Boosey and Hawkes, Inc.
— 1st Theme — R34
— 2nd Theme — R35

Preludes, Pft.
Op. 3, No. 2,
(Famous C Sharp Minor)
Copyright renewal assigned
1925 to G. Schirmer, Inc.
— 1st Theme — R36
— 2nd Theme — R37

Op. 23, No. 1
Copyright renewal assigned
1925 to G. Schirmer, Inc. — R38

No. 2 — R39

No. 3 — R40
No. 4 — R41
No. 5 — 1st Theme — R42
2nd Theme — R43
No. 6 — R44
No. 7 — R45
No. 8 — R46
No. 9 — R47
No. 10 — R48
Op. 32, No. 5
By permission of the copyright owner, Boosey and Hawkes, Inc.
No. 10 — R49
No. 10 — R50
No. 12 — R51
Serenade, Op. 3, No. 5
Copyright by Charles Foley, New York — R52
Sonata in G Minor, Op. 19, Vcl. & Pft.
By permission of International Music Co.
1st Movement 1st Theme — R53
1st Movement 2nd Theme — R54
2nd Movement 1st Theme — R55
2nd Movement 2nd Theme — R56
2nd Movement 3rd Theme — R57
3rd Movement — R58
4th Movement 1st Theme — R59

4th Movement / 2nd Theme — R60

Suite No. 2, Op. 17, Pfts., 4 Hands
By permission of International Music Co.
1st Movement / Intro. — R61

2nd Movement / Valse / 1st Theme — R62

2nd Movement / 2nd Theme — R63

2nd Movement / 3rd Theme — R64

3rd Movement / Romance — R65

4th Movement / Tarantelle (Italian Folksong) — R66

Symphony No. 2 in E Minor, Op. 27
By permission of the copyright owner, Boosey and Hawkes, Inc.
1st Movement / 1st Theme — R67

1st Movement / 2nd Theme — R68

2nd Movement / 1st Theme — R69

2nd Movement / 2nd Theme — R70

3rd Movement / Intro. — R71

3rd Movement / 1st Theme — R72

3rd Movement / 2nd Theme — R73

4th Movement / 1st Theme — R74

4th Movement / 2nd Theme — R75

Waltz, Op. 10, No. 2, Pft.
By permission of the copyright owner, Boosey and Hawkes, Inc.
— R76

RAFF, Joseph Joachim (1822-1882)

Cavatina, Op. 85, No. 3, Vn. & Pft. — R77

La Fileuse, Op. 157, No. 2, Pft. — R78

RAMEAU, Jean Philippe (1683-1764)

Castor et Pollux, Opera	Gavotte No. 1	R79
	Gavotte No. 2	R80
	Minuet No. 1	R81
	Minuet No. 2	R82
	Passepied No. 1	R83
	Passepied No. 2	R84
Dardanus, Opera	Rigaudon No. 1	R85
	Air en Rondeau	R86
	Rigaudon No. 2	R87
Les Fêtes de Hebe Opera	Tambourin	R88
	Musette	R89
La Follette, Harpsi.		R90
Gavotte Variée, Harpsi.		R91
L'Indifferente, Harpsi.		R92
La Joyeuse, Harpsi.	1st Theme	R93
	1st Theme	R94
Minuet No. 1, Harpsi.		R95
Minuet No. 2, Harpsi.		R96
Pièces de Clavecin en Concert, No. 3, Fl., Vn. & Harpsi.	La Timide	R97

Tambourin No. 1 — R98
Tambourin No. 2 — R99
No. 4   La Pantomime — R100
L'Indiscrète — R101
No. 5   La Forqueray — R102
La Cupis — R103
La Marais — R104
Platée, Opera   Minuet No. 1 — R105
Minuet No. 2 — R106
La Poule, Harpsi. — R107
Les Sauvages, Harpsi. — R108
Suite in E Minor, Harpsi.   Allemande — R109
Gigue en Rondeau No. 1 — R110
Gigue en Rondeau No. 2 — R111
Le Rappel des Oiseaux — R112
Rigaudon No. 1 — R113
Rigaudon No. 2 — R114
Musette en Rondeau — R115
Tambourin — R116
La Villageoise — R117

Les Tendres Plaintes, Harpsi. — R118

Les Tourbillons, Harpsi. — R119

Les Tricotets, Harpsi. — R120

Les Triolets, Harpsi. — R121

La Triompante, Harpsi. — R122

RAVEL, Maurice (1875-1937)

Alborada Del Graciosa (Miroirs No. 4), Pft.
By permission of Associated Music Publishers, Inc.
Theme, A — R123
Theme, B — R124

Bolero, Orch.
Permission for reprint granted by Durand & Cie, Paris. Elkan-Vogel Co. Inc. Philadelphia, Copyright Owners.
Theme, A — R125
Theme, B — R126

Concerto, Pft. & Orch.
Permission for reprint granted by Durand & Cie, Paris. Elkan-Vogel Co., Inc. Philadelphia, Copyright Owners.
1st Movement 1st Theme — R127
1st Movement 2nd Theme — R128
2nd Movement — R129
3rd Movement 1st Theme — R130
3rd Movement 2nd Theme — R131

Concerto for the Left Hand, Pft. & Orch.
Permission for reprint granted by Durand & Cie, Paris. Elkan-Vogel Co., Inc. Philadelphia, Copyright Owners.
1st Theme, A — R132
1st Theme, B — R133
2nd Theme — R134

Daphnis et Chloe, Ballet Suite No. 1, Orch.
Permission for reprint granted by Durand & Cie, Paris. Elkan-Vogel Co., Inc. Philadelphia, Copyright Owners.
1st Theme — R135
2nd Theme — R136

3rd Theme   R137

4th Theme   R138

5th Theme   R139

Daphnis et Chloe, Ballet Suite No. 2, Orch.
Permission for reprint granted by Durand & Cie, Paris. Elkan-Vogel Co., Inc. Philadelphia, Copyright Owners,

1st Theme, A   R140

1st Theme, B   R141

2nd Theme   R142

3rd Theme   R143

4th Theme   R144

5th Theme   R145

6th Theme   R146

Gaspard de la Nuit, Pft.
Permission for reprint granted by Durand & Cie, Paris. Elkan-Vogel Co., Inc. Philadelphia, Copyright Owners,

No. 1 Ondine   R147

No. 2 La Gibet   R148

No. 3 Scarbo   R149

Introduction and Allegro, Harp, Str. Quart., Fl. & Cl.
Permission for reprint granted by Durand & Cie, Paris. Elkan-Vogel Co., Inc., Philadelphia, Copyright Owners.

Intro. 1st Theme, A   R150

1st Theme, B   R151

2nd Theme   R152

Allegro 1st Theme   R153

2nd Theme   R154

Jeux D'Eau, Pft.
Copyright 1930 by Edward B. Marks Music Co. Copyright Assigned 1932 to Edward B. Marks Music Corp. Used by Permission

1st Theme   R155

2nd Theme   R156

Ma Mère L'Oye,
(Mother Goose Suite)
Orch.
Permission for
reprint granted
by Durand & Cie,
Paris. Elkan-Vogel Co.,
Inc., Philadelphia,
Copyright
Owners.

Pavane of the
Sleeping Beauty
(Pavane de la
Belle au Bois Dormant)   R157

Hop O' My Thumb
(Petit Poucet)   R158

Empress of the Pagodas
(Laideronnette,
Impératrice des Pagodes)   R159

Beauty and the Beast
(Les Entretiens
de la Belle et de la Bête)   R160

The Enchanted Garden
(La Jardin Féerique)   R161

Pavane for a Dead Infanta,
Small Orch. or Pft.
By permission of Associated
Music Publishers, Inc.   R162

Quartet in F,
Str.
By permission of
International Music Co.

1st Movement
1st Theme   R163

1st Movement
2nd Theme   R164

2nd Movement
Intro.   R165

2nd Movement
1st Theme   R166

2nd Movement
2nd Theme   R167

3rd Movement
1st Theme   R168

3rd Movement
2nd Theme   R169

4th Movement   R170

Rapsodie Espagnole,
Orch.
Permission for reprint
granted by Durand &
Cie, Paris. Elkan-Vogel
Co., Inc. Philadelphia,
Copyright Owners,

1st Movement
Prélude à la Nuit   R171

2nd Movement
Malagueña
Intro.   R172

2nd Movement
1st Theme   R173

2nd Movement
2nd Theme   R174

3rd Movement
Habañera
1st Theme   R175

3rd Movement
2nd Theme   R176

Sonatine, Pft.
Permission for reprint
granted by Durand &
Cie, Paris. Elkan-Vogel
Co., Inc. Philadelphia,
Copyright Owners.

Le Tombeau de Couperin,
Pft. or Orch.
Permission for reprint
granted by Durand &
Cie, Paris. Elkan-Vogel
Co., Inc. Philadelphia,
Copyright Owners.

13*

Tzigane, Vn. & Orch.
Permission for reprint granted
by Durand & Cie, Paris.
Elkan-Vogel Co., Inc.
Philadelphia, Copyright
Owners.

Intro. Cadenza   R197

1st Theme   R198

1st Theme   R199

2nd Theme   R200

3rd Theme   R201

La Valse, Orch.
Permission for reprint granted
by Durand & Cie, Paris.
Elkan-Vogel Co., Inc.
Philadelphia, Copyright
Owners.

1st Theme   R202

2nd Theme   R203

3rd Theme   R204

4th Theme   R205

5th Theme   R206

6th Theme   R207

7th Theme   R208

8th Theme   R209

**Valses Nobles et
Sentimentales
Pft. or Orch.**
Permission for reprint granted
by Durand & Cie, Paris.
Elkan-Vogel Co., Inc.
Philadelphia, Copyright
Owners.

No. 1   R210

No. 2   R211

No. 3   R212

No. 4   R213

No. 5   R214

No. 6   R215

No. 7   R216

No. 8 — R217

REBIKOFF, Vladimir (1866-1920)

The Christmas Tree, Opera — Dance of the Dolls, 1st Theme — R218

2nd Theme — R219

March of the Gnomes, 1st Theme — R220

2nd Theme — R221

Dance of the Chinese Dolls — R222

REGER, Max (1873-1916)

Balletmusik, Op. 130
By Permission of C. F. Peters, Clayton F. Summy Co., Chicago, — Waltz — R223

Finale — R224

Gavotte, Op. 82, No 5, Pft.
By permission of Associated Music Publishers, Inc. — R225

Konzert im Alten Stil, Op. 123, Orch.
By permission of Associated Music Publishers, Inc. — 1st Movement — R226

2nd Movement — R227

3rd Movement — R228

Quintet, in A, Op. 146, Cl. & Str. Quart.
By permission of Associated Music Publishers, Inc. — 1st Movement, 1st Theme — R229

1st Movement, 2nd Theme — R230

2nd Movement, 1st Theme — R231

2nd Movement, 2nd Theme — R232

3rd Movement — R233

4th Movement — R234

Romance, Op. 87, No. 2, Vn. & Pft. — R235

Serenade, Op. 77a, Fl., Vn. & Vla.
1st Movement — R236
2nd Movement — R237
3rd Movement 1st Theme — R238
3rd Movement 2nd Theme — R239

Suite in A Minor, Op. 193a, Vn. & Pft.
By permission of Associated Music Publishers, Inc.
1st Movement Präludium — R240
2nd Movement Gavotte 1st Theme — R241
2nd Movement 2nd Theme — R242
3rd Movement Aria — R243
4th Movement Burleske — R244
5th Movement Minuet 1st Theme — R245
5th Movement 2nd Theme — R246
6th Movement Gigue — R247

RESPIGHI, Ottorino (1879-1936)

Adagio con Variazioni, Vcl. & Pft. — R248

Antiche Danze Ed Arie Per Liuto.
Copyright 1920 by G. Ricordi & Co., Inc.
Suite No 1, Orch.
1st Movement Balletto "Il Conte Orlando" (After Simone Molinaro) — R249
2nd Movement Gagliarda (After Vincenzo Galilei) 1st Theme — R250
2nd Movement 2nd Theme — R251
3rd Movement Villanella (After Ignoto) 1st Theme — R252
3rd Movement 2nd Theme — R253

4th Movement
Passo Mezzo e Mascherada (Ignoto)
1st Theme — R254

4th Movement
2nd Theme — R255

4th Movement
3rd Theme — R256

4th Movement
4th Theme — R257

Suite No. 2, Orch.
Copyright 1924 by
G. Ricordi & Co.,
Inc.
1st Movement
Laura Soave
(After Carosio)
1st Theme — R258

1st Movement
2nd Theme — R259

1st Movement
3rd Theme — R260

2nd Movement
Danza Rustica (After Besardo) — R261

3rd Movement
1st Theme — R262
Campanae Parisienses (Author Unknown)

3rd Movement
2nd Theme — R263
Aria (After Mersenne Marin)

4th Movement
Bergamasca (After Bernardo Gianoncelli) — R264

Suite No. 3, Orch.
Copyright 1932
by G. Ricordi Italiana
& Co., Inc.
1st Movement
(After Ignoto) — R265

2nd Movement
Arie di Corte (After Besardo)
1st Theme — R266

2nd Movement
2nd Theme — R267

3rd Movement
Siciliano (After Ignoto) — R268

4th Movement
Passacaglia (After Roncalli) — R269

Fountains of Rome, Orch.
Copyright 1918 by G. Ricordi & Co., Inc.
The Fountain of Valle Giulia at Dawn
1st Theme — R270

2nd Theme — R271

The Triton Fountain at Morning — R272

The Fountains of Trevi at Mid-day — R273

The Villa Medici Fountain at Sunset
1st Theme — R274

2nd Theme — R275

Notturno, Pft. — R276

Pines of Rome, Orch.
Copyright 1925 by G. Ricordi & Co., Inc.
The Pines of the Villa Borghese
1st Theme — R277

2nd Theme — R278

3rd Theme — R279

Pines Near a Catacomb — R280

Pines of the Gianicolo
1st Theme — R281

2nd Theme — R282

Pines of the Appian Way
1st Theme — R283

2nd Theme — R284

Rossiniana,
Suite for Orch.
1st Movement
Capri and Taormina
(Barcarola & Siciliana)
1st Theme — R285

1st Movement
2nd Theme — R286

2nd Movement
Lament
1st Theme — R287

2nd Movement
2nd Theme — R288

3rd Movement
Intermezzo
1st Theme — R289

3rd Movement
2nd Theme — R290

4th Movement
Tarantella & Procession
1st Theme — R291

4th Movement
2nd Theme — R292

Trittico Botticelliano,
Chamber Orch.
Copyright 1928 by G.
Ricordi & Co., Inc.
1st Movement
La Primavera
1st Theme — R293

1st Movement
2nd Theme — R294

2nd Movement
Adoration of the Magi
1st Theme — R295

2nd Movement
2nd Theme — R296

3rd Movement
The Birth of Venus
1st Theme — R297

3rd Movement
2nd Theme — R298

REYER, Ernest (1823-1909)

Sigurd, Overture
By permission of
the copyright owner,
Heugel & Cie, Paris.

1st Theme — R299

2nd Theme — R300

3rd Theme — R301

REZNIČEK, Emil Nikolaus von (1860-1945)

Donna Diana, Overture
By permission of Associated
Music Publishers, Inc.

1st Theme — R302

2nd Theme — R303

RIEGGER, Wallingford (1885-1961)

New Dance, 2 Pfts.
Copyright 1940 by Arrow
Music Press, Inc., N. Y.

— R303a

Accompanying Figure
A — R303b

Accompanying Figure
B — R303c

RIMSKY-KORSAKOFF, Nicolas (1844-1908)

Antar Symphony, Op. 9

1st Movement
Intro.
1st Theme — R304

1st Movement
Intro.
2nd Theme — R305

1st Movement
1st Theme — R306

1st Movement / 2nd Theme — R307
1st Movement / 3rd Theme — R308
2nd Movement / 1st Theme — R309
2nd Movement / 2nd Theme — R310
3rd Movement / 1st Theme — R311
3rd Movement / 2nd Theme — R312
4th Movement — R313

Capriccio Espagnol, Op. 34, Orch.
By permission of Associated Music Publishers, Inc.

Intro. and Alborada — R314
Variations — R315
Scene and Gypsy Song / 1st Theme — R316
2nd Theme — R317
Fandango Asturiano — R318

Le Coq D'Or, Suite Orch.
By permission of Associated Music Publishers, Inc.

1st Movement / 1st Theme — R319
1st Movement / 2nd Theme — R320
1st Movement / 3rd Theme — R321
2nd Movement — R322
3rd Movement / 1st Theme — R323
3rd Movement / 2nd Theme — R324
3rd Movement / 3rd Theme — R325
3rd Movement / 4th Theme — R326

La Grande Paque Russe, Overture, Op. 36
By permission of Associated Music Publishers, Inc.

1st Theme — R327
2nd Theme — R328
3rd Theme — R329
4th Theme — R330
5th Theme — R331

May Night, Overture
By permission of Associated Music Publishers, Inc.

1st Theme — R332
2nd Theme — R333
3rd Theme — R334

Mlada, Ballet
By permission of Associated Music Publishers, Inc.

1st Theme Cortège des Nobles — R335
2nd Theme — R336

Scheherezade, Op. 35, Orch.
By permission of Associated Music Publishers, Inc.

1st Movement The Sea & Sinbad's Ship Intro. A — R337
1st Movement Intro. B — R338
1st Movement 1st Theme — R339
1st Movement 2nd Theme — R340
1st Movement 3rd Theme — R341
2nd Movement The Story of the Kalander Prince 1st Theme, A — R342
2nd Movement 1st Theme, B — R343
2nd Movement 2nd Theme — R344
3rd Movement The Young Prince & the Young Princess 1st Theme — R345
3rd Movement 2nd Theme — R346

4th Movement
Festival at Bagdad — R347

Snow Maiden,
(Snegourotchka), Opera — Dance of the Buffoons 1st Theme — R348

2nd Theme — R349

3rd Theme — R350

Tale of the Invisible City of Kitezh, Opera — Battle of Kershenetz 1st Theme — R351

2nd Theme — R352

Tsar Saltan, Opera — Flight of the Bumble Bee 1st Theme — R353

2nd Theme — R354

The Tsar's Bride, Overture
By permission of Associated Music Publishers, Inc. — 1st Theme — R355

2nd Theme — R356

3rd Theme — R357

ROSAS, J. (1868-1894)

Over the Waves, Waltzes — 1st Theme — R358

2nd Theme — R359

ROSSINI, Gioacchino Antonio (1792-1868)

The Barber of Seville, Overture — Intro. — R360

1st Theme — R361

2nd Theme — R362

3rd Theme — R363

La Boutique Fantasque, Ballet — 1st Movement Overture 1st Theme — R364

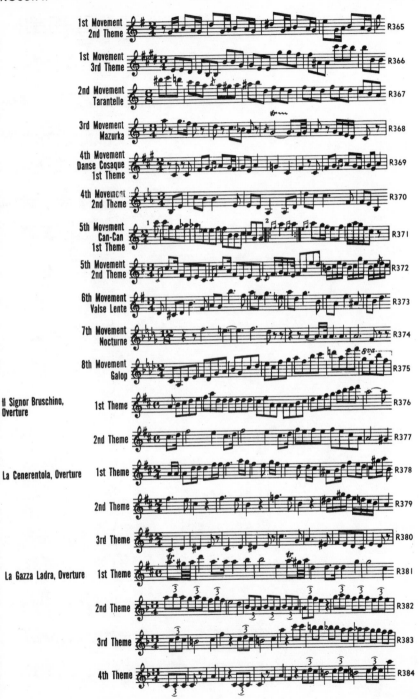

1st Movement / 2nd Theme — R365

1st Movement / 3rd Theme — R366

2nd Movement / Tarantelle — R367

3rd Movement / Mazurka — R368

4th Movement / Danse Cosaque / 1st Theme — R369

4th Movement / 2nd Theme — R370

5th Movement / Can-Can / 1st Theme — R371

5th Movement / 2nd Theme — R372

6th Movement / Valse Lente — R373

7th Movement / Nocturne — R374

8th Movement / Galop — R375

Il Signor Bruschino, Overture / 1st Theme — R376

2nd Theme — R377

La Cenerentola, Overture / 1st Theme — R378

2nd Theme — R379

3rd Theme — R380

La Gazza Ladra, Overture / 1st Theme — R381

2nd Theme — R382

3rd Theme — R383

4th Theme — R384

L'Italiana In Algeri, Overture 1st Theme — R385

2nd Theme — R386

Semiramide, Overture 1st Theme — R387

2nd Theme — R388

3rd Theme — R389

Tancredi, Overture 1st Theme — R390

2nd Theme — R391

William Tell Opera — Overture 1st Theme — R392

2nd Theme — R393

Act 3 Soldier's Ballet 1st Theme — R394

2nd Theme — R395

ROUSSEL, Albert (1869-1937)

Le Festin de L'Araignée, Ballet, Op. 17 — Prelude 1st Theme — R396
Permission for reprint granted by Durand & Cie, Paris. Elkan-Vogel Co., Inc. Philadelphia, Copyright Owners.

2nd Theme — R397

Entrée des Fourmis — R398

Danse du Papillon — R399

Danse de l'Éphémère 1st Theme — R400

2nd Theme — R401

Funerailles de l'Éphémère — R402

La Naissance de la Lyre, Op. 24, Orch. — Danse des Nymphes 1st Theme — R403
Permission for reprint granted by Durand & Cie, Paris. Elkan-Vogel Co., Inc. Philadelphia, Copyright Owners.

2nd Theme — R404

Sinfonietta, Op. 52, Str. Orch.
Permission for reprint granted by Durand & Cie, Paris. Elkan-Vogel Co., Inc. Philadelphia, Copyright Owners.

1st Movement 1st Theme — R405

1st Movement 2nd Theme — R406

2nd Movement — R407

3rd Movement 1st Theme — R408

3rd Movement 2nd Theme — R409

Symphony No. 3 in G Minor, Op. 42
Permission for reprint granted by Durand & Cie, Paris. Elkan-Vogel Co., Inc. Philadelphia, Copyright Owners.

1st Movement 1st Theme — R410

1st Movement 2nd Theme — R411

2nd Movement 1st Theme — R412

2nd Movement 2nd Theme — R413

3rd Movement 1st Theme — R414

3rd Movement 2nd Theme — R415

4th Movement 1st Theme — R416

4th Movement 2nd Theme — R417

Symphony No. 4, Op. 53
Permission for reprint granted by Durand & Cie, Paris. Elkan-Vogel Co., Inc. Philadelphia, Copyright Owners,

1st Movement 1st Theme — R418

1st Movement 2nd Theme — R419

2nd Movement — R420

3rd Movement 1st Theme — R421

3rd Movement 2nd Theme — R422

4th Movement 1st Theme — R423

RUBINSTEIN, Anton (1829-1894)

Barcarolle, Op. 30, No. 1, Pft.
By permission of Associated Music Publishers, Inc.
1st Theme — R424
2nd Theme — R425

Concerto No. 4 in D Minor, Op. 70, Pft. & Orch.
By permission of Associated Music Publishers, Inc.
1st Movement 1st Theme, A — R426
1st Movement 1st Theme, B — R427
1st Movement 2nd Theme — R428
2nd Movement — R429
3rd Movement 1st Theme — R430
3rd Movement 2nd Theme — R431

Cracovienne, Op. 5, No. 3, Pft.
1st Theme — R432
2nd Theme — R433

Etude, Op. 23, No. 2, Pft. "Staccato"
1st Theme — R434
2nd Theme — R435

Feramors (Lalla Rookh) Opera
By permission of Associated Music Publishers, Inc.
Bridal March 1st Theme — R436
2nd Theme — R437

Kamennoi-Ostrow, Op. 10, No. 22, Pft.
1st Theme — R438
2nd Theme — R439

Melody in F, Op. 3, No. 1, Pft.
1st Theme — R440
2nd Theme — R441

Romance, Op. 44, No. 1, Pft. 1st Theme — R442

2nd Theme — R443

Toreador et Andalouse,
Op. 103, No. 7, from Bal
Costumé, Pft., 4 Hands
By permission of Associated
Music Publishers, Inc.

1st Theme — R444

2nd Theme — R445

Valse in F, Pft.
By permission of Associated
Music Publishers, Inc.

— R446

Valse Caprice, Pft.
By permission of Associated
Music Publishers, Inc.

1st Theme — R447

2nd Theme — R448

3rd Theme — R449

SACCHINI, Antonio (1730-1786)

Sonata in F
Harpsi.

1st Movement — S1

2nd Movement
1st Theme — S2

2nd Movement
2nd Theme — S3

SAINT-SAËNS, Camille (1835-1921)

Caprice Arabe, Op. 96,
2 Pfts.
Permission for reprint granted
by Durand & Cie, Paris.
Elkan-Vogel Co., Inc.
Philadelphia, Copyright
Owners.

1st Theme — S4

2nd Theme — S5

3rd Theme — S6

Carnaval des Animaux,
Orch. & 2 Pfts.
Permission for reprint granted
by Durand & Cie, Paris.
Elkan-Vogel Co., Inc.
Philadelphia, Copyright
Owners.

March Royale
du Lion — S7

Poules et Coqs — S8

Tortues (Theme from
Orpheus in Hades — Offenbach) — S9

L'Éléphant — S10

Kangorous — S11

Aquarium   S12

Le Coucou au Fond des Bois   S13

Fossiles   S14

The Swan   S15

Finale   S16

Concertos

No. 1 in
A Minor, Op. 33,
Vcl. & Orch.
Permission for reprint
granted by Durand &
Cie, Paris. Elkan-Vogel
Co., Inc. Philadelphia,
Copyright Owners,

1st Movement 1st Theme   S17

1st Movement 2nd Theme   S18

2nd Movement   S19

3rd Movement 1st Theme   S20

3rd Movement 2nd Theme   S21

3rd Movement Coda   S22

No. 2 in G Minor,
Op. 22, Pft. & Orch.
Permission for reprint
granted by Durand &
Cie, Paris. Elkan-Vogel
Co., Inc. Philadelphia,
Copyright Owners,

1st Movement 1st Theme   S23

1st Movement 2nd Theme   S24

2nd Movement 1st Theme   S25

2nd Movement 2nd Theme   S26

3rd Movement 1st Theme   S27

3rd Movement 2nd Theme   S28

No. 4 in C Minor,
Op. 44, Pft. & Orch.
Permission for reprint
granted by Durand &
Cie, Paris. Elkan-Vogel
Co., Inc. Philadelphia,
Copyright Owners,

1st Movement 1st Theme   S29

1st Movement 2nd Theme, A   S30

1st Movement 2nd Theme, B   S31

2nd Movement 1st Theme — S32

2nd Movement 2nd Theme — S33

3rd Movement — S34

No. 3 in B Minor, Op. 61, Vn. & Orch.
Copyright 1905 by Carl Fischer, Inc., N. Y.

1st Movement 1st Theme — S35

1st Movement 2nd Theme — S36

2nd Movement 1st Theme — S37

2nd Movement 2nd Theme — S38

3rd Movement 1st Theme, A — S39

3rd Movement 1st Theme, B — S40

3rd Movement 2nd Theme — S41

3rd Movement 3rd Theme — S42

Concertstück, Op. 20, Vn. & Orch.
By permission of J. Hamelle Music Publishers, Paris.

Intro. — S43

1st Theme — S44

2nd Theme — S45

3rd Theme — S46

Danse Macabre, Op. 40, Orch. or 2 Pfts.
Permission for reprint granted by Durand & Cie, Paris. Elkan-Vogel Co., Inc. Philadelphia, Copyright Owners.

1st Theme — S47

2nd Theme — S48

Elégie, Op. 143, Vn. & Pft.
Permission for reprint granted by Durand & Cie, Paris. Elkan-Vogel Co., Inc. Philadelphia, Copyright Owners.

1st Theme — S49

2nd Theme — S50

Havanaise, Op. 83, Vn. & Orch.
Permission for reprint granted by Durand & Cie, Paris. Elkan-Vogel Co., Inc. Philadelphia, Copyright Owners.

1st Theme — S51

2nd Theme — S52
3rd Theme — S53

Henry VIII
Ballet Music
Permission for reprint
granted by Durand &
Cie, Paris. Elkan-Vogel
Co., Inc., Philadelphia,
Copyright Owners.

Entry of the Clans
1st Theme — S54
2nd Theme — S55
Scotch Idyll — S56
Dance of the Gypsy
1st Theme — S57
2nd Theme — S58
Scherzetto — S59
Gigue & Finale
1st Theme — S60
2nd Theme — S61
3rd Theme — S62

Introduction & Rondo
Capriccioso, Op. 28, Vn. & Orch.
Copyright renewal assigned
1928 to G. Schirmer, Inc.

Intro. — S63
1st Theme — S64
2nd Theme — S65
3rd Theme — S66

La Jeunesse d'Hercule,
Op. 50, Orch.
Permission for reprint
granted by Durand &
Cie, Paris. Elkan-Vogel
Co., Inc. Philadelphia,
Copyright Owners.

1st Theme — S67
2nd Theme — S68
3rd Theme — S69
4th Theme — S70

Marche Héroique,
Op. 34, Orch.
Permission for reprint granted
by Durand & Cie, Paris. Elkan-Vogel Co., Inc.
Philadelphia, Copyright Owners.

1st Theme — S71

2nd Theme S72

3rd Theme S73

Phaëton, Op. 39, Orch.
Permission for reprint granted
by Durand & Cie, Paris.
Elkan-Vogel Co., Inc.
Philadelphia, Copyright
Owners.

1st Theme S74

2nd Theme S75

3rd Theme S76

Romance, Op. 36, Fr. Horn & Orch.
Permission for reprint granted
by Durand & Cie, Paris. Elkan-Vogel
Co., Inc. Philadelphia, Copyright
Owners.

S77

**Le Rouet d'Omphale,
Op. 31, Orch.**
Permission for reprint granted
by Durand & Cie, Paris.
Elkan-Vogel Co., Inc.
Philadelphia, Copyright
Owners.

1st Theme S78

2nd Thème S79

**Samson et Dalila,
Opera, Op. 47**
Copyright 1892
by G. Schirmer, Inc.

**Bacchanale
1st Theme** S80

**2nd Theme,
A** S81

**2nd Theme,
B** S82

3rd Theme S83

4th Theme S84

Scherzo, Op. 87, 2 Pfts.
By permission of
International Music Co.

Intro. S85

1st Theme S86

2nd Theme S87

3rd Theme S88

**Septet, Op. 65, Tpt.,
Str. Quin. & Pft.**
Permission for reprint
granted by Durand &
Cie, Paris. Elkan-Vogel
Co., Inc. Philadelphia,
Copyright Owners,

**1st Movement
Préambule** S89

**2nd Movement
Minuet
1st Theme** S90

**2nd Movement
2nd Theme** S91

Sonatas

No. 1 in C Minor, Op. 32, Vcl. & Pft.

Permission for reprint granted by Durand & Cie, Paris. Elkan-Vogel Co., Inc. Philadelphia, Copyright Owners.

No. 2 in F, Op. 123, Vcl. & Pft.

Permission for reprint granted by Durand & Cie, Paris. Elkan-Vogel Co., Inc. Philadelphia, Copyright Owners.

No. 1, Op. 75, Vn. & Pft.

Permission for reprint granted by Durand & Cie, Paris. Elkan-Vogel Co., Inc. Philadelphia, Copyright Owners,

3rd Movement Intermède — S92
4th Movement Gavotte & Finale — S93
1st Movement Intro. — S94
1st Movement 1st Theme — S95
1st Movement 2nd Theme — S96
2nd Movement — S97
3rd Movement 1st Theme — S98
3rd Movement 2nd Theme — S99
1st Movement Intro. — S100
1st Movement 1st Theme — S101
1st Movement 2nd Theme — S102
2nd Movement Scherzo con Variazione — S103
3rd Movement Romance — S104
4th Movement 1st Theme — S105
4th Movement 2nd Theme — S106
1st Movement 1st Theme — S107
1st Movement 2nd Theme — S108
1st Movement 3rd Theme — S109
2nd Movement 1st Theme — S110
2nd Movement 2nd Theme — S111

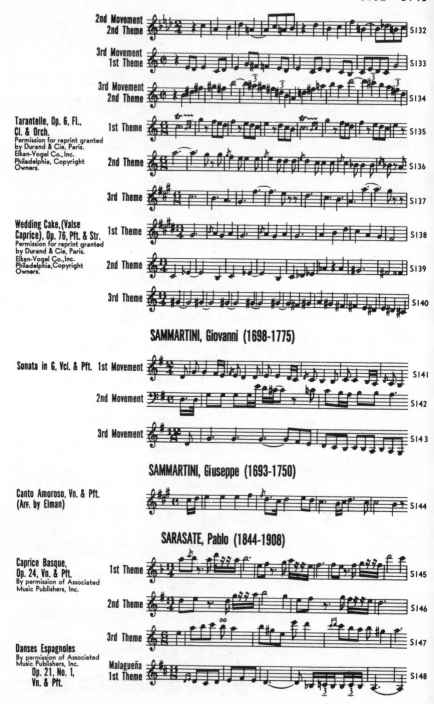

2nd Movement 2nd Theme — S132

3rd Movement 1st Theme — S133

3rd Movement 2nd Theme — S134

Tarantelle, Op. 6, Fl., Cl. & Orch.
Permission for reprint granted by Durand & Cie, Paris. Elkan-Vogel Co., Inc. Philadelphia, Copyright Owners.

1st Theme — S135

2nd Theme — S136

3rd Theme — S137

Wedding Cake, (Valse Caprice), Op. 76, Pft. & Str.
Permission for reprint granted by Durand & Cie, Paris. Elkan-Vogel Co., Inc. Philadelphia, Copyright Owners.

1st Theme — S138

2nd Theme — S139

3rd Theme — S140

SAMMARTINI, Giovanni (1698-1775)

Sonata in G, Vcl. & Pft. 1st Movement — S141

2nd Movement — S142

3rd Movement — S143

SAMMARTINI, Giuseppe (1693-1750)

Canto Amoroso, Vn. & Pft.
(ARR. by Elman) — S144

SARASATE, Pablo (1844-1908)

Caprice Basque, Op. 24, Vn. & Pft.
By permission of Associated Music Publishers, Inc.

1st Theme — S145

2nd Theme — S146

3rd Theme — S147

Danses Espagnoles
By permission of Associated Music Publishers, Inc.
Op. 21, No. 1, Vn. & Pft.

Malagueña 1st Theme — S148

4th Theme — S169

5th Theme — S170

6th Theme — S171

SATIE, Erik (1866-1925)

Gnossiennes, Pft. Copyright by Editions
No. 1   Salabert Editions Salabert,
22 Rue Chaucat, Paris
Salabert, Inc., I East 57
St., N. Y.   — S172

No. 2 — S173

No. 3 — S174

Gymnopédies, Pft. Copyright by Editions
No. 1   Salabert Editions Salabert,
22 Rue Chaucat, Paris   — S175
No. 2   Salabert, Inc., I East 57
St., N. Y.   — S176

No. 3 — S177

Parade Ballet
Copyright by Editions Salabert Rag-Time
Editions Salabert, 22 Rue Chaucat, Paris
Salabert, Inc., I East 57 St., N. Y.   — S178
Trois Petites Pièces   De L'Enfance
Montées, (after   de Pantagruel   — S179
Rabelais), Orch.
Copyright by Editions Salabert
Editions Salabert, 22 Rue Chaucat, Paris
Salabert, Inc.,   Marche de Cocagne
I East 57 St., N. Y.   — S180

Jeux de Gargantua — S181

SAUVEPLANE, Henri (1892-   )

Habañera, Vn. & Pft. — S182

SCARLATTI, Alessandro (1660-1725)

Fuga, Pft. — S183

SCARLATTI, Domenico (1685-1757)

Sonatas, Harpsi.
Longo 22 in E Minor — S184

Longo 23 in E   S185

Longo 33 in B Minor   S186

Longo 58 in D Minor "Gavotte"   S187

Longo 104 in C   S188

Longo 107 in D   S189

Longo 108 in D Minor   S190

Longo 129 in G   S191

Longo 142 in E Flat   S192

Longo 152 in A   S193

Longo 205 in C   S194

Longo 208 in D   S195

Longo 232 in G   S196

Longo 239 in A Minor   S197

Longo 243 in A Minor, "Pastorale"   S198

Longo 256 in C Sharp Minor   S199

Longo 257 in E   S200

Longo 261 in D   S201

Longo 263 in B Minor   S202

Longo 294 in F Sharp Minor,   S203

Longo 338 in G Minor "Burlesca"   S204

Longo 345 in A — S205

Longo 352 in C Minor — S206

Longo 375 in E, — S207

Longo 382 in F Minor — S208

Longo 384 in F — S209

Longo 387 in G — S210

Longo 395 in A — S211

Longo 407 in C Minor — S212

Longo 411 in D — S213

Longo 413 in D Minor "Pastorale" — S214

Longo 422 in D Minor "Toccata" — S215

Longo 429 in A Minor — S216

Longo 434 in B Flat — S217

Longo 438 in F Minor — S218

Longo 449 in B Minor — S219

Longo 463 in D "Tempo di Ballo" — S220

Longo 465 in D — S221

Longo 474 in F — S222

Longo 475 in F Minor — S223

Longo 479 in F — S224

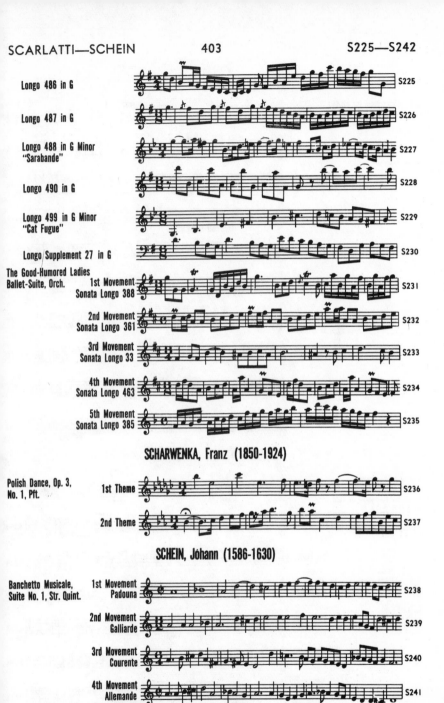

Longo 486 in G — S225

Longo 487 in G — S226

Longo 488 in G Minor "Sarabande" — S227

Longo 490 in G — S228

Longo 499 in G Minor "Cat Fugue" — S229

Longo Supplement 27 in G — S230

The Good-Humored Ladies Ballet-Suite, Orch. — 1st Movement Sonata Longo 388 — S231

2nd Movement Sonata Longo 361 — S232

3rd Movement Sonata Longo 33 — S233

4th Movement Sonata Longo 463 — S234

5th Movement Sonata Longo 385 — S235

SCHARWENKA, Franz (1850-1924)

Polish Dance, Op. 3, No. 1, Pft. — 1st Theme — S236

2nd Theme — S237

SCHEIN, Johann (1586-1630)

Banchetto Musicale, Suite No. 1, Str. Quint. — 1st Movement Padouna — S238

2nd Movement Galliarde — S239

3rd Movement Courente — S240

4th Movement Allemande — S241

5th Movement Tripla — S242

SCHELLING, Ernest (1876-1939)

Impressions from an Artist's
Life (Variations), Orch. & Pft.
By permission of Associated
Music Publishers, Inc.

Theme   S243

A Victory Ball, Orch.
By permission of Associated
Music Publishers, Inc.

1st Theme   S244

2nd Theme   S245

3rd Theme   S246

4th Theme
A   S247

4th Theme
B   S248

4th Theme
C   S249

5th Theme   S250

6th Theme   S251

7th Theme   S252

SCHMITT, Florent (1870-1958)

Rapsodie Viennoise,
Op. 53, No. 3, Orch.
Permission for reprint granted
by Durand & Cie, Paris.
Elkan-Vogel Co., Inc.
Philadelphia, Copyright
Owners.

1st Theme   S253

2nd Theme   S254

3rd Theme   S255

Reflets d'Allemagne,
Orch.
Copyright by Editions
Salabert Editions Salabert,
22 Rue Chaucat, Paris
Salabert, Inc.,
1 East 57 St., N. Y.

1st Movement
Nuremberg   S256

2nd Movement
Dresden   S257

3rd Movement
Werder   S258

4th Movement
Munich
1st Theme   S259

4th Movement
2nd Theme   S260

SCHOBERT, Johann (c. 1720-1767)

Sonata in F,
Op. 8, Pft.

1st Movement — S261

2nd Movement — S262

3rd Movement
Polonaise — S263

4th Movement
1st Theme — S264

4th Movement
2nd Theme — S265

SCHÖNBERG, Arnold (1874-1951)

Six Little Piano Pieces,
Op. 19
By permission of Associated
Music Publishers, Inc.

No. 1 — S266

No. 2 — S267

No. 3 — S268

No. 4 — S269

No. 5 — S270

Verklärte Nacht, Op. 4,
Str. Sextet

1st Theme — S271

2nd Theme — S272

3rd Theme — S273

4th Theme — S274

5th Theme — S275

SCHREKER, Franz (1878-1934)

Birthday of the Infanta, 1st Movement
Orch.   "Reigen" (Rounds)
By permission of   1st Theme
Associated Music
Publishers, Inc. — S276

1st Movement
2nd Theme — S277

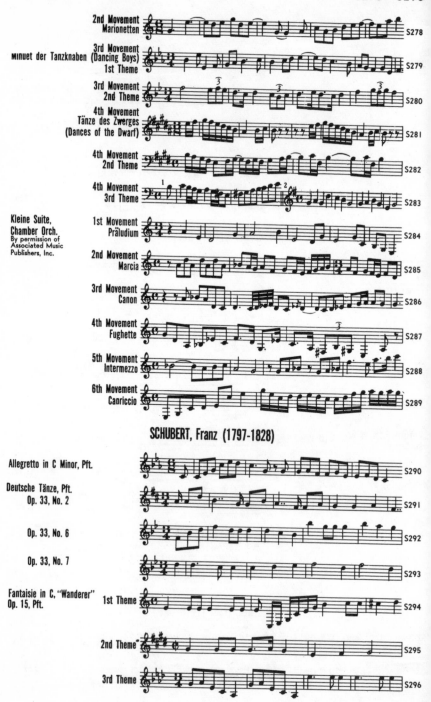

2nd Movement
Marionetten — S278

Minuet der Tanzknaben (Dancing Boys)
3rd Movement
1st Theme — S279

3rd Movement
2nd Theme — S280

4th Movement
Tänze des Zwerges
(Dances of the Dwarf) — S281

4th Movement
2nd Theme — S282

4th Movement
3rd Theme — S283

Kleine Suite,
Chamber Orch.
By permission of
Associated Music
Publishers, Inc.

1st Movement
Präludium — S284

2nd Movement
Marcia — S285

3rd Movement
Canon — S286

4th Movement
Fughette — S287

5th Movement
Intermezzo — S288

6th Movement
Capriccio — S289

SCHUBERT, Franz (1797-1828)

Allegretto in C Minor, Pft. — S290

Deutsche Tänze, Pft.
Op. 33, No. 2 — S291

Op. 33, No. 6 — S292

Op. 33, No. 7 — S293

Fantaisie in C, "Wanderer"
Op. 15, Pft. 1st Theme — S294

2nd Theme — S295

3rd Theme — S296

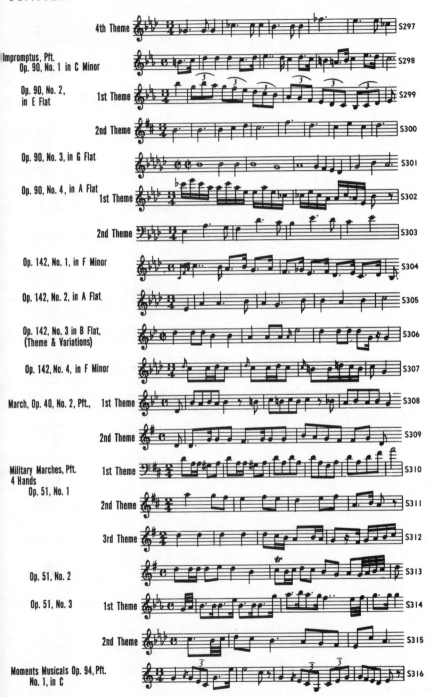

4th Theme — S297

Impromptus, Pft.
Op. 90, No. 1 in C Minor — S298

Op. 90, No. 2, in E Flat — 1st Theme — S299

2nd Theme — S300

Op. 90, No. 3, in G Flat — S301

Op. 90, No. 4, in A Flat — 1st Theme — S302

2nd Theme — S303

Op. 142, No. 1, in F Minor — S304

Op. 142, No. 2, in A Flat — S305

Op. 142, No. 3 in B Flat, (Theme & Variations) — S306

Op. 142, No. 4, in F Minor — S307

March, Op. 40, No. 2, Pft., — 1st Theme — S308

2nd Theme — S309

Military Marches, Pft. 4 Hands — Op. 51, No. 1 — 1st Theme — S310

2nd Theme — S311

3rd Theme — S312

Op. 51, No. 2 — S313

Op. 51, No. 3 — 1st Theme — S314

2nd Theme — S315

Moments Musicals Op. 94, Pft. No. 1, in C — S316

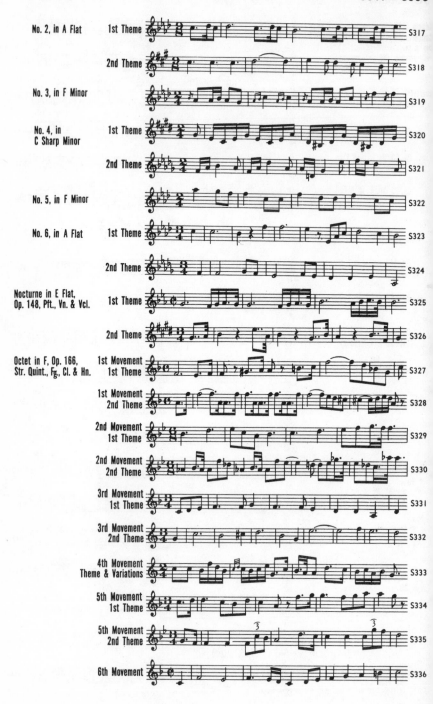

No. 2, in A Flat — 1st Theme — S317

2nd Theme — S318

No. 3, in F Minor — S319

No. 4, in C Sharp Minor — 1st Theme — S320

2nd Theme — S321

No. 5, in F Minor — S322

No. 6, in A Flat — 1st Theme — S323

2nd Theme — S324

Nocturne in E Flat, Op. 148, Pft., Vn. & Vcl. — 1st Theme — S325

2nd Theme — S326

Octet in F, Op. 166, Str. Quint., Fg., Cl. & Hn. — 1st Movement 1st Theme — S327

1st Movement 2nd Theme — S328

2nd Movement 1st Theme — S329

2nd Movement 2nd Theme — S330

3rd Movement 1st Theme — S331

3rd Movement 2nd Theme — S332

4th Movement Theme & Variations — S333

5th Movement 1st Theme — S334

5th Movement 2nd Theme — S335

6th Movement — S336

Adagio & Rondo
Concertante in F,
Pft. & Str.

1st Movement — S337

2nd Movement — S338

Quartets
No. 4, in C,
Str.

1st Movement — S339

2nd Movement — S340

3rd Movement — S341

4th Movement — S342

No. 6, in D, Str.

1st Movement — S343

2nd Movement — S344

3rd Movement — S345

4th Movement — S346

No. 8, in B Flat,
Op. 168, Str.

1st Movement — S347

2nd Movement
1st Theme — S348

2nd Movement
2nd Theme — S349

3rd Movement
1st Theme — S350

3rd Movement
2nd Theme — S351

4th Movement — S352

No. 9, in G Minor,
Str.

1st Movement — S353

2nd Movement — S354

3rd Movement — S355

4th Movement — S356

14*

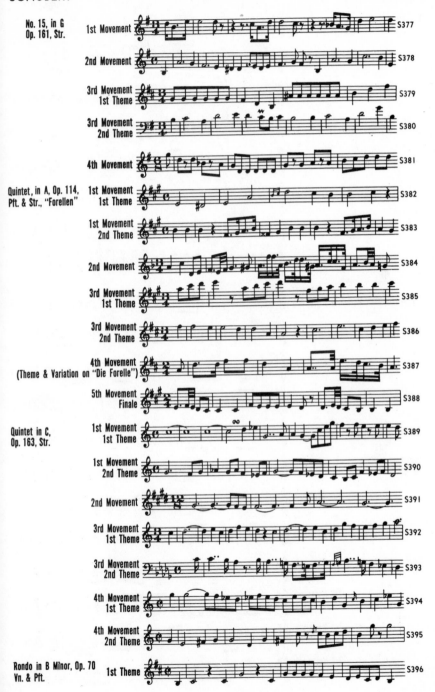

SCHUBERT

No. 15, in G
Op. 161, Str. — 1st Movement — S377

2nd Movement — S378

3rd Movement
1st Theme — S379

3rd Movement
2nd Theme — S380

4th Movement — S381

Quintet, in A, Op. 114,
Pft. & Str., "Forellen" — 1st Movement
1st Theme — S382

1st Movement
2nd Theme — S383

2nd Movement — S384

3rd Movement
1st Theme — S385

3rd Movement
2nd Theme — S386

4th Movement
(Theme & Variation on "Die Forelle") — S387

5th Movement
Finale — S388

Quintet in C,
Op. 163, Str. — 1st Movement
1st Theme — S389

1st Movement
2nd Theme — S390

2nd Movement — S391

3rd Movement
1st Theme — S392

3rd Movement
2nd Theme — S393

4th Movement
1st Theme — S394

4th Movement
2nd Theme — S395

Rondo in B Minor, Op. 70
Vn. & Pft. — 1st Theme — S396

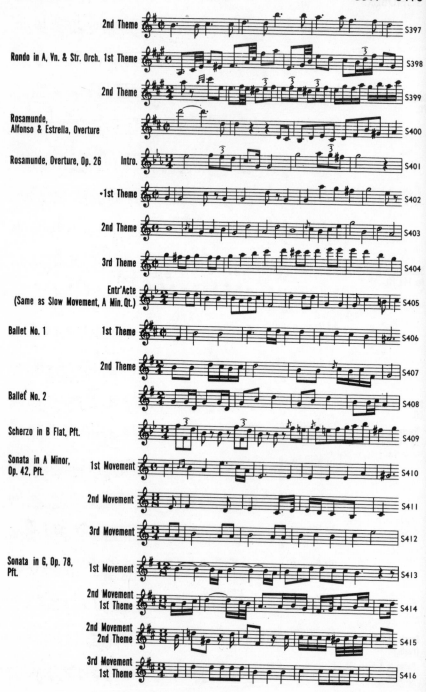

2nd Theme — S397

Rondo in A, Vn. & Str. Orch. 1st Theme — S398

2nd Theme — S399

Rosamunde, Alfonso & Estrella, Overture — S400

Rosamunde, Overture, Op. 26   Intro. — S401

•1st Theme — S402

2nd Theme — S403

3rd Theme — S404

Entr'Acte (Same as Slow Movement, A Min. Qt.) — S405

Ballet No. 1   1st Theme — S406

2nd Theme — S407

Ballet No. 2 — S408

Scherzo in B Flat, Pft. — S409

Sonata in A Minor, Op. 42, Pft.   1st Movement — S410

2nd Movement — S411

3rd Movement — S412

Sonata in G, Op. 78, Pft.   1st Movement — S413

2nd Movement 1st Theme — S414

2nd Movement 2nd Theme — S415

3rd Movement 1st Theme — S416

3rd Movement 2nd Theme	S417
4th Movement	S418
Sonata in A, Op. 120, Pft. — 1st Movement 1st Theme	S419
1st Movement 2nd Theme	S420
2nd Movement	S421
3rd Movement 1st Theme	S422
3rd Movement 2nd Theme	S423
Sonata in A Minor, Op. 143, Pft. — 1st Movement	S424
2nd Movement	S425
3rd Movement 1st Theme	S426
3rd Movement 2nd Theme	S427
Sonata in B, Op. 147, Pft. — 1st Movement 1st Theme	S428
1st Movement 2nd Theme	S429
1st Movement 3rd Theme	S430
2nd Movement	S431
3rd Movement	S432
4th Movement 1st Theme	S433
4th Movement 2nd Theme	S434
Sonata in B Flat, Pft. (Posth.) — 1st Movement 1st Theme	S435
1st Movement 2nd Theme	S436

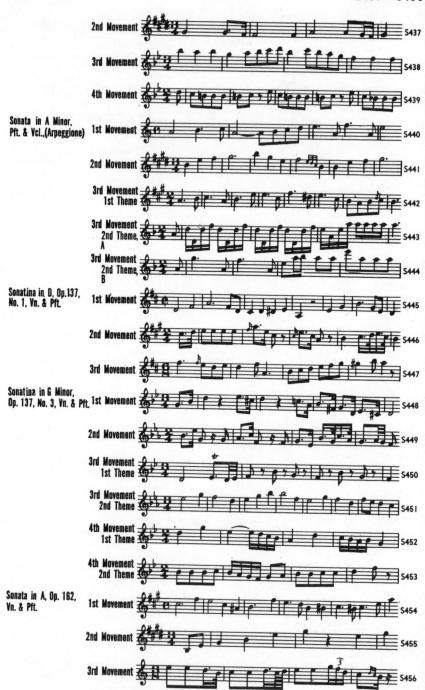

2nd Movement — S437

3rd Movement — S438

4th Movement — S439

Sonata in A Minor,
Pft. & Vcl.,(Arpeggione) 1st Movement — S440

2nd Movement — S441

3rd Movement
1st Theme — S442

3rd Movement
2nd Theme,
A — S443

3rd Movement
2nd Theme,
B — S444

Sonatina in D, Op.137,
No. 1, Vn. & Pft. 1st Movement — S445

2nd Movement — S446

3rd Movement — S447

Sonatina in G Minor,
Op. 137, No. 3, Vn. & Pft. 1st Movement — S448

2nd Movement — S449

3rd Movement
1st Theme — S450

3rd Movement
2nd Theme — S451

4th Movement
1st Theme — S452

4th Movement
2nd Theme — S453

Sonata in A, Op. 162,
Vn. & Pft. 1st Movement — S454

2nd Movement — S455

3rd Movement — S456

SCHUBERT

415

S457—S476

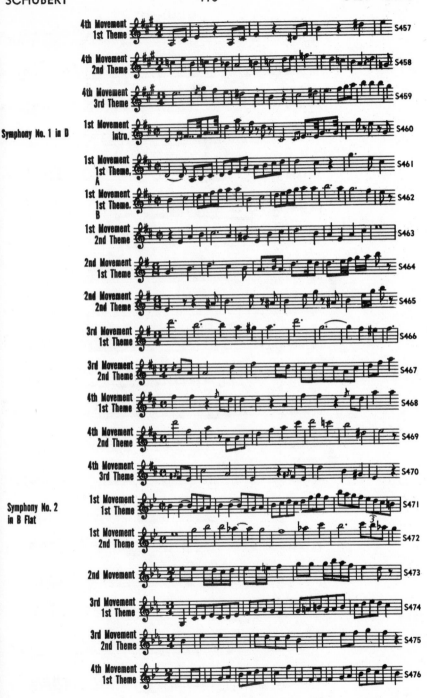

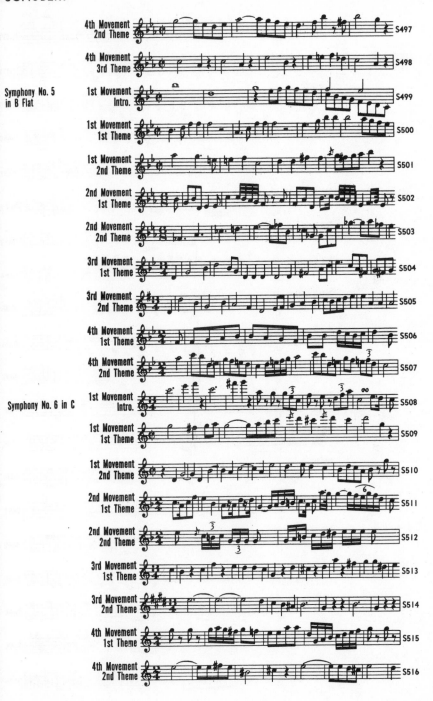

4th Movement / 2nd Theme — S497

4th Movement / 3rd Theme — S498

Symphony No. 5 in B Flat

1st Movement / Intro. — S499

1st Movement / 1st Theme — S500

1st Movement / 2nd Theme — S501

2nd Movement / 1st Theme — S502

2nd Movement / 2nd Theme — S503

3rd Movement / 1st Theme — S504

3rd Movement / 2nd Theme — S505

4th Movement / 1st Theme — S506

4th Movement / 2nd Theme — S507

Symphony No. 6 in C

1st Movement / Intro. — S508

1st Movement / 1st Theme — S509

1st Movement / 2nd Theme — S510

2nd Movement / 1st Theme — S511

2nd Movement / 2nd Theme — S512

3rd Movement / 1st Theme — S513

3rd Movement / 2nd Theme — S514

4th Movement / 1st Theme — S515

4th Movement / 2nd Theme — S516

SCHUBERT — 419

Trio in B Flat, Op. 99, Vn., Pft. & Vcl.

- 2nd Movement, 1st Theme — S537
- 2nd Movement, 2nd Theme — S538
- 1st Movement, 1st Theme — S539
- 1st Movement, 2nd Theme — S540
- 2nd Movement — S541
- 3rd Movement, 1st Theme — S542
- 3rd Movement, 2nd Theme — S543
- 4th Movement, 1st Theme — S544
- 4th Movement, 2nd Theme — S545

Trio in E Flat, Op. 100, Vn., Pft. & Vcl.

- 1st Movement, 1st Theme — S546
- 1st Movement, 2nd Theme — S547
- 1st Movement, 3rd Theme — S548
- 2nd Movement — S549
- 3rd Movement — S550
- 4th Movement, 1st Theme — S551
- 4th Movement, 2nd Theme — S552

Trio in B Flat, (1817), Vn., Vla. & Vcl.

- 1st Movement — S553
- 2nd Movement — S554
- 3rd Movement — S555
- 4th Movement — S556

Trio in B Flat, Vn., Vla. & Vcl.
(One Movement)

Waltzes, Pft.
Op. 9, No. 1

Op. 9, No. 2

Op. 9, No. 12

Op. 50, No. 13

Op. 77, No. 9

Op. 77, No. 10

SCHUMAN, William (1910-   )

American Festival
Overture, Orch.
Copyright 1941 by
G. Schirmer, Inc.

1st Theme,
A

1st Theme,
B

2nd Theme
Fugue Theme

3rd Theme
Counter Theme

4th Theme

Symphony for Strings
Copyright 1943
by G. Schirmer, Inc.

1st Movement
1st Theme,
A

1st Movement
1st Theme,
B

1st Movement
2nd Theme,
A

1st Movement
2nd Theme,
B

2nd Movement
Intro.

2nd Movement
1st Theme

2nd Movement
2nd Theme

Symphony No. 3
Part I
Passacaglia & Fugue
Copyright 1942 by
G. Schirmer, Inc.

Part II
Chorale & Toccata

3rd Movement
1st Theme — S576

3rd Movement
2nd Theme — S577

1st Theme
Passacaglia — S578

2nd Theme
Fugue — S579

1st Theme
Chorale — S580

2nd Theme
Toccata — S581

SCHUMANN, Robert (1810-1856)

Abegg Variations, Op. 1, Pft. — S582

Abendlied (Evening Song),
Op. 85, No. 12, Pft., 4 Hands — S583

Des Abends, Op. 12, No. 1, Pft. — S584

Album for the Young,
Op. 68, Pft.

Soldiers' March — S584a

The Wild Horseman — S584b

Folk Song — S584c

The Happy Farmer — S584d

Sicilienne — S584e

Little Romance — S584f

The Strange Man — S584g

Italian Sailors' Song — S584h

Arabeske, Op. 18, Pft.

1st Theme — S585

2nd Theme — S586

3rd Theme — S587

Aufschwung (Soaring), Op. 12, No. 2, Pft. — 1st Theme — S588

2nd Theme — S589

Carnaval, Op. 9, Pft. — Préambule — S590

Pierrot — S591

Arlequin — S592

Valse Noble — S593

Eusebius — S594

Florestan — S595

Lettres Dansantes — S596

Chopin — S597

Estrella — S598

Reconnaissance — S599

March of the Davidsbündler — S600

Concerto in A Minor, Op. 129, Vcl. & Orch. — 1st Movement 1st Theme — S601

1st Movement 2nd Theme — S602

1st Movement 3rd Theme — S603

2nd Movement — S604

3rd Movement 1st Theme — S605

3rd Movement 2nd Theme — S606

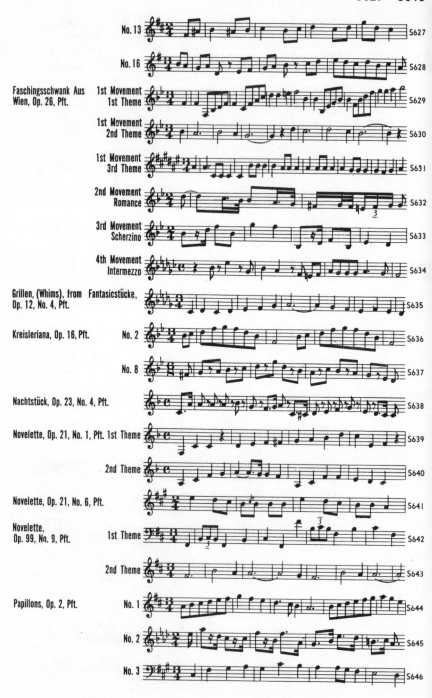

2nd Movement
1st Theme
Scherzo — S667

2nd Movement
2nd Theme
Intermezzo — S668

3rd Movement — S669

4th Movement — S670

Quartet in F,
Op. 41, No. 2, Str.

1st Movement
1st Theme — S671

1st Movement
2nd Theme — S672

2nd Movement — S673

3rd Movement
1st Theme — S674

3rd Movement
2nd Theme — S675

4th Movement
1st Theme — S676

4th Movement
2nd Theme,
A — S677

4th Movement
2nd Theme,
B — S678

Quartet in A, Op. 41,
No. 3, Str.

1st Movement
1st Theme — S679

1st Movement
2nd Theme — S680

2nd Movement
1st Theme — S681

2nd Movement
2nd Theme — S682

2nd Movement
3rd Theme — S683

3rd Movement
1st Theme — S684

3rd Movement
2nd Theme — S685

4th Movement
1st Theme — S686

SCHUMANN

Quartet in E Flat, p. 47, Pft. & Str.

Quintet in E Flat, Op. 44, Pft. & Str.

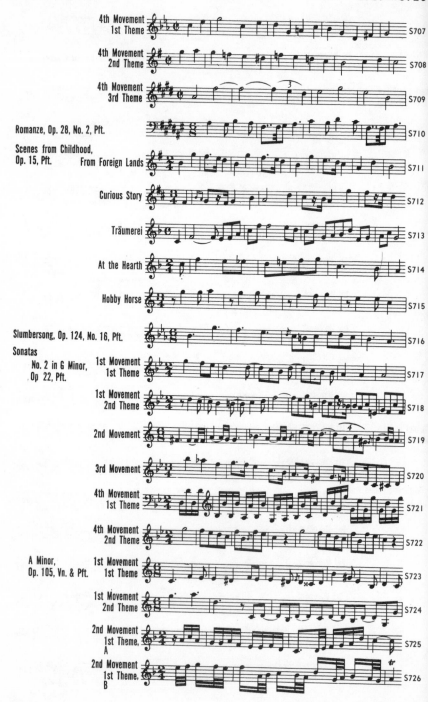

4th Movement 1st Theme — S707

4th Movement 2nd Theme — S708

4th Movement 3rd Theme — S709

Romanze, Op. 28, No. 2, Pft. — S710

Scenes from Childhood, Op. 15, Pft.   From Foreign Lands — S711

Curious Story — S712

Träumerei — S713

At the Hearth — S714

Hobby Horse — S715

Slumbersong, Op. 124, No. 16, Pft. — S716

Sonatas
No. 2 in G Minor, Op 22, Pft.   1st Movement 1st Theme — S717

1st Movement 2nd Theme — S718

2nd Movement — S719

3rd Movement — S720

4th Movement 1st Theme — S721

4th Movement 2nd Theme — S722

A Minor, Op. 105, Vn. & Pft.   1st Movement 1st Theme — S723

1st Movement 2nd Theme — S724

2nd Movement 1st Theme, A — S725

2nd Movement 1st Theme, B — S726

2nd Movement, 2nd Theme   S727

3rd Movement, 1st Theme   S728

3rd Movement, 2nd Theme   S729

3rd Movement, 3rd Theme   S730

D Minor, Op. 121, Vn. & Pft.

1st Movement, Intro.   S731

1st Movement, 1st Theme   S732

1st Movement, 2nd Theme   S733

2nd Movement, 1st Theme   S734

2nd Movement, 2nd Theme   S735

2nd Movement, 3rd Theme   S736

3rd Movement, 1st Theme   S737

3rd Movement, 2nd Theme   S738

4th Movement, 1st Theme   S739

4th Movement, 2nd Theme   S740

Symphonic Etudes, in C Sharp Minor, Op. 13, Pft.

Theme   S741

Etude I   S742

Etude II   S743

Etude III   S744

Etude VI   S745

Finale, 1st Theme   S746

2nd Theme — S747

Symphony No. 1 in
B Flat, Op. 38, "Spring"

1st Movement
Intro. — S748

1st Movement
1st Theme — S749

1st Movement
2nd Theme — S750

1st Movement
3rd Theme — S751

1st Movement
4th Theme — S752

1st Movement
5th Theme — S753

2nd Movement — S754

2nd Movement
2nd Theme — S755

3rd Movement
1st Theme — S756

3rd Movement
2nd Theme — S757

3rd Movement
3rd Theme — S758

3rd Movement
4th Theme — S759

4th Movement
Intro. — S760

4th Movement
1st Theme — S761

4th Movement
2nd Theme — S762

4th Movement
3rd Theme — S763

Symphony No. 2
in C, Op. 61

1st Movement
Intro.
A 1 — S764

1st Movement
Intro.
A 2 — S765

1st Movement
Intro.
B — S766

1st Movement / 1st Theme — S767
1st Movement / 2nd Theme — S768
1st Movement / 3rd Theme — S769
2nd Movement / 1st Theme — S770
2nd Movement / 2nd Theme — S771
2nd Movement / 3rd Theme — S772
2nd Movement / 4th Theme — S773
3rd Movement / 1st Theme — S774
3rd Movement / 2nd Theme — S775
4th Movement / Intro. — S776
4th Movement / 1st Theme — S777
4th Movement / 2nd Theme — S778
4th Movement / 3rd Theme — S779

Symphony No. 3 in E Flat, Op. 97, "Rhenish"

1st Movement / 1st Theme — S780
1st Movement / 2nd Theme — S781
2nd Movement / 1st Theme — S782
2nd Movement / 2nd Theme — S783
3rd Movement / 1st Theme — S784
3rd Movement / 2nd Theme — S785
4th Movement — S786

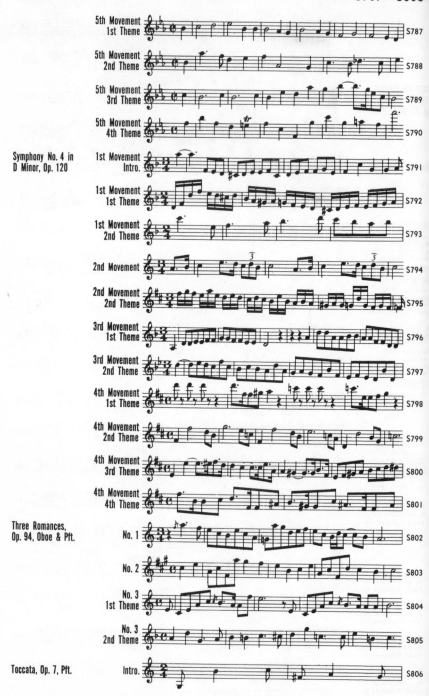

1st Theme   S807

2nd Theme   S808

ogel Als Prophet,
Bird as Prophet)
p. 82, No. 7, Pft.

1st Theme   S809

2nd Theme   S810

Warum? (Why?), Op. 12, No. 3, Pft.   S811

SCOTT, Cyril (1879-1971)

anse Nègre, Op. 58, No. 5, Pft.
copyright 1911 by
lkin & Co., Ltd.
y permission of Galaxy
Music Corporation, N. Y.

S812

otus Land, Op. 47,
No. 1, Pft.
Copyright 1905 by
lkin & Co., Ltd.
y permission of Galaxy
Music Corporation, N. Y.

1st Theme   S813

2nd Theme   S814

A Song from the East,
Op. 54, No. 2, Pft.
Copyright 1907
by Elkin & Co., Ltd.
By permission of Galaxy
Music Corporation, N. Y

S815

SCRIABIN, Alexander (1872-1915)

Etudes
By permisssion of The Boston Music Co.,
   Op. 2, No. 1, Pft. copyright owner.

S816

Op. 8, No. 10, Pft.
By permission of Associated
Music Publishers, Inc.

S817

Op. 8, No.12, Pft.
By permission of Associated
Music Publishers, Inc.

S818

Fantaisie, Op. 28, Pft.
By permission of Associated
Music Publishers, Inc.

1st Theme   S819

2nd Theme   S820

Mazurka, Op. 25, No. 3, Pft.
By permission of Associated
Music Publishers, Inc.

S821

Nocturne, Pft. (For Left Hand Alone)
By permission of Associated
Music Publishers, Inc.

S822

Poème, Op. 32, No. 1, Pft.
By permission of Associated
Music Publishers, Inc.

S823

Poème, Op. 32, No. 2, Pft.
By permission of Associated
Music Publishers, Inc.

S824

15

Poème D'Extase, Op. 34, Orch.
By permission of Associated Music Publishers, Inc.
1st Theme — S825

2nd Theme — S826

3rd Theme — S827

Preludes
Op. 9, No. 1, Pft.
(For Left Hand Alone)
By permission of Associated Music Publishers, Inc.
Op. 11, No. 2, Pft.
By permission of Associated Music Publishers, Inc.
— S828

— S829

No. 9, Pft. — S830

No. 10, Pft. — S831

Sonata, No. 4, Op. 30, Pft.
By permission of International Music Co.
1st Movement — S832

2nd Movement — S833

Symphony No. 3, Op. 43 "Le Divin Poème"
By permission of Associated Music Publishers, Inc.
Intro. — S834

1st Movement Luttes 1st Theme — S835

1st Movement 2nd Theme — S836

2nd Movement Voluptés — S837

3rd Movement Jeu Divin 1st Theme — S838

3rd Movement 2nd Theme — S839

Waltz, Op. 38, Pft.
By permission of Associated Music Publishers, Inc.
— S840

SGAMBATI, Giovanni (1841-1914)

Serenata Napoletana, Op. 24, No. 2, Vn. & Pft.
1st Theme, A — S841

1st Theme, B — S842

2nd Theme — S843

Vecchio Minuetto, Op. 18, Pft. — S844

SHOSTAKOVICH, Dmitri (1906-   )

Concerto, Op. 35, Pft. & Orch.
By permission of Broude Brothers

1st Movement 1st Theme — S845

1st Movement 2nd Theme — S846

2nd Movement — S847

3rd Movement Finale 1st Theme — S848

3rd Movement 2nd Theme — S849

3rd Movement 3rd Theme — S850

The Golden Age, Op. 22, Ballet
Copyright 1941 by Leeds Music Corp., N. Y. Reprinted here by permisssion of the copyright owner.

1st Theme Polka — S851

2nd Theme — S852

3rd Theme — S853

Quartet, Op. 49, Str.
By permission of International Music Co.

1st Movement 1st Theme — S854

1st Movement 2nd Theme — S855

2nd Movement — S856

3rd Movement 1st Theme — S857

3rd Movement 2nd Theme — S858

4th Movement 1st Theme — S859

4th Movement 2nd Theme — S860

Quintet, Op. 57, Pft. & Str.

1st Movement Prelude 1st Theme — S861

1st Movement 2nd Theme — S862

2nd Movement
Fugue — S863

3rd Movement
Scherzo
1st Theme — S864

3rd Movement
2nd Theme — S865

4th Movement
Intermezzo — S866

5th Movement
Finale
1st Theme, A — S867

5th Movement
1st Theme, B — S868

5th Movement
2nd Theme — S869

5th Movement
3rd Theme — S870

Sonata, Op. 40
Cello & Pft.
Copyright 1947 by Leeds
Music Corp., N. Y.
Reprinted here by
permission of the
copyright owner.

1st Movement
1st Theme — S870a

1st Movement
2nd Theme — S870b

2nd Movement
1st Theme — S870c

2nd Movement
2nd Theme — S870d

3rd Movement
1st Theme — S870e

3rd Movement
2nd Theme — S870f

4th Movement — S870g

Symphony No. 1 in F,
Op. 10
Copyright 1946 by
Leeds Music Corp., N. Y.
Reprinted here by
permission of the
copyright owner.

1st Movement
Intro. — S871

1st Movement
1st Theme — S872

1st Movement
2nd Theme — S873

2nd Movement
1st Theme — S874

2nd Movement
2nd Theme — S875

438

Symphony No. 6, Op. 53
Copyright 1946 by Leeds
Music Corp., N. Y.
Reprinted here by
permisssion of the
copyright owner.

1st Movement 1st Theme — S896
1st Movement 2nd Theme — S897
2nd Movement 1st Theme — S898
2nd Movement 2nd Theme — S899
3rd Movement 1st Theme — S900
3rd Movement 2nd Theme — S901
3rd Movement 3rd Theme — S902

Symphony No. 7, Op. 60
Copyright 1945 by Leeds
Music Corp., N. Y.
Reprinted here by
permisssion of the
copyright owner.

1st Movement 1st Theme — S903
1st Movement 2nd Theme — S904
1st Movement 3rd Theme — S905
2nd Movement 1st Theme — S906
2nd Movement 2nd Theme — S907
2nd Movement 3rd Theme — S908
3rd Movement 1st Theme — S909
3rd Movement 2nd Theme — S910
3rd Movement 3rd Theme — S911
4th Movement 1st Theme — S912
4th Movement 2nd Theme — S913

Symphony No. 9, Op. 70

1st Movement 1st Theme — S914
1st Movement 2nd Theme — S915

2nd Movement 1st Theme — S916

2nd Movement 2nd Theme — S917

3rd Movement 1st Theme — S918

3rd Movement 2nd Theme — S919

4th Movement — S920

5th Movement 1st Theme — S921

5th Movement 2nd Theme — S922

Three Fantastic Dances, Op. 1, Pft.
Copyright 1944 and 1945 by Leeds Music Corp., N. Y. Reprinted here by permisssion of the copyright owner.

No. 1 — S923

No. 2 — S924

No. 3 — S925

Two Pieces for String Octet, Op. 11
Copyright 1946 by Leeds Music Corp., N. Y. Reprinted here by permissionn of the copyright owner.

No. 1 Prelude 1st Theme — S925a

2nd Theme — S925b

No. 2 Scherzo 1st Theme — S925c

2nd Theme — S925d

SIBELIUS, Jean (1865-1957)

The Bard, Op. 64, Orch.
By permission of Associated Music Publishers, Inc.

1st Theme — S926

2nd Theme — S927

Concerto, Op. 47, Vn. & Orch.
By permission of International Music Co.

1st Movement 1st Theme — S928

1st Movement 2nd Theme, A — S929

1st Movement 2nd Theme, B — S930

2nd Movement Intro. — S931

2nd Movement — S932

3rd Movement 1st Theme — S933

3rd Movement 2nd Theme — S934

En Saga, Op. 9, Orch.
By permission of Associated
Music Publishers, Inc.
1st Theme — S935

2nd Theme — S936

3rd Theme — S937

4th Theme — S938

5th Theme — S939

6th Theme — S940

Finlandia, Op. 26,
No. 7, Orch.
By permission of Associated
Music Publishers, Inc.
1st Theme — S941

2nd Theme — S942

3rd Theme — S943

In Memoriam, Op. 59
(Funeral March), Orch.
By permission of Associated
Music Publishers, Inc. — S944

Karelia, Op. 11,
Suite for Orch.
By permission of Associated
Music Publishers, Inc.
1st Movement Intermezzo — S945

2nd Movement Ballade — S946

3rd Movement Alla Marcia 1st Theme — S947

3rd Movement 2nd Theme — S948

King Christian II, Op. 27,
Suite for Orch.
By permission of Associated
Music Publishers, Inc.
Nocturne 1st Theme — S949

2nd Theme — S950

Elégie and Musette
1st Theme
Elégie   S951

2nd Theme
Musette   S952

Serenade
1st Theme   S953

2nd Theme   S954

Ballade
1st Theme   S955

2nd Theme   S956

Lemminkäinen's Homeward
Journey, Op. 22, No. 4
Orch.   1st Theme   S957
By permission of Associated
Music Publishers, Inc.

2nd Theme   S958

3rd Theme   S959

Nightride and Sunrise,
Op. 55, Orch.   1st Theme   S960

2nd Theme   S961

3rd Theme   S962

The Oceanides,
Op. 73, Orch.   1st Theme   S963
By permission of Associated
Music Publishers, Inc.

2nd Theme   S964

Pelléas et Mélisande,
(Incidental Music)   Mélisande   S965
Op. 46, Orch.

A Spring in the Park   S966

Pastorale   S967

Entr'acte   S968

Death of Mélisande   S969

Pohjola's Daughter,
Op. 49, Orch.   1st Theme   S970
Copyright by Lienau   A
Licensed by SESAC, Inc., N. Y.

15*

1st Theme, B — S971

2nd Theme — S972

3rd Theme — S973

4th Theme — S974

4th Theme — S975

5th Theme — S976

Quartet, Op. 56, Str.
"Voces Intimae"
By permission of Associated
Music Publishers, Inc.

1st Movement 1st Theme, A — S977

1st Movement 1st Theme, B — S978

1st Movement 2nd Theme — S979

2nd Movement 1st Theme — S980

2nd Movement 2nd Theme — S981

3rd Movement 1st Theme, A — S982

3rd Movement 1st Theme, B — S983

4th Movement 1st Theme — S984

4th Movement 2nd Theme — S985

4th Movement 3rd Theme — S986

5th Movement 1st Theme — S987

5th Movement 2nd Theme — S988

5th Movement 3rd Theme — S989

Rakastava, (The Lover),
Op. 14, Suite for Orch.
By permission of Associated
Music Publishers, Inc.

1st Movement — S990

Symphony No. 2
in D, Op. 43
By permission of Associated
Music Publishers, Inc.

Symphony No. 3
in C, Op. 52
Copyright by Lienau,
Licensed by SESAC
Inc., N. Y.

1st Movement / 1st Theme	S1011
1st Movement / 2nd Theme	S1012
1st Movement / 3rd Theme	S1013
2nd Movement / Intro.	S1014
2nd Movement / 1st Theme	S1015
2nd Movement / 2nd Theme	S1016
3rd Movement / 1st Theme	S1017
3rd Movement / 2nd Theme	S1018
3rd Movement / 3rd Theme	S1019
4th Movement / 1st Theme	S1020
4th Movement / 2nd Theme	S1021
4th Movement / 3rd Theme	S1022
4th Movement / 4th Theme	S1023
1st Movement / 1st Theme	S1024
1st Movement / 2nd Theme	S1025
1st Movement / 3rd Theme	S1026
2nd Movement	S1027
3rd Movement / 1st Theme	S1028
3rd Movement / 2nd Theme	S1029
3rd Movement / 3rd Theme	S1030

Symphony No. 4
in A Minor, Op. 63
By permission of Associated
Music Publishers, Inc.

1st Movement
1st Theme
S1031

1st Movement
2nd Theme
S1032

1st Movement
3rd Theme
S1033

2nd Movement
1st Theme
S1034

2nd Movement
2nd Theme
S1035

2nd Movement
3rd Theme
S1036

2nd Movement
4th Theme
S1037

2nd Movement
5th Theme
S1038

3rd Movement
1st Theme
S1039

3rd Movement
2nd Theme
S1040

4th Movement
1st Theme
S1041

4th Movement
2nd Theme
S1042

4th Movement
3rd Theme
S1043

4th Movement
4th Theme
S1044

4th Movement
5th Theme
S1045

Symphony No. 5
in E Flat, Op. 82
By permission of Associated
Music Publishers, Inc.

1st Movement
1st Theme
S1046

1st Movement
2nd Theme
S1047

1st Movement
3rd Theme
S1048

1st Movement
4th Theme
S1049

1st Movement
5th Theme
S1050

SIBELIUS

446

S1051—S1070

2nd Movement Intro. — S1051
2nd Movement 1st Theme — S1052
2nd Movement 2nd Theme — S1053
3rd Movement 1st Theme — S1054
3rd Movement 2nd Theme — S1055
3rd Movement 3rd Theme — S1056

Symphony No. 6
in D Minor, Op. 104
By permission of Associated
Music Publishers, Inc.

1st Movement 1st Theme — S1057
1st Movement 2nd Theme — S1058
1st Movement 3rd Theme — S1059
1st Movement 4th Theme — S1060
1st Movement 5th Theme — S1061
1st Movement 6th Theme — S1062
2nd Movement 1st Theme — S1063
2nd Movement 2nd Theme — S1064
2nd Movement 3rd Theme — S1065
3rd Movement 1st Theme — S1066
3rd Movement 2nd Theme — S1067
3rd Movement 3rd Theme — S1068
3rd Movement 4th Theme — S1069
4th Movement 1st Theme — S1070

SIBELIUS

4th Movement 2nd Theme — S1071

4th Movement 3rd Theme — S1072

4th Movement 4th Theme — S1073

Symphony No. 7 in C, Op. 105
By permission of Associated Music Publishers, Inc.

1st Theme — S1074

2nd Theme — S1075

3rd Theme A — S1076

3rd Theme B — S1077

4th Theme — S1078

5th Theme — S1079

6th Theme — S1080

7th Theme — S1081

8th Theme — S1082

9th Theme — S1083

10th Theme — S1084

11th Theme — S1085

Tapiola, Op. 112, Orch.
By permission of Associated Music Publishers, Inc.

1st Theme — S1086

2nd Theme — S1087

3rd Theme — S1088

Valse Triste (from Kuolema), Op. 44 Orch.
Copyright 1926 by G. Schirmer, Inc.

1st Theme — S1089

2nd Theme — S1090

| 3rd Theme | S1091 |
| 4th Theme | S1092 |

SINDING, Christian (1856-1941)

Marche Grotesque, Op. 32, No. 1, Pft.

Rustle of Spring
(Frühlingsrauschen),
Op. 32, No. 3, Pft.
Copyright renewal assigned
1931 to G. Schirmer, Inc.

1st Theme, A — S1094

1st Theme, B — S1095

SMETANA, Bedřich (1824-1884)

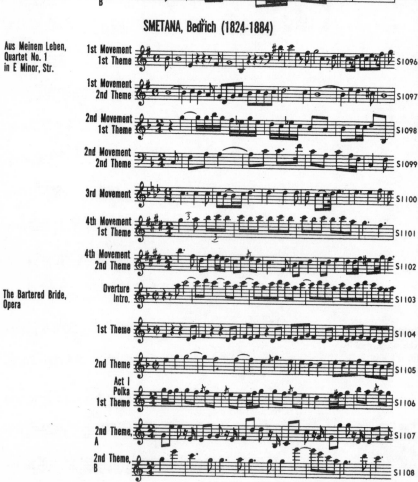

Aus Meinem Leben,
Quartet No. 1
in E Minor, Str.

1st Movement 1st Theme	S1096
1st Movement 2nd Theme	S1097
2nd Movement 1st Theme	S1098
2nd Movement 2nd Theme	S1099
3rd Movement	S1100
4th Movement 1st Theme	S1101
4th Movement 2nd Theme	S1102

The Bartered Bride,
Opera

Overture Intro.	S1103
1st Theme	S1104
2nd Theme	S1105
Act I Polka 1st Theme	S1106
2nd Theme, A	S1107
2nd Theme, B	S1108

2nd Movement 2nd Theme — S1129

2nd Movement 3rd Theme — S1130

3rd Movement 1st Theme — S1131

3rd Movement 2nd Theme — S1132

SOLER, Padre Antonio (1729-1783)

Sonatas
F, Harpsi. — S1133

A Minor, Harpsi. — S1134

D, Harpsi. — S1135

SOUSA, John Philip (1854-1932)

El Capitan, March
1st Theme — S1136
2nd Theme — S1137
3rd Theme — S1138
4th Theme — S1139

Hail to the Spirit of Liberty, March
1st Theme — S1140
2nd Theme — S1141
3rd Theme — S1142

The High School Cadets, March
1st Theme — S1143
2nd Theme — S1144
3rd Theme — S1145
4th Theme — S1146

King Cotton, March
Published and copyrighted
(renewal 1923) by The John
Church Co. Used by
permission.

1st Theme S1147

2nd Theme S1148

3rd Theme S1149

The Liberty Bell, March

1st Theme S1150

2nd Theme S1151

3rd Theme S1152

Manhattan Beach, March

1st Theme S1153

2nd Theme S1154

3rd Theme S1155

4th Theme S1156

Semper Fidelis, March

1st Theme S1157

2nd Theme S1158

3rd Theme S1159

4th Theme S1160

Stars and Stripes Forever, March
Published and copyrighted
(renewal 1925) by The John
Church Co. Used by
permission.

1st Theme S1161

2nd Theme S1162

3rd Theme S1163

4th Theme S1164

The Thunderer, March

1st Theme S1165

2nd Theme S1166

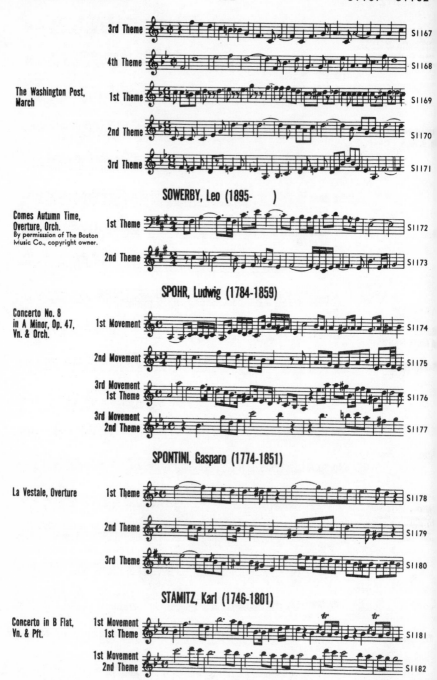

3rd Theme   S1167

4th Theme   S1168

The Washington Post, March

1st Theme   S1169

2nd Theme   S1170

3rd Theme   S1171

SOWERBY, Leo (1895-   )

Comes Autumn Time, Overture, Orch.
By permisssion of The Boston Music Co., copyright owner.

1st Theme   S1172

2nd Theme   S1173

SPOHR, Ludwig (1784-1859)

Concerto No. 8 in A Minor, Op. 47, Vn. & Orch.

1st Movement   S1174

2nd Movement   S1175

3rd Movement 1st Theme   S1176

3rd Movement 2nd Theme   S1177

SPONTINI, Gasparo (1774-1851)

La Vestale, Overture

1st Theme   S1178

2nd Theme   S1179

3rd Theme   S1180

STAMITZ, Karl (1746-1801)

Concerto in B Flat, Vn. & Pft.

1st Movement 1st Theme   S1181

1st Movement 2nd Theme   S1182

2nd Movement — S1183

3rd Movement
1st Theme — S1184

3rd Movement
2nd Theme — S1185

Orchestra-Quartet in F,
Op. 4, No. 4

1st Movement
1st Theme — S1186

1st Movement
2nd Theme — S1187

2nd Movement
1st Theme — S1188

2nd Movement
2nd Theme — S1189

3rd Movement
1st Theme — S1190

3rd Movement
2nd Theme — S1191

Sonata in D, Viola
d'Amore & Harpsi.

1st Movement — S1192

2nd Movement — S1193

3rd Movement — S1194

4th Movement — S1195

STILL, William Grant (1895-   )

1st Movement
1st Theme,
A — S1196

1st Movement
1st Theme,
B — S1197

1st Movement
2nd Theme — S1198

2nd Movement
Intro. — S1199

2nd Movement — S1200

3rd Movement
1st Theme — S1201

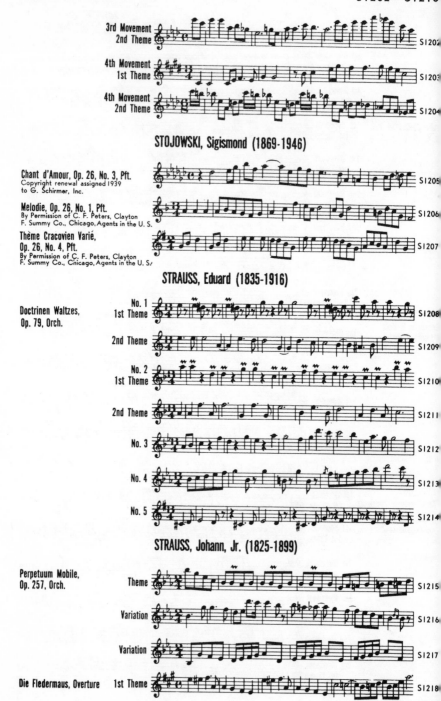

3rd Movement 2nd Theme — S1202

4th Movement 1st Theme — S1203

4th Movement 2nd Theme — S1204

STOJOWSKI, Sigismond (1869-1946)

Chant d'Amour, Op. 26, No. 3, Pft.
Copyright renewal assigned 1939 to G. Schirmer, Inc. — S1205

Melodie, Op. 26, No. 1, Pft.
By Permission of C. F. Peters, Clayton F. Summy Co., Chicago, Agents in the U. S. — S1206

Thème Cracovien Varié, Op. 26, No. 4, Pft.
By Permission of C. F. Peters, Clayton F. Summy Co., Chicago, Agents in the U. S. — S1207

STRAUSS, Eduard (1835-1916)

Doctrinen Waltzes, Op. 79, Orch.

No. 1 1st Theme — S1208

2nd Theme — S1209

No. 2 1st Theme — S1210

2nd Theme — S1211

No. 3 — S1212

No. 4 — S1213

No. 5 — S1214

STRAUSS, Johann, Jr. (1825-1899)

Perpetuum Mobile, Op. 257, Orch.

Theme — S1215

Variation — S1216

Variation — S1217

Die Fledermaus, Overture 1st Theme — S1218

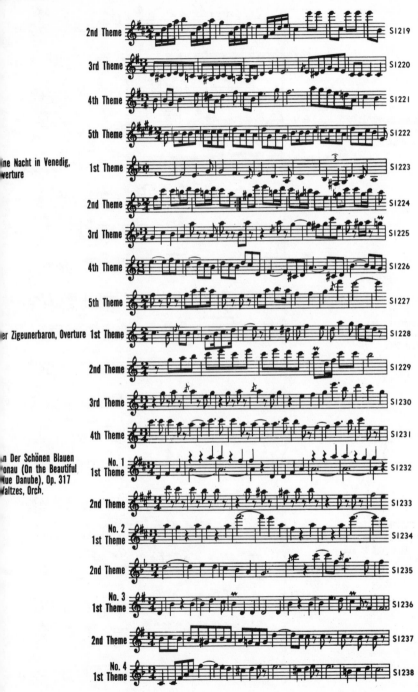

2nd Theme S1219

3rd Theme S1220

4th Theme S1221

5th Theme S1222

ine Nacht in Venedig,
verture

1st Theme S1223

2nd Theme S1224

3rd Theme S1225

4th Theme S1226

5th Theme S1227

er Zigeunerbaron, Overture 1st Theme S1228

2nd Theme S1229

3rd Theme S1230

4th Theme S1231

an Der Schönen Blauen
onau (On the Beautiful
lue Danube), Op. 317
Waltzes, Orch.

No. 1
1st Theme S1232

2nd Theme S1233

No. 2
1st Theme S1234

2nd Theme S1235

No. 3
1st Theme S1236

2nd Theme S1237

No. 4
1st Theme S1238

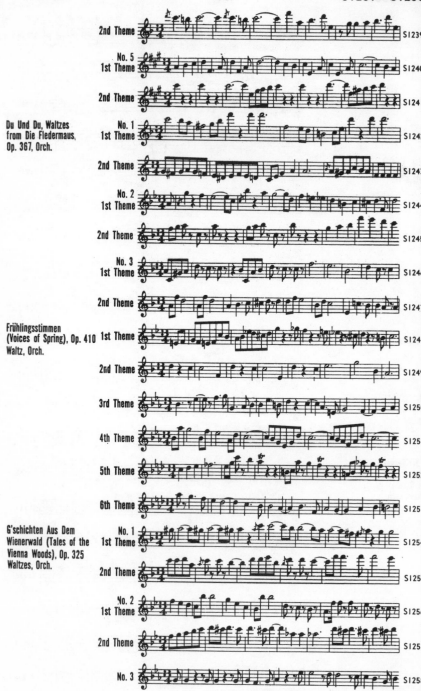

2nd Theme — S1239

No. 5 1st Theme — S1240

2nd Theme — S1241

Du Und Du, Waltzes from Die Fledermaus, Op. 367, Orch.
No. 1 1st Theme — S1242

2nd Theme — S1243

No. 2 1st Theme — S1244

2nd Theme — S1245

No. 3 1st Theme — S1246

2nd Theme — S1247

Frühlingsstimmen (Voices of Spring), Op. 410 Waltz, Orch.
1st Theme — S1248

2nd Theme — S1249

3rd Theme — S1250

4th Theme — S1251

5th Theme — S1252

6th Theme — S1253

G'schichten Aus Dem Wienerwald (Tales of the Vienna Woods), Op. 325 Waltzes, Orch.
No. 1 1st Theme — S1254

2nd Theme — S1255

No. 2 1st Theme — S1256

2nd Theme — S1257

No. 3 — S1258

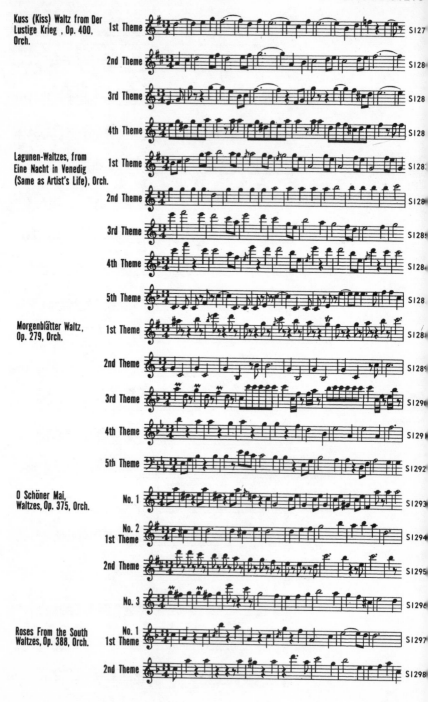

Kuss (Kiss) Waltz from Der Lustige Krieg , Op. 400, Orch. — 1st Theme — S127

2nd Theme — S128

3rd Theme — S128

4th Theme — S128

Lagunen-Waltzes, from Eine Nacht in Venedig (Same as Artist's Life), Orch. — 1st Theme — S128

2nd Theme — S128

3rd Theme — S128

4th Theme — S128

5th Theme — S128

Morgenblätter Waltz, Op. 279, Orch. — 1st Theme — S128

2nd Theme — S128

3rd Theme — S1290

4th Theme — S129

5th Theme — S1292

O Schöner Mai, Waltzes, Op. 375, Orch. — No. 1 — S1293

No. 2 1st Theme — S1294

2nd Theme — S1295

No. 3 — S1296

Roses From the South Waltzes, Op. 388, Orch. — No. 1 1st Theme — S1297

2nd Theme — S1298

No. 2 — S1299

No. 3 1st Theme — S1300

2nd Theme — S1301

No. 4 1st Theme — S1302

2nd Theme — S1303

Schatz Waltzer, (Treasure Waltzes), Op. 418, Orch.

No. 1 — S1304

No. 2 — S1305

No. 3 — S1306

No. 4 1st Theme — S1307

2nd Theme — S1308

Thousand and One Nights, Op. 346 Waltzes, Orch.

No. 1 1st Theme — S1309

2nd Theme — S1310

3rd Theme — S1311

No. 2 — S1312

No. 3 — S1313

Wein, Weib und Gesang (Wine, Women and Song), Op. 333, Waltzes, Orch.

No. 1 1st Theme — S1314

2nd Theme — S1315

No. 2 1st Theme — S1316

2nd Theme — S1317

No. 3 — S1318

No. 4   S1319

Wiener-Blut, Op. 354
Waltzes, Orch.

No. 1
1st Theme   S1320

2nd Theme   S1321

No. 2   S1322

No. 3
1st Theme   S1323

2nd Theme   S1324

No. 4   S1325

Wiener-Bonbons, Op. 307
Waltzes, Orch.

No. 1
1st Theme   S1326

2nd Theme   S1327

No. 2   S1328

No. 3
1st Theme   S1329

2nd Theme   S1330

No. 4   S1331

No. 5
1st Theme   S1332

2nd Theme   S1333

STRAUSS, Johann, Sr. (1804-1849)

Radetsky March, Orch.

1st Theme   S1334

2nd Theme   S1335

STRAUSS, Joseph (1827-1870)

Dorfschwalben Aus
Oesterreich (Village
Swallows of Austria), Op. 164
Waltzes, Orch.

No. 1
1st Theme   S1336

2nd Theme   S1337

No. 2   S1338

No. 3   S1339

No. 4   S1340

No. 5   S1341

Sphärenklange, Op. 235
Waltzes, Orch.

No. 1
1st Theme   S1342

2nd Theme   S1343

No. 2   S1344

No. 3   S1345

No. 4   S1346

No. 5   S1347

Wiener Kinder, Op. 61
Waltzes, Orch.

No. 1   S1348

No. 2   S1349

No. 3   S1350

No. 4   S1351

No. 5   S1352

STRAUSS, Richard. (1864-1949)

Alpensinfonie, Op. 64
Orch.
By permission of Associated
Music Publishers. Inc.

1st Theme   S1353

2nd Theme   S1354

3rd Theme   S1355

STRAUSS

4th Theme — S1356

5th Theme — S1357

6th Theme — S1358

7th Theme — S1359

8th Theme — S1360

9th Theme — S1361

10th Theme — S1362

11th Theme — S1363

12th Theme — S1364

Also Sprach Zarathustra
(Thus Spake Zarathustra),
Op. 30, Orch.

Intro. — S1365

1st Theme — S1366

2nd Theme — S1367

3rd Theme, A — S1368

3rd Theme, B — S1369

4th Theme — S1370

5th Theme, A — S1371

5th Theme, B — S1372

6th Theme — S1373

7th Theme, A — S1374

7th Theme, B — S1375

us Italien,
mphonic Fantasy,
p. 16

In the Campagna
(Auf der Campagna)
1st Theme

2nd Theme

3rd Theme

In the Roman Ruins
(In Roms Ruinen)
1st Theme

2nd Theme

3rd Theme

4th Theme

5th Theme

The Beach at Sorrento
(Am Strande von Sorrent)
1st Theme

2nd Theme

3rd Theme

4th Theme

Neapolitan Folk Life
(Neapolitanisches Volksleben)
1st Theme
A

1st Theme
B

2nd Theme

3rd Theme

4th Theme

Der Bürger Als
Edelmann, Op. 60,
Orch.
By permission of the
copyright owner,
Boosey and Hawkes, Inc.

Overture
1st Theme

2nd Theme

Minuet

S1376
S1377
S1378
S1379
S1380
S1381
S1382
S1383
S1384
S1385
S1386
S1387
S1388
S1389
S1390
S1391
S1392
S1393
S1394
S1395

The Fencing Master
1st Theme — S1396

2nd Theme — S1397

Entry & Dance of the Tailors
1st Theme — S1398

2nd Theme — S1399

Minuet of Lully
1st Theme — S1400

2nd Theme — S1401

Courante
1st Theme, A — S1402

1st Theme, B — S1403

2nd Theme — S1404

Entrance of Cleonte
1st Theme — S1405

2nd Theme — S1406

Intermezzo
(Prelude to Act II) — S1407

The Dinner
1st Theme — S1408

2nd Theme — S1409

3rd Theme — S1410

4th Theme — S1411

5th Theme — S1412

6th Theme
Dance of the Kitchen Boys — S1413

Burleske, Pft. & Orch. 1st Theme — S1414

2nd Theme — S1415

STRAUSS

3rd Theme — S1416
4th Theme — S1417
5th Theme — S1418

Don Juan, Op. 20, Orch.
1st Theme — S1419
2nd Theme — S1420
3rd Theme — S1421
4th Theme — S1422
5th Theme — S1423
6th Theme — S1424

Don Quixote, Op. 35, Orch.
1st Theme — S1425
2nd Theme — S1426
3rd Theme — S1427
4th Theme — S1428
5th Theme, A — S1429
5th Theme, B — S1430

Ein Heldenleben, Op. 40, Orch.
By permission of Associated Music Publishers, Inc.
1st Theme — S1431
2nd Theme, A — S1432
2nd Theme, B — S1433
2nd Theme, C — S1434
3rd Theme — S1435

4th Theme — S1436

5th Theme — S1437

6th Theme — S1438

7th Theme — S1439

8th Theme — S1440

9th Theme — S1441

Rêverie, Op. 9, No. 4, Pft. or Pft. & Vn. — S1442

Der Rosenkavalier, Waltz Themes, Op. 59.
By permission of the copyright owner, Boosey and Hawkes, Inc. — S1443

— S1444

— S1445

— S1446

— S1447

Salome, Opera, Op. 54
By permission of the copyright owner, Boosey and Hawkes, Inc.

Dance of the Seven Veils 1st Theme — S1448

2nd Theme — S1449

3rd Theme — S1450

4th Theme — S1451

5th Theme — S1452

Sonata in E Flat, Op. 18, Vn. & Pft.

1st Movement 1st Theme A — S1453

1st Movement 1st Theme B — S1454

1st Movement 2nd Theme — S1455

1st Movement 3rd Theme — S1456

2nd Movement Improvisation — S1457

3rd Movement Finale 1st Theme — S1458

3rd Movement 2nd Theme — S1459

3rd Movement 3rd Theme — S1460

Sinfonia Domestica, Op. 53
By permission of Associated Music Publishers, Inc.

1st Movement 1st Theme, A — S1461

1st Theme, B — S1462

2nd Theme, A — S1463

2nd Theme, B — S1464

3rd Theme — S1465

4th Theme Cradle Song — S1466

5th Theme — S1467

Till Eulenspiegels Lustige Streiche, Op. 28, Orch.

1st Theme — S1468

2nd Theme — S1469

3rd Theme (Variant of First Theme) — S1470

4th Theme — S1471

5th Theme — S1472

6th Theme — S1473

7th Theme — S1474

Tod Und Verklärung (Death and Transfiguration), Op. 24, Orch.

1st Theme — S1475

2nd Theme — S1476

3rd Theme — S1477

4th Theme — S1478

5th Theme — S1479

STRAVINSKY, Igor (1882-1971)

Apollon Musagètes, Ballet
By permission of the copyright owner, Boosey and Hawkes, Inc.

Birth of Apollo, Prologue
1st Theme, A — S1480

1st Theme, B — S1481

2nd Theme — S1482

Variation of Apollo — S1483

Pas d'Action
1st Theme — S1484

2nd Theme — S1485

Variation of Calliope — S1486

Variation of Polymnie — S1487

Variation of Terpsichore — S1488

Pas de Deux — S1489

Coda — S1490

Apotheosis — S1491

Le Baiser de la Fée, Ballet on Tschaikovsky Themes
By permission of the copyright owner, Boosey and Hawkes, Inc.

1st Movement
Berceuse de la Tempête
1st Theme — S1492

1st Movement
2nd Theme — S1493

2nd Movement
Fête au Village
1st Theme — S1494

Capriccio
Pft. & Orch.
By permission of the
copyright owner,
Boosey and Hawkes, Inc.

2nd Movement
1st Theme,
B — S1514

2nd Movement
2nd Theme — S1515

2nd Movement
3rd Theme — S1516

3rd Movement
1st Theme — S1517

3rd Movement
2nd Theme — S1518

3rd Movement
3rd Theme,
A — S1519

3rd Movement
3rd Theme,
B — S1520

3rd Movement
Coda — S1521

Chant du Rossignol
Poème Symphonique,
Orch.
By permission of the
copyright owner,
Boosey and Hawkes, Inc.

1st Movement
1st Theme — S1521a

1st Movement
2nd Theme — S1521b

2nd Movement
Marche Chinoise
1st Theme — S1521c

2nd Movement
2nd Theme — S1521d

Jeu du Rossignol Mécanique
3rd Movement
1st Theme — S1521e

3rd Movement
2nd Theme — S1521f

Concerto,
Pft. & Orch.
By permission of the
copyright owner,
Boosey and Hawkes, Inc.

1st Movement — S1522

2nd Movement
1st Theme — S1573

2nd Movement
2nd Theme — S1524

3rd Movement
1st Theme — S1525

3rd Movement
2nd Theme — S1526

3rd Movement
3rd Theme — S1527

Concerto in D, Vn. & Orch.
By permission of Associated Music Publishers, Inc.

1st Movement 1st Theme — S1528

1st Movement 2nd Theme, A — S1529

1st Movement 2nd Theme, B — S1530

2nd Movement Aria, A — S1531

3rd Movement Aria, B — S1532

4th Movement Intro. — S1533

4th Movement Theme — S1534

Dumbarton Oaks Concerto, Chamber Orch.
By permission of Associated Music Publishers, Inc.

1st Movement 1st Theme — S1534a

1st Movement 2nd Theme — S1534b

1st Movement 3rd Theme — S1534c

2nd Movement — S1534d

3rd Movement 1st Theme — S1534e

3rd Movement 1st Theme — S1534f

3rd Movement 2nd Theme — S1534g

The Fire Bird Ballet Suite, Orch.
By permission of the copyright holders, J. & W. Chester, Ltd., 11 Great Marlborough Street, London, W. 1.

Intro. — S1535

Ronde des Princesses 1st Theme — S1536

2nd Theme — S1537

Dance of Kastchei — S1538

Berceuse — S1539

Finale — S1540

**Octet for Fl., Cl.,
2 Fg., 2 Trpts.,
2 Tromb.**
By permission of the
copyright owner,
Boosey and Hawkes, Inc.

**Pastorale
Vn. & Pft.**
By permission of the copyright
owner, Boosey and Hawkes, Inc.

**Petrouchka, Suite
Ballet, Orch.**
By permission of the
copyright owner,
Boosey and Hawkes, Inc

1st Movement Intro. — S1541
1st Movement 1st Theme — S1542
1st Movement 2nd Theme — S1543
2nd Movement Theme & Variations — S1544
3rd Movement Finale — S1545
Intro. — S1546
Theme — S1547
Tableau 1 1st Theme — S1548
2nd Theme — S1549
3rd Theme — S1550
4th Theme — S1551
Le Tour de Passe-passe — S1552
Danse Russe 1st Theme — S1553
2nd Theme — S1554
3rd Theme — S1555
Tableau 2 Chez Petrouchka 1st Theme — S1556
2nd Theme, A — S1557
2nd Theme, B — S1558
Tableau 3 Chez le Maure — S1559
Danse de la Ballerina — S1560

16*

Games of the Rival Cities 1st Theme — S1581

2nd Theme — S1582

Procession of the Wise Men — S1583

Dance of the Earth — S1584

Part II, The Sacrifice Intro. — S1585

Mysterious Circles of the Adolescents — S1586

Evocation of the Ancestors — S1587

Ritual of the Ancestors — S1588

Sacrificial Dance, Motive A — S1589

Motives B & C — S1590

Suite No. 1, Small Orch.
By permission of the copyright holders, J. & W. Chester, Ltd., 11 Great Marlborough Street, London, W. 1.

1st Movement Andante — S1591

2nd Movement Napolitana — S1592

3rd Movement Española — S1593

4th Movement Balalaika — S1594

Suite No. 2 Small Orch.
By permission of the copyright holders, J. & W. Chester, Ltd., 11 Great Marlborough Street, London, W. 1.

1st Movement March — S1595

2nd Movement Waltz — S1596

3rd Movement Polka — S1597

4th Movement Galop — S1598

Symphony in Three Movements
By permission of Associated Music Publishers, Inc.

1st Movement 1st Theme — S1599

1st Movement 2nd Theme — S1600

1st Movement 3rd Theme   S1601

1st Movement 4th Theme   S1602

2nd Movement 1st Theme   S1603

2nd Movement 2nd Theme   S1604

2nd Movement 3rd Theme   S1605

3rd Movement 1st Theme   S1606

3rd Movement 2nd Theme   S1607

3rd Movement 3rd Theme   S1608

SUK, Joseph (1874-1935)

Serenade, Op. 6
Str. Orch.
By permission of
Associated Music
Publishers, Inc.

1st Movement 1st Theme   S1609

1st Movement 2nd Theme   S1610

2nd Movement 1st Theme   S1611

2nd Movement 2nd Theme   S1612

3rd Movement 1st Theme   S1613

3rd Movement 2nd Theme   S1614

4th Movement   S1615

SUPPÉ, Franz von (1819-1895)

Banditenstreiche,
Overture

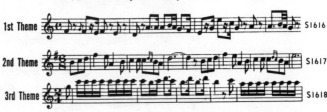

1st Theme   S1616

2nd Theme   S1617

3rd Theme   S1618

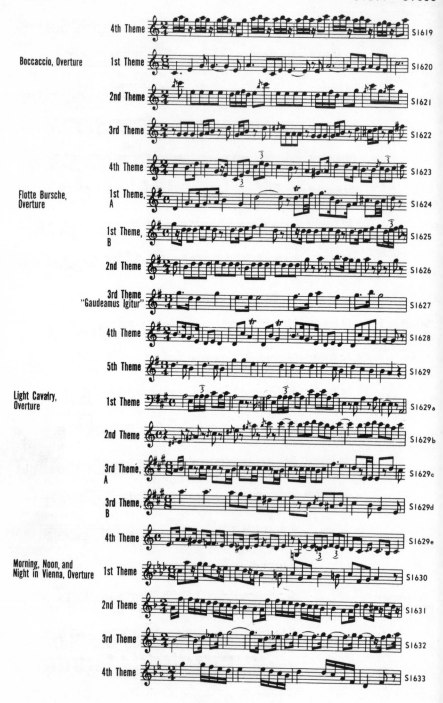

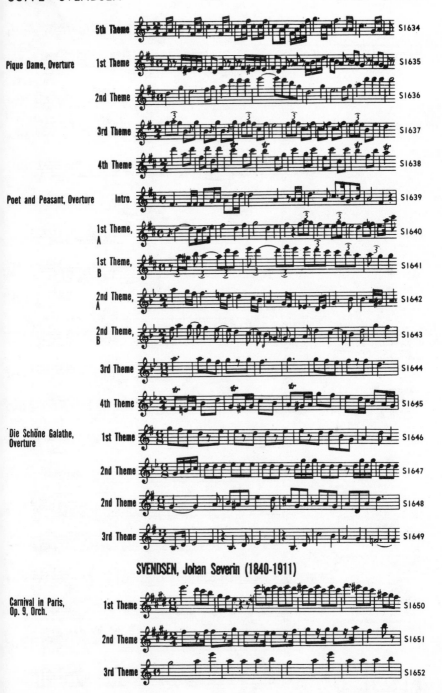

SVENDSEN, Johan Severin (1840-1911)

Festival Polonaise,
Op. 12, Orch.
By permission of Associated
Music Publishers, Inc.   1st Theme   S1653

2nd Theme   S1654

3rd Theme   S1655

Norwegian Artists'
Carnival, Op. 14, Orch.   1st Theme   S1656

2nd Theme
Italian Folk Song   S1657

3rd Theme
Norwegian Dance Tune   S1658

Romance, Op. 26, Vn. & Pft.   1st Theme   S1659

2nd Theme   S1660

SZYMANOWSKI, Karol (1883-1937)

The Fountain of Arethusa,
Op. 30, No. 1, Vn. & Pft.
By permission of Associated
Music Publishers, Inc.   1st Theme   S1661

2nd Theme   S1662

Mazurkas, Pft.
By permission of Associated
Music Publishers, Inc.
Op. 50, No. 1   1st Theme   S1663

2nd Theme   S1664

Op. 50, No. 2   1st Theme   S1665

2nd Theme   S1666

Notturno, Op. 28,
No. 1, Vn. & Pft.
By permission of Associated
Music Publishers, Inc.   1st Theme   S1667

2nd Theme   S1668

Romance, Op. 23,
Vn. & Pft.
By permission of Associated
Music Publishers, Inc.   1st Theme   S1669

2nd Theme   S1670

Tarantella, Op. 28,
No. 2, Vn. & Pft.
By permission of Associated
Music Publishers, Inc.   1st Theme   S1671

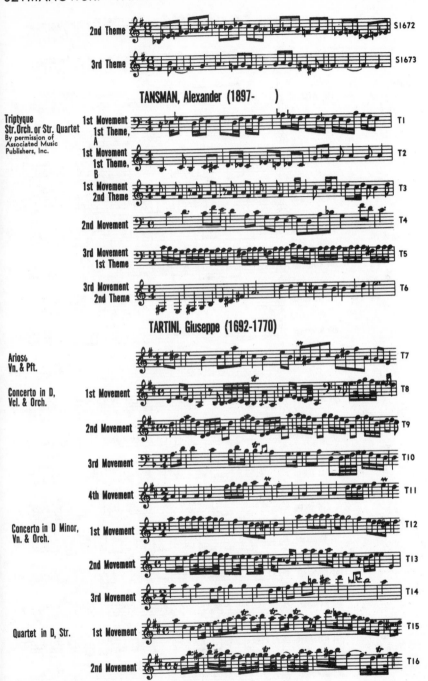

Triptyque
Str. Orch. or Str. Quartet
By permission of
Associated Music
Publishers, Inc.

Ariost
Vn. & Pft.

Concerto in D,
Vcl. & Orch.

Concerto in D Minor,
Vn. & Orch.

Quartet in D, Str.

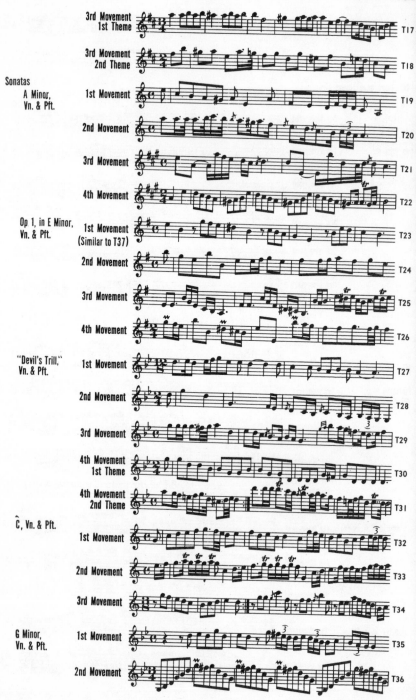

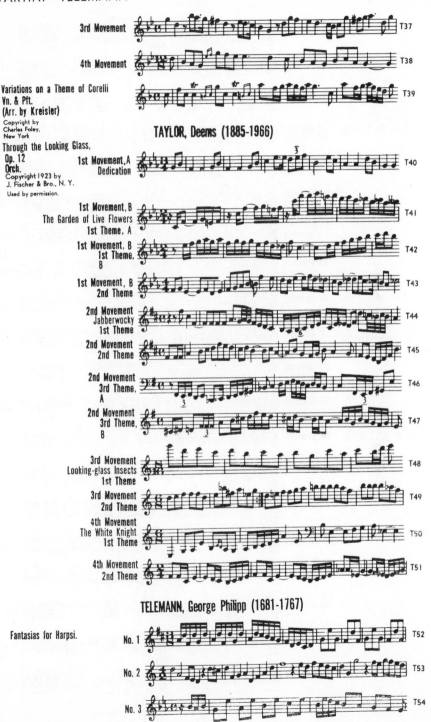

3rd Movement   T37

4th Movement   T38

Variations on a Theme of Corelli
Vn. & Pft.
(Arr. by Kreisler)

T39

TAYLOR, Deems (1885-1966)

Through the Looking Glass,
Op. 12
Orch.

1st Movement, A
Dedication

T40

1st Movement, B
The Garden of Live Flowers
1st Theme, A   T41

1st Movement, B
1st Theme,
B   T42

1st Movement, B
2nd Theme   T43

2nd Movement
Jabberwocky
1st Theme   T44

2nd Movement
2nd Theme   T45

2nd Movement
3rd Theme,
A   T46

2nd Movement
3rd Theme,
B   T47

3rd Movement
Looking-glass Insects
1st Theme   T48

3rd Movement
2nd Theme   T49

4th Movement
The White Knight
1st Theme   T50

4th Movement
2nd Theme   T51

TELEMANN, George Philipp (1681-1767)

Fantasias for Harpsi.

No. 1   T52

No. 2   T53

No. 3   T54

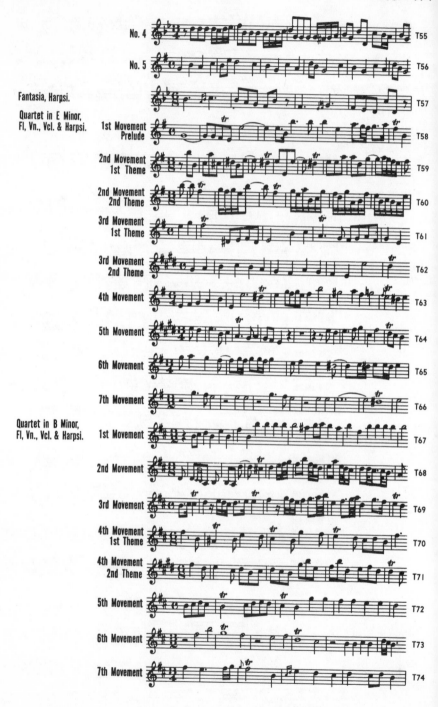

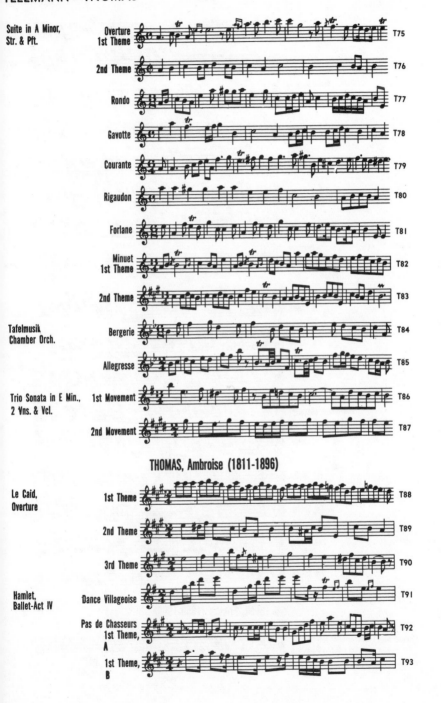

Suite in A Minor, Str. & Pft. — Overture 1st Theme — T75

2nd Theme — T76

Rondo — T77

Gavotte — T78

Courante — T79

Rigaudon — T80

Forlane — T81

Minuet 1st Theme — T82

2nd Theme — T83

Tafelmusik Chamber Orch. — Bergerie — T84

Allegresse — T85

Trio Sonata in E Min., 2 Vns. & Vcl. — 1st Movement — T86

2nd Movement — T87

THOMAS, Ambroise (1811-1896)

Le Caid, Overture — 1st Theme — T88

2nd Theme — T89

3rd Theme — T90

Hamlet, Ballet-Act IV — Dance Villageoise — T91

Pas de Chasseurs 1st Theme, A — T92

1st Theme, B — T93

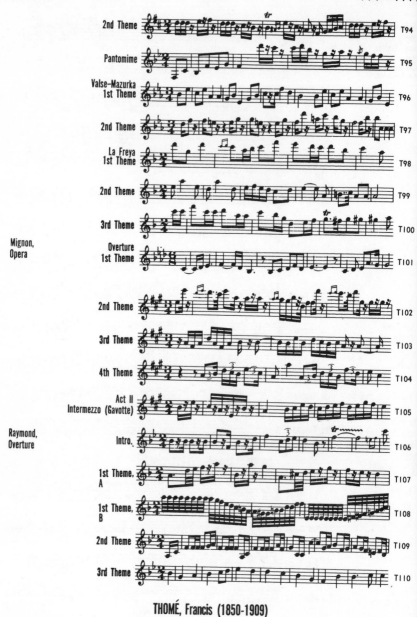

2nd Theme — T94
Pantomime — T95
Valse-Mazurka 1st Theme — T96
2nd Theme — T97
La Freya 1st Theme — T98
2nd Theme — T99
3rd Theme — T100

Mignon, Opera
Overture 1st Theme — T101
2nd Theme — T102
3rd Theme — T103
4th Theme — T104
Act II Intermezzo (Gavotte) — T105

Raymond, Overture
Intro. — T106
1st Theme, A — T107
1st Theme, B — T108
2nd Theme — T109
3rd Theme — T110

THOMÉ, Francis (1850-1909)

Simple Confession
(Simple Aveu) — T111

THOMSON, Virgil (1896-   )

No. 1
Intro.
1st Theme — TIIIa

2nd Theme — TIIIb

No. 2
Mac's Dance — TIIIc

No. 3
Motorist and Mac — TIIId

No. 4
Truck Drivers' Dance — TIIIe

2nd Theme — TIIIf

No. 7
Tango — TIIIg

No. 8
Waltz
1st Theme — TIIIh

2nd Theme — TIIIi

No. 9
The Big Apple — TIIIj

No. 11
The Chase — TIIIk

1st Movement
Prelude
1st Theme — TII2

1st Movement
2nd Theme — TII3

2nd Movement
Pastorale
(Grass) — TII4

3rd Movement
Cattle — TII5

4th Movement
Blues (Speculation)
1st Theme — TII6

4th Movement
2nd Theme — TII7

5th Movement
Drought
(6th Movement repeats
previous Themes) — TII8

1st Movement
1st Theme — TII8a

TOCH, Ernst (1887-1964)

3rd Movement 2nd Theme — T121

5th Movement — T122

Pinocchio Overture
By permission of Associated Music Publishers, Inc.

1st Theme — T122a

2nd Theme — T122b

3rd Theme — T122c

TSCHAIKOVSKY, Peter Ilyich (1840-1893)

Capriccio Italien, Op. 45 Orch. — 1st Theme — T123

2nd Theme — T124

3rd Theme — T125

4th Theme — T126

Chanson Triste, Op. 40, No. 2, Pft. — T127

Chant Sans Paroles Op. 2, No. 3, Pft. — T128

Chant Sans Paroles Op. 40, No. 6, Pft. — T129

Concerto No. 1, in B Flat Minor, Op. 23, Pft. & Orch. — 1st Movement 1st Theme — T130

1st Movement 2nd Theme — T131

1st Movement 3rd Theme — T132

2nd Movement 1st Theme — T133

2nd Movement 2nd Theme — T134

3rd Movement 1st Theme — T135

3rd Movement 2nd Theme — T136

Concerto No. 2 in G
Op. 44, Pft. & Orch.

1st Movement
1st Theme — T136a

1st Movement
2nd Theme,
A — T136b

1st Movement
2nd Theme,
B — T136c

2nd Movement
1st Theme,
A — T136d

2nd Movement
1st Theme,
B — T136e

3rd Movement
1st Theme — T136f

3rd Movement
2nd Theme — T136g

Concerto in D,
Op. 35, Vn. & Orch.

1st Movement
1st Theme — T137

1st Movement
2nd Theme — T138

1st Movement
3rd Theme — T139

2nd Movement
1st Theme — T140

2nd Movement
2nd Theme — T141

3rd Movement
1st Theme — T142

3rd Movement
2nd Theme — T143

Dolly's Funeral, from
Children's Album,
Op. 39, No. 7, Pft. — T144

Francesca da Rimini,
Op. 32, Orch.

1st Theme — T145

2nd Theme — T146

3rd Theme — T147

Humoresque,
Op. 10, No. 2, Pft.

1st Theme — T148

2nd Theme — T149

Marche Slave, Op. 31,
Orch. — 1st Theme — T150

2nd Theme — T151

3rd Theme — T152

* 4th Theme — T153 *

Soldiers' March Op. 39, No 5,
from Children's Album, Pft. — T154

Waltz from Eugen Onegin,
2nd Act — T155

Polonaise from Eugen Onegin,
3rd Act — T156

Hamlet, Fantasy Overture,
Op. 67 — 1st Theme — T157

2nd Theme — T158

3rd Theme — T159

Romeo and Juliet,
Fantasy Overture — 1st Theme — T160

2nd Theme — T161

3rd Theme — T162

4th Theme — T163

1812, Festival Overture,
Op. 49 — 1st Theme — T164

2nd Theme — T165

3rd Theme — T166

4th Theme — T167

Quartet in D, Op. 11,
Str. — 1st Movement — T168

2nd Movement
1st Theme — T169

For Melodie, T153a, see Page 526.

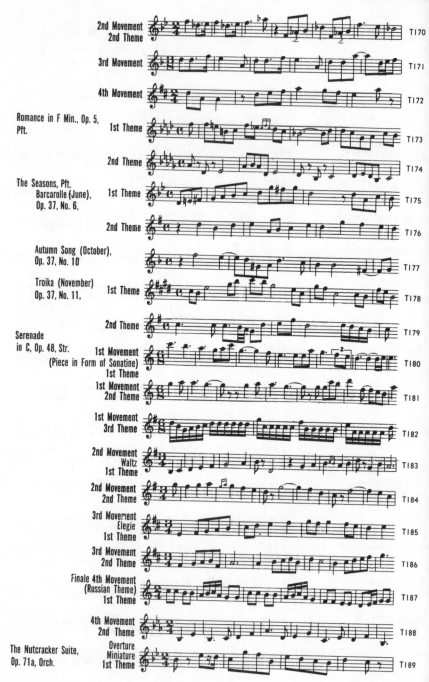

2nd Movement
2nd Theme   T170

3rd Movement   T171

4th Movement   T172

Romance in F Min., Op. 5,
Pft.   1st Theme   T173

2nd Theme   T174

The Seasons, Pft.
Barcarolle (June),   1st Theme   T175
Op. 37, No. 6,

2nd Theme   T176

Autumn Song (October),
Op. 37, No. 10   T177

Troika (November)   1st Theme   T178
Op. 37, No. 11,

2nd Theme   T179

Serenade
in C, Op. 48, Str.   1st Movement
(Piece in Form of Sonatine)   T180
1st Theme

1st Movement
2nd Theme   T181

1st Movement
3rd Theme   T182

2nd Movement
Waltz   T183
1st Theme

2nd Movement
2nd Theme   T184

3rd Movement
Elegie   T185
1st Theme

3rd Movement
2nd Theme   T186

Finale 4th Movement
(Russian Theme)   T187
1st Theme

4th Movement
2nd Theme   T188

The Nutcracker Suite,   Overture
Op. 71a, Orch.   Miniature   T189
1st Theme

5th Movement / Waltz — T210

Swan Lake, / Suite from the / Ballet, Op. 20a, Orch.

1st Movement / Intro. — T211

2nd Movement / Waltz — T212

3rd Movement / Dance of the Swans — T213

4th Movement / Hungarian Dance and Czardas / 1st Theme — T214

4th Movement / 2nd Theme — T215

Symphony No. 1, / Op. 13 / "Rêverie d'Hiver"

1st Movement / 1st Theme, / A — T216

1st Movement / 1st Theme, / B — T217

1st Movement / 2nd Theme — T218

2nd Movement / 1st Theme — T219

2nd Movement / 2nd Theme, / A — T220

2nd Movement / 2nd Theme, / B — T221

3rd Movement / 1st Theme — T222

3rd Movement / 2nd Theme — T223

4th Movement / 1st Theme — T224

4th Movement / 2nd Theme — T225

Symphony No. 2, / in C Minor, Op. 17, / "Little Russia"

1st Movement / 1st Theme — T226

1st Movement / 2nd Theme — T227

1st Movement / 3rd Theme, / A — T228

1st Movement / 3rd Theme, / B — T229

Symphony No. 4,
in F Minor.
Op. 36

Symphony No. 5,
in E Minor,
Op. 64

Symphony No. 6,
in B Minor, Op. 74
"Pathétique"
By permission of
Associated Music
Publishers, Inc.

4th Movement / 2nd Theme — T290

Theme & Variations, Op. 19, No. 6, Pft. — T291

Trio in A Min., Op. 50, Pft., Vn. & Vcl. — 1st Movement / 1st Theme — T292

1st Movement / 2nd Theme — T293

2nd Movement / Theme & Variations — T294

TURINA, Joaquín (1882-1950)

Danzas Fantásticas, Orch. or Pft. — Ensueño / 1st Theme, A — T295

1st Theme, B — T296

2nd Theme — T297

3rd Theme — T298

Orgia / 1st Theme — T299

2nd Theme — T300

Fandanguillo, Guitar
By permission of Associated Music Publishers, Inc. — 1st Theme — T301

2nd Theme — T302

Femmes d'Espagne (Mujeres Españolas)
Copyright by Editions Salabert
Editions Salabert, 22 Rue Chaucat, Paris Salabert, Inc., I East 57 St., N. Y. — L'Andalouse Sentimentale 1st Theme — T303

2nd Theme — T304

3rd Theme — T305

La Oración del Torero Quart., Str. — 1st Theme — T306

2nd Theme — T307

3rd Theme — T308

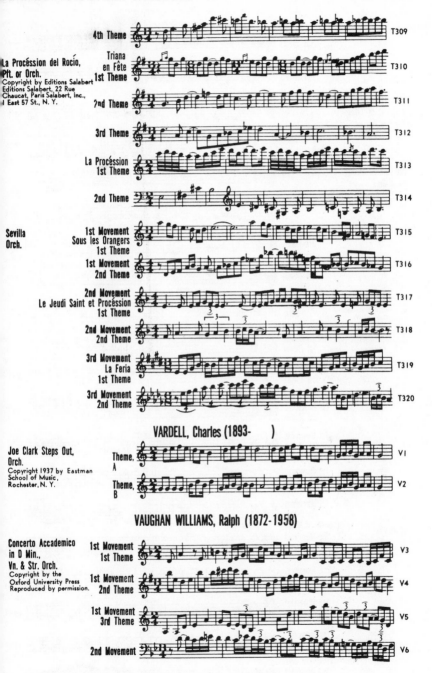

4th Theme T309

La Procéssion del Rocío,
Pft. or Orch.
Copyright by Editions Salabert
Editions Salabert, 22 Rue
Chaucat, Paris Salabert, Inc.,
I East 57 St., N. Y.

Triana
en Fête
1st Theme T310

2nd Theme T311

3rd Theme T312

La Procéssion
1st Theme T313

2nd Theme T314

Sevilla
Orch.

1st Movement
Sous les Orangers
1st Theme T315

1st Movement
2nd Theme T316

2nd Movement
Le Jeudi Saint et Procession
1st Theme T317

2nd Movement
2nd Theme T318

3rd Movement
La Feria
1st Theme T319

3rd Movement
2nd Theme T320

VARDELL, Charles (1893-   )

Joe Clark Steps Out,
Orch.
Copyright 1937 by Eastman
School of Music,
Rochester, N. Y.

Theme,
A V1

Theme,
B V2

VAUGHAN WILLIAMS, Ralph (1872-1958)

Concerto Accademico
in D Min.,
Vn. & Str. Orch.
Copyright by the
Oxford University Press
Reproduced by permission.

1st Movement
1st Theme V3

1st Movement
2nd Theme V4

1st Movement
3rd Theme V5

2nd Movement V6

3rd Movement 2nd Theme — V27
3rd Movement 3rd Theme — V28
4th Movement 1st Theme — V29
4th Movement 2nd Theme — V30

Symphony No. 4, in F Minor
Copyright by the Oxford University Press Reproduced by permission.

1st Movement 1st Theme — V31
1st Movement 2nd Theme — V32
1st Movement 3rd Theme — V33
1st Movement 4th Theme — V34
2nd Movement — V35
3rd Movement 1st Theme — V36
3rd Movement 2nd Theme — V37
3rd Movement 3rd Theme — V38
4th Movement 1st Theme, A — V39
4th Movement 1st Theme, B — V40
4th Movement 2nd Theme — V41

The Wasps (Aristophanes) Orch.

1st Movement Overture 1st Theme — V42
1st Movement 2nd Theme — V43
1st Movement 3rd Theme — V44
2nd Movement Entr'acte — V45
3rd Movement March Past of the Kitchen Utensils 1st Theme — V46

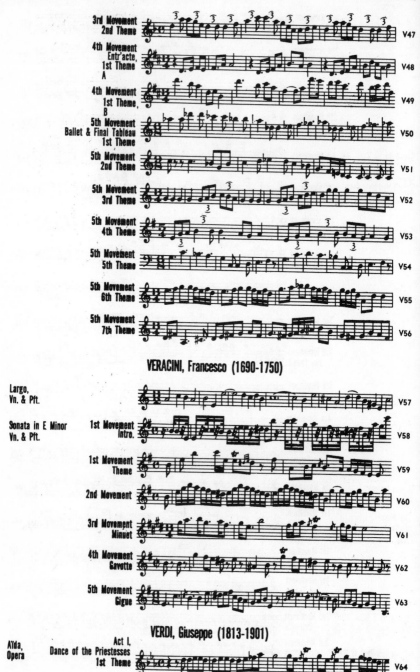

3rd Movement
2nd Theme — V47

4th Movement
Entr'acte,
1st Theme
A — V48

4th Movement
1st Theme,
B — V49

5th Movement
Ballet & Final Tableau
1st Theme — V50

5th Movement
2nd Theme — V51

5th Movement
3rd Theme — V52

5th Movement
4th Theme — V53

5th Movement
5th Theme — V54

5th Movement
6th Theme — V55

5th Movement
7th Theme — V56

VERACINI, Francesco (1690-1750)

Largo,
Vn. & Pft. — V57

Sonata in E Minor
Vn. & Pft.   1st Movement
Intro. — V58

1st Movement
Theme — V59

2nd Movement — V60

3rd Movement
Minuet — V61

4th Movement
Gavotte — V62

5th Movement
Gigue — V63

VERDI, Giuseppe (1813-1901)

Aïda,
Opera   Act I,
Dance of the Priestesses
1st Theme — V64

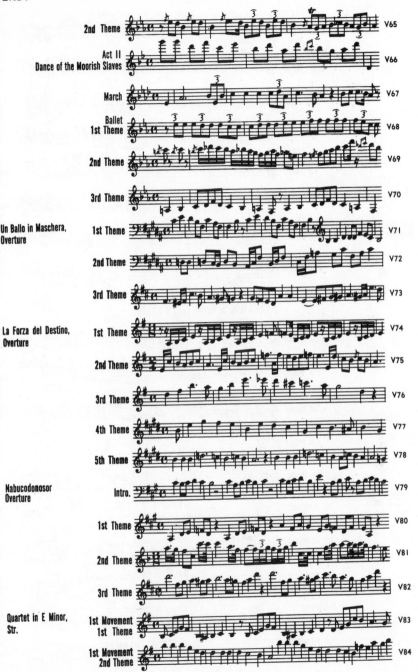

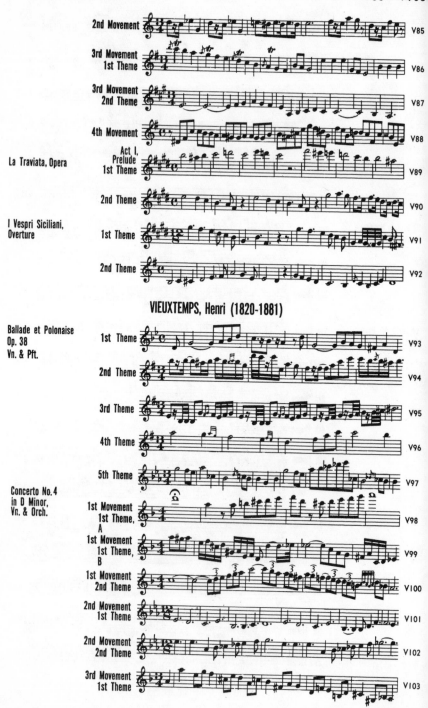

2nd Movement — V85

3rd Movement 1st Theme — V86

3rd Movement 2nd Theme — V87

4th Movement — V88

La Traviata, Opera

Act I, Prelude 1st Theme — V89

2nd Theme — V90

I Vespri Siciliani, Overture

1st Theme — V91

2nd Theme — V92

VIEUXTEMPS, Henri (1820-1881)

Ballade et Polonaise Op. 38 Vn. & Pft.

1st Theme — V93

2nd Theme — V94

3rd Theme — V95

4th Theme — V96

5th Theme — V97

Concerto No. 4 in D Minor, Vn. & Orch.

1st Movement 1st Theme, A — V98

1st Movement 1st Theme, B — V99

1st Movement 2nd Theme — V100

2nd Movement 1st Theme — V101

2nd Movement 2nd Theme — V102

3rd Movement 1st Theme — V103

3rd Movement 2nd Theme — V104

4th Movement 1st Theme — V105

4th Movement 2nd Theme — V106

VILLA-LOBOS, Heitor (1887-1959)

Bachianas-Brasileiras, No. 4, Pft. — 1st Theme — V107

2nd Theme — V108

3rd Theme — V109

Saudades das Selvas Brasileiras, Pft. By permission of Associated Music Publishers, Inc. — No. 1 — V110

No. 2 — V111

VINCI, Leonardo (1690-1730)

Sonata in D, Fl. & Harpsi. — 1st Movement — V112

2nd Movement — V113

3rd Movement — V114

4th Movement — V115

5th Movement — V116

VIOTTI, Giovanni (1753-1824)

Concerto No. 22, in A Minor, Vn. & Orch. — 1st Movement 1st Theme — V117

1st Movement 2nd Theme — V118

1st Movement 3rd Theme — V119

2nd Movement 1st Theme — V120

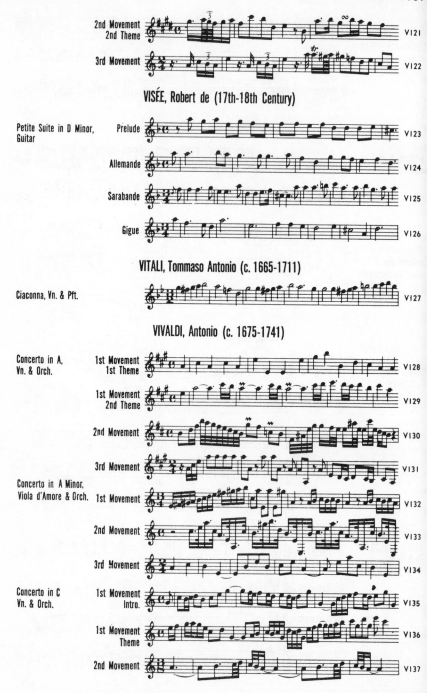

2nd Movement
2nd Theme — V121

3rd Movement — V122

VISÉE, Robert de (17th-18th Century)

Petite Suite in D Minor,
Guitar — Prelude — V123

Allemande — V124

Sarabande — V125

Gigue — V126

VITALI, Tommaso Antonio (c. 1665-1711)

Ciaconna, Vn. & Pft. — V127

VIVALDI, Antonio (c. 1675-1741)

Concerto in A,
Vn. & Orch. — 1st Movement
1st Theme — V128

1st Movement
2nd Theme — V129

2nd Movement — V130

3rd Movement — V131

Concerto in A Minor,
Viola d'Amore & Orch. — 1st Movement — V132

2nd Movement — V133

3rd Movement — V134

Concerto in C
Vn. & Orch. — 1st Movement
Intro. — V135

1st Movement
Theme — V136

2nd Movement — V137

	3rd Movement	V138
Concerto in C Minor, Vn. & Orch.	1st Movement	V139
	2nd Movement	V140
	3rd Movement	V141
Concerto in G Minor, Op. 6, No. 1, Vn. & Orch.	1st Movement	V142
	2nd Movement	V143
	3rd Movement	V144
Concerto in G Minor, Vn. & Str. Orch.	1st Movement	V145
	2nd Movement	V146
	3rd Movement	V147
Concerto Grosso in G Minor, Op. 3, No. 2 (L'Estro Armonico) Orch.	1st Movement	V148
	2nd Movement	V149
	3rd Movement	V150
Concerto Grosso in A Minor, Op. 3, No. 6 (L'Estro Armonico)	1st Movement	V151
	2nd Movement	V152
	3rd Movement	V153
Concerto Grosso in A Minor, Op. 3, No. 8 2 Vns. & Orch.	1st Movement	V154
	2nd Movement	V155
	3rd Movement	V156
Concerto Grosso in D, Op. 3, No. 9 Orch.	1st Movement	V157

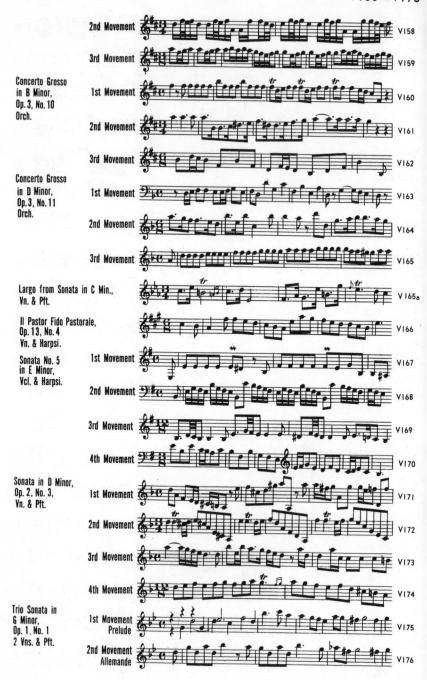

2nd Movement	V158
3rd Movement	V159
Concerto Grosso in B Minor, Op. 3, No. 10 Orch. — 1st Movement	V160
2nd Movement	V161
3rd Movement	V162
Concerto Grosso in D Minor, Op. 3, No. 11 Orch. — 1st Movement	V163
2nd Movement	V164
3rd Movement	V165
Largo from Sonata in C Min., Vn. & Pft.	V165a
Il Pastor Fido Pastorale, Op. 13, No. 4 Vn. & Harpsi.	V166
Sonata No. 5 in E Minor, Vcl. & Harpsi. — 1st Movement	V167
2nd Movement	V168
3rd Movement	V169
4th Movement	V170
Sonata in D Minor, Op. 2, No. 3, Vn. & Pft. — 1st Movement	V171
2nd Movement	V172
3rd Movement	V173
4th Movement	V174
Trio Sonata in G Minor, Op. 1, No. 1 2 Vns. & Pft. — 1st Movement Prelude	V175
2nd Movement Allemande	V176

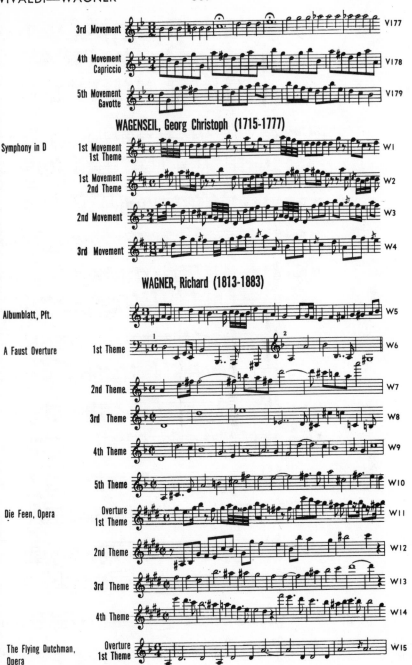

3rd Movement — V177

4th Movement Capriccio — V178

5th Movement Gavotte — V179

WAGENSEIL, Georg Christoph (1715-1777)

Symphony in D

1st Movement 1st Theme — W1

1st Movement 2nd Theme — W2

2nd Movement — W3

3rd Movement — W4

WAGNER, Richard (1813-1883)

Albumblatt, Pft. — W5

A Faust Overture

1st Theme — W6

2nd Theme — W7

3rd Theme — W8

4th Theme — W9

5th Theme — W10

Die Feen, Opera

Overture 1st Theme — W11

2nd Theme — W12

3rd Theme — W13

4th Theme — W14

The Flying Dutchman, Opera

Overture 1st Theme — W15

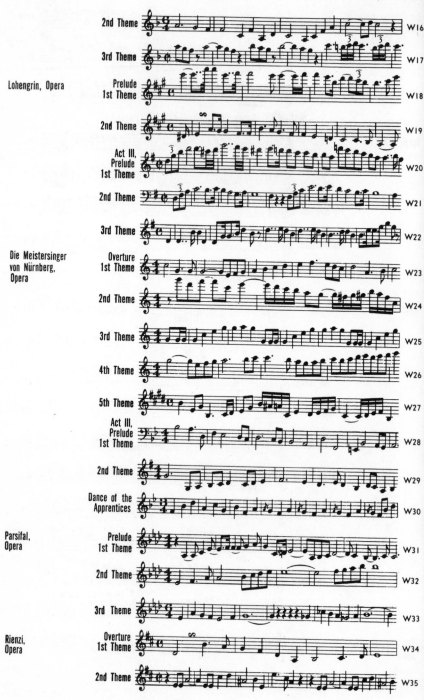

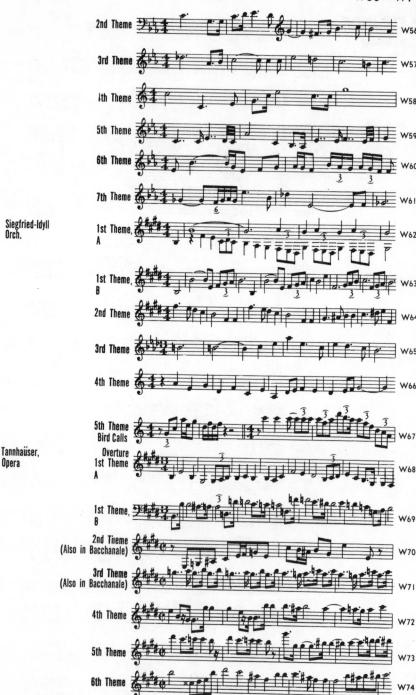

2nd Theme — W56
3rd Theme — W57
lth Theme — W58
5th Theme — W59
6th Theme — W60
7th Theme — W61

Siegfried-Idyll
Orch.

1st Theme,
A — W62
1st Theme,
B — W63
2nd Theme — W64
3rd Theme — W65
4th Theme — W66
5th Theme
Bird Calls — W67

Tannhaüser,
Opera

Overture
1st Theme
A — W68
1st Theme,
B — W69
2nd Theme
(Also in Bacchanale) — W70
3rd Theme
(Also in Bacchanale) — W71
4th Theme — W72
5th Theme — W73
6th Theme — W74

7th Theme — W75

8th Theme — W76

Act II,
March
Intro. — W77

1st Theme — W78

2nd Theme — W79

3rd Theme — W80

Bacchanale
(Venusberg Music)
1st Theme — W81

2nd Theme — W82

3rd Theme — W83

4th Theme — W84

Tristan und Isolde, Opera   Prelude
1st Theme — W85

2nd Theme — W86

Act III
Prelude
1st Theme — W87

2nd Theme — W88

3rd Theme — W89

Love Death
1st Theme — W90

2nd Theme — W91

WALDTEUFEL, Emil (1837-1915)

Dolores Waltzes
Op. 170, Orch.
Courtesy Carl Fischer,
Inc., N.Y.

No. 1
1st Theme — W92

2nd Theme — W93

Espana, Waltzes
Op. 286, Orch.
Courtesy Carl Fischer,
Inc., N. Y.

Estudiantina, Waltzes
Op. 191, Orch.
Courtesy Carl Fischer,
Inc., N. Y.

Frühlingskinder Waltz (Violettes), Op. 148 Orch.

1st Theme

2nd Theme

3rd Theme

4th Theme

Ganz Allerliebst (Très Jolie), Waltz Op. 159, Orch.

1st Theme

2nd Theme

3rd Theme

4th Theme

Immer Oder Nimmer (Toujours ou Jamais), Waltzes Op. 156, Orch.

No. 1

No. 2 1st Theme

2nd Theme

No. 3 1st Theme

2nd Theme

No. 4

Mein Traum, Waltzes, Op. 151, Orch.

No. 1

No. 2 1st Theme

2nd Theme

No. 3 1st Theme

2nd Theme

No. 4

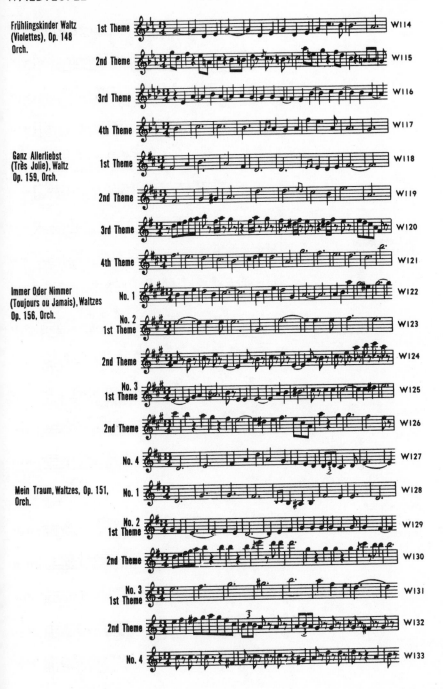

W114
W115
W116
W117
W118
W119
W120
W121
W122
W123
W124
W125
W126
W127
W128
W129
W130
W131
W132
W133

Sirenenzauber (Sirens)
Waltzes, Op. 154
Orch.

No. 1
1st Theme — W134

2nd Theme — W135

No. 2
1st Theme — W136

2nd Theme — W137

No. 3
1st Theme — W138

2nd Theme — W139

No. 4 — W140

The Skaters, Waltzes
Op. 183, Orch.
Courtesy Carl Fischer,
Inc., N. Y.

No. 1
1st Theme — W141

2nd Theme — W142

No. 2
1st Theme — W143

2nd Theme — W144

No. 3
1st Theme — W145

2nd Theme — W146

No. 4 — W147

WALLACE, William Vincent (1812-1865)

Maritana,
Overture

1st Theme — W148

2nd Theme — W149

3rd Theme — W150

4th Theme — W151

5th Theme — W152

WALTON, William Turner (1902-   )

Concerto Viola & Orch.
Copyright by the Oxford University Press.
Reproduced by permission.

1st Movement 1st Theme — W153

1st Movement 2nd Theme — W154

2nd Movement 1st Theme — W155

2nd Movement 2nd Theme — W156

2nd Movement 3rd Theme — W157

3rd Movement 1st Theme — W158

3rd Movement 2nd Theme — W159

Concerto Vn. & Orch.
Copyright by the Oxford University Press.
Reproduced by permission.

1st Movement 1st Theme — W160

1st Movement 2nd Theme — W161

2nd Movement 1st Theme, A — W162

2nd Movement 1st Theme, B — W163

2nd Movement 2nd Theme — W164

2nd Movement 3rd Theme — W165

3rd Movement 1st Theme — W166

3rd Movement 2nd Theme — W167

Crown Imperial, Coronation March, Orch.
Copyright by the Oxford University Press.
Reproduced by permission.

1st Theme — W168

2nd Theme — W169

3rd Theme — W170

4th Theme — W171

Façade, Suite No. 1, Orch.
Copyright by the Oxford University Press.
Reproduced by permission.

Polka 1st Theme

W172

2nd Theme

W173

3rd Theme

W174

Valse 1st Theme

W175

2nd Theme

W176

A Swiss Yodeling Song 1st Theme

W177

2nd Theme (Parody on William Tell)

W178

3rd Theme

W179

Tango-Pasodoble 1st Theme

W180

2nd Theme

W181

Tarantella-Sevillana 1st Theme

W182

2nd Theme

W183

Façade, Suite No. 2, Orch.
Copyright by the Oxford University Press.
Reproduced by permission.

Fanfare

W184

Scotch Rhapsody 1st Theme

W185

2nd Theme

W186

Country Dance

W187

Noche Española 1st Theme

W188

2nd Theme

W189

Popular Song

W190

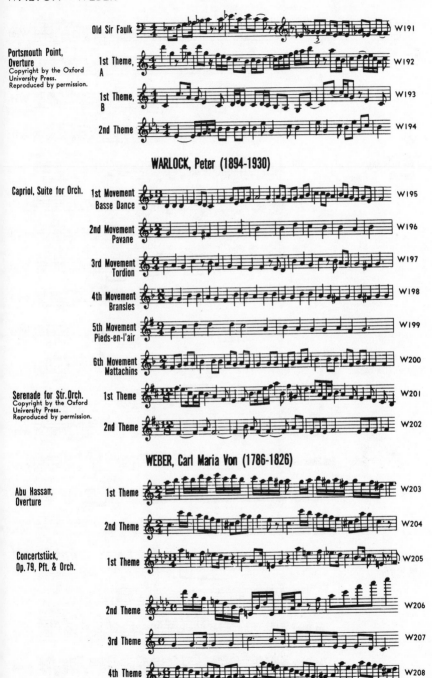

Old Sir Faulk — W191

Portsmouth Point, Overture
Copyright by the Oxford University Press. Reproduced by permission.
1st Theme, A — W192

1st Theme, B — W193

2nd Theme — W194

WARLOCK, Peter (1894-1930)

Capriol, Suite for Orch.
1st Movement Basse Dance — W195

2nd Movement Pavane — W196

3rd Movement Tordion — W197

4th Movement Bransles — W198

5th Movement Pieds-en-l'air — W199

6th Movement Mattachins — W200

Serenade for Str. Orch.
Copyright by the Oxford University Press. Reproduced by permission.
1st Theme — W201

2nd Theme — W202

WEBER, Carl Maria Von (1786-1826)

Abu Hassan, Overture
1st Theme — W203

2nd Theme — W204

Concertstück, Op. 79, Pft. & Orch.
1st Theme — W205

2nd Theme — W206

3rd Theme — W207

4th Theme — W208

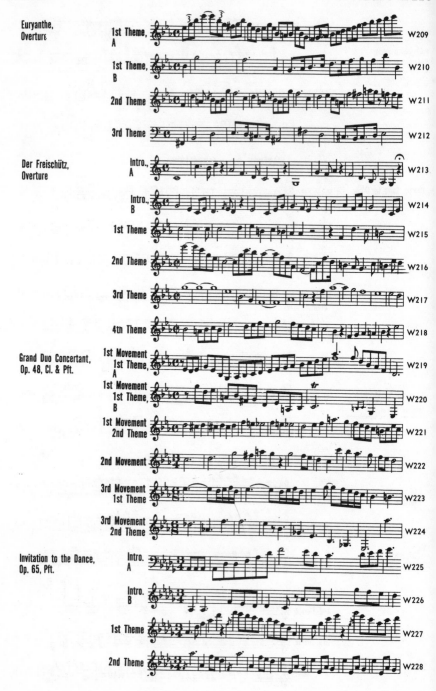

WEBER

Euryanthe, Overture
- 1st Theme, A — W209
- 1st Theme, B — W210
- 2nd Theme — W211
- 3rd Theme — W212

Der Freischütz, Overture
- Intro., A — W213
- Intro., B — W214
- 1st Theme — W215
- 2nd Theme — W216
- 3rd Theme — W217
- 4th Theme — W218

Grand Duo Concertant, Op. 48, Cl. & Pft.
- 1st Movement 1st Theme, A — W219
- 1st Movement 1st Theme, B — W220
- 1st Movement 2nd Theme — W221
- 2nd Movement — W222
- 3rd Movement 1st Theme — W223
- 3rd Movement 2nd Theme — W224

Invitation to the Dance, Op. 65, Pft.
- Intro. A — W225
- Intro. B — W226
- 1st Theme — W227
- 2nd Theme — W228

3rd Theme — W229
4th Theme — W230
5th Theme — W231
Jubel-Ouvertüre
Intro.
1st Theme — W232
2nd Theme — W233
1st Theme — W234
2nd Theme — W235
3rd Theme — W236
4th Theme
God Save the King — W237
Oberon,
Overture
Intro. — W238
1st Theme — W239
2nd Theme — W240
3rd Theme — W241
Peter Schmoll
und Seine Nachbarn,
Overture
Intro. — W242
1st Theme — W243
2nd Theme — W244
Polacca Brillante,
Op. 72, Pft.
1st Theme — W245
2nd Theme — W246
Preciosa,
Overture
1st Theme — W247
2nd Theme — W248

4th Movement
3rd Theme — W 269

WEINBERGER, Jaromir (1896-1967)

Schwanda, Opera
By permission of Associated
Music Publishers, Inc.

Polka — W270

Fugue — W271

Under the Spreading
Chestnut Tree,
(Variations and
Fugue on an
old English tune),
Orch.
By permission of Associated
Music Publishers, Inc.

1st Theme
Theme for Variations — W 272

2nd Theme
Theme for Fugue — W 273

WIENIAWSKI, Henri (1835-1880)

Concerto No. 2
in D Minor, Op. 22,
Vn. & Orch.

1st Movement
1st Theme — W274

1st Movement
2nd Theme — W275

2nd Movement
Romance — W276

3rd Movement
1st Theme — W277

3rd Movement
2nd Theme — W278

Dudziarz (Mazurka),
Op. 19, No. 2
Vn. & Pft.

1st Theme — W279

2nd Theme — W280

Kuiawiak, Op. 3,
Vn. & Pft.

Intro. — W281

1st Theme — W282

2nd Theme — W283

3rd Theme — W284

Legende, Op. 17
Vn. & Pft.

1st Theme — W285

2nd Theme — W286

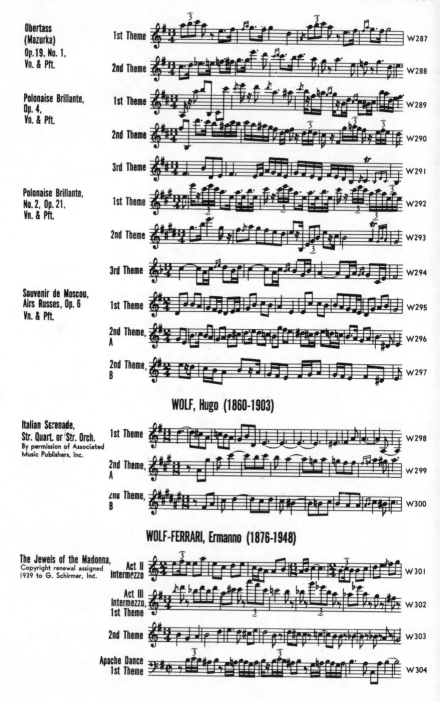

Obertass (Mazurka) Op. 19, No. 1, Vn. & Pft.
1st Theme — W287
2nd Theme — W288

Polonaise Brillante, Op. 4, Vn. & Pft.
1st Theme — W289
2nd Theme — W290
3rd Theme — W291

Polonaise Brillante, No. 2, Op. 21, Vn. & Pft.
1st Theme — W292
2nd Theme — W293
3rd Theme — W294

Souvenir de Moscou, Airs Russes, Op. 6 Vn. & Pft.
1st Theme — W295
2nd Theme, A — W296
2nd Theme, B — W297

WOLF, Hugo (1860-1903)

Italian Serenade, Str. Quart. or Str. Orch.
By permission of Associated Music Publishers, Inc.
1st Theme — W298
2nd Theme, A — W299
2nd Theme, B — W300

WOLF-FERRARI, Ermanno (1876-1948)

The Jewels of the Madonna,
Copyright renewal assigned 1939 to G. Schirmer, Inc.
Act II Intermezzo — W301
Act III Intermezzo, 1st Theme — W302
2nd Theme — W303
Apache Dance 1st Theme — W304

2nd Theme — W305

The Secret of Suzanne,
Overture
Copyright 1910 by
Josef Weinberger, Leipzig.

1st Theme — W306

2nd Theme — W307

3rd Theme — W308

YSAŸE, Théo (1865-1918)

Variations, Op. 10,
2 Pfts.
By permission of Associated
Music Publishers, Inc.

Theme — Y1

ZANDONAI, Riccardo (1883-1944)

Giulietta E Romeo
Symphonic Episode, Orch.
Copyright 1928
by G. Ricordi & Co., Inc.

1st Theme — Z1

2nd Theme — Z2

3rd Theme — Z3

ZARZYCKI, Alexander (1834-1895)

Mazurka, Op. 26,
Vn. & Pft.
Copyright 1899
by Carl Fischer, Inc., N. Y.

1st Theme — Z4

2nd Theme — Z5

3rd Theme — Z6

ZIMBALIST, Efrem (1889-   )

Quartet in E Minor,
Str.
Copyright 1938
by G. Schirmer, Inc.

1st Movement — Z7

2nd Movement
1st Theme — Z8

2nd Movement
2nd Theme — Z9

3rd Movement
1st Theme — Z10

3rd Movement
2nd Theme — Z11

4th Theme — Z12

TRANSPOSITION KEY

C	D	E	F	G	A	B	C	
C♯	D♯	E♯	F♯	G♯	A♯	B♯	C♯	} enharmonic[x]
D♭	E♭	F	G♭	A♭	B♭	C	D♭	
D	E	F♯	G	A	B	C♯	D	
E♭	F	G	A♭	B♭	C	D	E♭	
E	F♯	G♯	A	B	C♯	D♯	E	
F	G	A	B♭	C	D	E	F	
F♯	G♯	A♯	B	C♯	D♯	E♯	F♯	} enharmonic[x]
G♭	A♭	B♭	C♭	D♭	E♭	F	G♭	
G	A	B	C	D	E	F♯	G	
A♭	B♭	C	D♭	E♭	F	G	A♭	
A	B	C♯	D	E	F♯	G♯	A	
B♭	C	D	E♭	F	G	A	B♭	
B	C♯	D♯	E	F♯	G♯	A♯	B	} enharmonic[x]
C♭	D♭	E♭	F♭	G♭	A♭	B♭	C♭	

x Sounding the same but written differently.

This chart, though not necessary to the use of the notation key, should be helpful to the reader in explaining key relationships. For example, the fifth note in the key of C is G, its equivalent in the key of A is E.

HOW TO USE
THE NOTATION INDEX*

To identify a given theme, play it in the key of C and look it up under its note sequence using the following alphabet as a guide:

A Ab A♯ **B** Bb B♯ **C** Cb C♯ **D** Db D♯
E Eb E♯ **F** Fb F♯ **G** Gb G♯

Double flats follow flats; double sharps follow sharps.

The letter and number to the right of the definition indicate the place in the alphabetic section of the book where the theme may be found in its original key with the name of the composition and the composer.

Trills, turns, grace notes, and other embellishments are not taken into consideration here. However, it must be remembered that the appoggiatura is a regular note. In rare cases the grace note may be of such nature as to give the aural impression of being a regular note, in which case it is included in this section.

Keys are, in the main, determined by the harmonic structure of the opening bars, not by the cadence. The phrase that begins in C and goes to G is considered to be in C. Themes that may be analyzed in two keys are listed under both keys. There are themes that defy key definition. However, if the melodic line carries a key implication of its own, if only for the first few notes, that key is used. If the theme carries no such implication, then, for the sake of convenience, the first note is assumed to be C and the rest transposed accordingly.

Memory plays strange tricks and it is possible that the desired theme may be remembered inaccurately. We have occasionally listed a theme incorrectly as well as correctly if there is a popular misconception about it.

Each definition has been carried to six places except in the case of duplication. Duplicates are continued to a point of difference, but in no case to more than eleven places. When a note is repeated many times, for space conservation an exponent is used, *i.e.* $G\ G\ G\ G\ G\ G = G^6$.

H. B.

* Publisher's note: The Notation Index was conceived by Harold Barlow.

Fugue in G Minor, Organ
"The Little Fugue" Bach

B99a

Symphony No.2, Op. 63
Elgar

By permission of
Novello & Co., Ltd.,
London.

1st Movement
1st Theme.
A

E73a

1st Movement
1st Theme.
B

E73b

1st Movement
2nd Theme.
A

E73c

1st Movement
2nd Theme
B

E73d

2nd Movement
Intro.

E73e

2nd Movement
1st Theme

E73f

2nd Movement
2nd Theme

E73g

3rd Movement
1st Theme

E73h

3rd Movement
2nd Theme

E73i

4th Movement
1st Theme

E73j

4th Movement
2nd Theme

E73k

Mélodie, Op. 42, No. 3
from Souvenir D'Un Lieu
Cher. Vn. & Pft.
Tschaikovsky

T153a

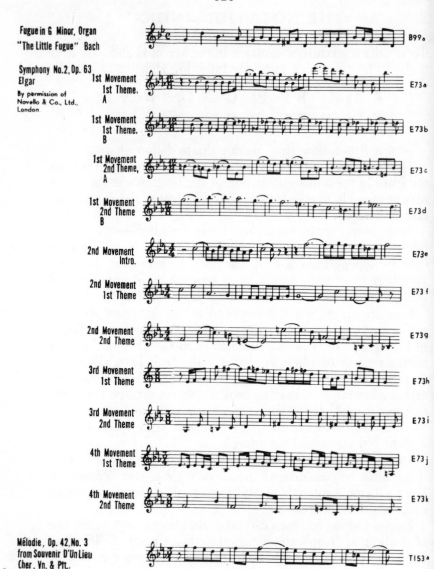

G G C D E D B	B1648	G G C G E E F F	B1103
G G C D E D C	T165	G G C G F E	M1004
G G C D E D G	G4	G G C G F Eb D	S168
G G C D E F D	M352	G G C G F Eb D	H852
G G C D E F G A	S254	G G C G F F E E	S1192
G G C D E F G G	W63	G G C G F F E G	H714
G G C D Eb D	R369	G G C G G A	T100
G G C D Eb F	V102	G G C G G C Eb	W54
G G C D Eb G	S1096	G G C G G C G	B1141
G G C E B C	M366	G G C G G D G G A	S402
G G C E C B	B910	G G C G G D G G E	B860
G G C E C F	B851	G G C G G E	W35
G G C E C G	H580	G G C G G G	B1117j
G G C E D B	C177	G G D B C C	B515
G G C E D C C	L31	G G D C A B	W62
G G C E D C E	S1437	G G D D C B	S818
G G C E D D	S2	G G D D C Bb	S1592
G G C E D G	B1632	G G D D D Eb	B161
G G C E F D	M821	G G D D Eb G	C531
G G C E F G A	H388	G G D E F A	M415
G G C E F G C	S1333	G G D E F E D C	M181
G G C E G C B	S1238	G G D E F E D E	C588
G G C E G C E	H384	G G D E F E E	L260
G G C E G E	P33	G G D Eb F Eb	L263
G G C E G F E D	D339	G G D Eb F G	P19
G G C E G F E F	M349	G G D Eb G F	V139
G G C E G F#	W240	G G D F E G	F21
G G C E G G	H647	G G D F Eb B	V103
G G C Eb Ab C	B315	G G D F Eb C	T157
G G C Eb Eb Ab	B486	G G D# E B C	B741
G G C Eb Eb D	C202	G G D# E E E	S745
G G C Eb G Bb	A38	G G E A G C	R286
G G C Eb G Eb	I 128	G G E C A C	D169
G G C F F G	H223	G G E C A G	B1529
G G C D D G	H578	G G E C B A	P49
G G C G A D	P353	G G E C B B	W13
G G C G B G	S621	G G E C C A	H626
G G C G C D	M231	G G E C C B	H527
G G C G C G F	P92	G G E C C G	S409
G G C G C G G	K96	G G E C E D	S505
G G C G D G	B984	G G E C E G C	M256
G G C G E C	B687	G G E C E G E	S1159
G G C G E E F E E	B1095	G G E C G A	S867
G G C G E E F E E	B1098	G G E C G C	M546

INDEX OF TITLES

645

PRINTED IN GREAT BRITAIN BY LOWE AND BRYDONE (PRINTERS) LTD., THETFORD, NORFOLK